DEVELOPMENTAL THEISM

Developmental Theism

From Pure Will to Unbounded Love

PETER FORREST

CLARENDON PRESS · OXFORD

BT
40
.F55
2007

OXFORD
UNIVERSITY PRESS

Great Clarendon Street, Oxford OX2 6DP

Oxford University Press is a department of the University of Oxford.
It furthers the University's objective of excellence in research, scholarship,
and education by publishing worldwide in

Oxford   New York

Auckland Cape Town Dar es Salaam Hong Kong Karachi
Kuala Lumpur Madrid Melbourne Mexico City Nairobi
New Delhi Shanghai Taipei Toronto

With offices in

Argentina Austria Brazil Chile Czech Republic France Greece
Guatemala Hungary Italy Japan Poland Portugal Singapore
South Korea Switzerland Thailand Turkey Ukraine Vietnam

Oxford is a registered trade mark of Oxford University Press
in the UK and in certain other countries

Published in the United States
by Oxford University Press Inc., New York

British Library Cataloguing in Publication Data

Data available

Library of Congress Cataloging in Publication Data

Forrest, Peter, 1948–
Developmental theism: from pure will to unbounded love / Peter Forrest.
p. cm.
Includes bibliographical references and index.
ISBN–13: 978–0–19–921458–7 (alk. paper)
ISBN–10: 0–19–921458–1 (alk. paper)
1. Philosophical theology.   I. Title.
BT40.F55 2007   231–dc22   2006036377

Typeset by Laserwords Private Limited, Chennai, India
Printed in Great Britain
on acid-free paper by
Biddles Ltd., King's Lynn, Norfolk

ISBN 978–0–19–921458–7

1 3 5 7 9 10 8 6 4 2

Preface

This book has developed out of the Wilde Lectures that I had the honour of giving in 2004. I have tried to retain as much of the vigour of the lecture format as possible, but readers should note that I have added an Introduction, an extra chapter (Chapter 3), and two appendices (to Chapters 5 and 9). The Introduction is largely a defence of my speculative method, which some find frivolous. Chapter 3 is effectively an overgrown appendix to Chapter 2. It resulted from the need to explain why I was not a dualist. The appendix to Chapter 5 concerns the classification dependence of appeals to simplicity. I added to Chapter 9 a discussion of the Real Presence in the Eucharist, with an appendix on transubstantiation and consubstantiation.

I would like to thank all those who have helped me, either by encouragement or by criticism, starting with Richard Swinburne, who was responsible for the invitation to give the lectures, and Brian Leftow, who inherited their organization from him. I owe a great deal to the comments of those who attended the lectures and the associated meetings of the Joseph Butler Society, especially Marilyn McCord Adams, Robert Adams, Joseph Jedwab, Brian Leftow, Howard Robinson, and Richard Swinburne. Peter Momtchiloff of Oxford University Press is to be thanked for his help and for the choice of readers, whose comments were most valuable. Finally, I would like to acknowledge my debt to my wife Felicity, who accompanied and supported me while I was giving the lectures—at some cost to her horticultural business.

Peter Forrest

University of New England, Australia, April 2006

To my beloved wife and children: Felicity, Joseph, Stephen, Alice, and Nicholas

Contents

Introduction

In this work I present a speculative philosophical theology based on three themes: that a version of materialism is a help, not a hindrance, in philosophical theology; that God develops; and that this development is on the whole kenotic—that is, an abandonment of power. Here is a synopsis:

> In the beginning there was a God that was not personal, which loved no one and which was not lovable, a God that was all-powerful and all-knowing. A sequence of acts resulted in a community of divine love, the Holy Trinity, and a world with many creatures who were autonomous agents. God loved us so much that one Divine Person become fully human and was willing to suffer to show us divine love. This is the development of God from Pure Will to Unbounded Love.

Although I shall provide arguments for this philosophical theology, they are, like most philosophical arguments, far from conclusive. Therefore something should be said about my motivation. Much of philosophy is the sketching of alternative hypotheses—of ways things might, for all we know, be. As a consequence of such sketches, philosophers present a range of not-too-improbable hypotheses, but without any hypothesis being established as more probable than not, and with the nagging worry that the best might still be out there, undiscovered. Given such a dismal prognosis, why not just give up? Moreover, the conclusions I tentatively reach are, in the words of one critic, 'radical, implausible, counterintuitive and heretical'. I admit, then, that all I am doing is speculating. But speculation is, I say, important, so as to distinguish the fairly probable from the highly improbable among the hypotheses on offer.

Here is a list of reasons—speculations about?—why speculation about God is important even though it does not provide us with conclusions that are more probable than not: sampling, defensive apologetics, bootstrapping, speculative theodicy, argument-generated comprehension, dialectics, and, if all else fails, providential agnosticism.

SAMPLING

If we try hard to find as many not-too-improbable hypotheses as we can, then we may think of them as a sample out of the population of all the not-too-improbable hypotheses. We may also have a rough idea of the comparative probabilities of these hypotheses. The probability of the existence of a loving God, relative to the (disjunction of) the hypotheses in the sample, is then a guide to the probability relative to (the disjunction of) all the hypotheses, including those we have not yet discovered. To be sure, the sample is not constructed to be random and is rather small, but it is hard think of a better way of assessing the probability of theism.

I have listed sampling first because it is, I hold, the most important justification for speculation, whether scientific, religious, or philosophical. As Bas van Fraassen (1980) has pointed out, reliance upon inference to the best explanation runs into the problem that we cannot survey all the relevant hypotheses. I used to take this threat more seriously than I do now, treating it as showing that, while not required for rationality, agnosticism was compatible with ideal rationality. And by agnosticism here I meant agnosticism about either God (Forrest 1996*a*: ch. 1) or neutrinos, etc. (Forrest 1994). While not denying that agnostics are on the whole rational men and women, I now withdraw this concession. Neither of the above kinds of agnosticism is ideally rational. For provided we have a society in which hypotheses may be investigated freely, then those that we have thought of may be taken as a sample of the whole range. The sample is biased, in that we have presumably considered only rather simple hypotheses, but assuming, as we should, that simpler hypotheses are significantly more probable than more complicated ones, this bias is moderate. I relish the conclusion that those who condemn speculation in general, and philosophy in particular, as frivolous unwittingly undermine the basis for our trust in the scientific theories that are not considered speculations.

But, you say, the sample is not merely biased in favour of simplicity, which is good, but biased in other ways, as shown by the sociology of knowledge—dreadful trade! This raises a rather subtle topic in the theory of sampling: namely, what is the difference between a random sample and one known to be biased but in ways that we cannot assess the impact of. In this case we have no way of knowing whether the accidents of the history of science, such as the religious beliefs of the scientists in question, help or hinder the pursuit of truth. The answer, I think, is that a sample biased in some unknown fashion is as good as a random sample of somewhat smaller size. (Smaller because the unknown biasing factors are likely to affect the different members of the sample similarly, thus reducing the effective range.)

The justification for philosophical speculation helps answer the question that David Stove used to ask, 'Why feed philosophers?' Why indeed, you might say, noting that we are a cantankerous bunch, often sadly lacking in common sense, given to being mavericks at best and sadly deluded narcissists at worst. I say that we should be not merely thrown the odd crust, but cherished, as one source of a wide range of speculations. Likewise, we should cherish the fraction of 1 per cent of physicists who go beyond the empirically supported theories. I call them mathematical metaphysicians, and welcome them as fellow philosophers.

DEFENSIVE APOLOGETICS

What we are otherwise inclined to accept is often brought into doubt by its apparent philosophical implausibility. Again, those who have accepted a religious tradition are subject not merely to disagreement but to ridicule. The fear that religious beliefs are somehow silly can be articulated by asking, 'How is this possible'? For instance, 'How is the Trinity possible?' When we ask that question, we are not asking for a mere proof of consistency, but rather for a metaphysical hypothesis that renders what seems outrageous quite acceptable, the sort of thing that Søren Kierkegaard disparaged as making Christianity reasonable.

One way to treat the hypothesis I develop is, then, as a piece of defensive apologetics, a way of showing either to oneself or to others that, in spite of St Paul and many others, Christianity is not folly. I expect to be taken to one side and gently reminded that this task has already been performed by abler philosophers. My response is that many people take it for granted that some sort of materialism is correct, and there is not much apologetics addressed to materialists. Although I think of materialism even in its defensible forms as just one more not-too-improbable speculation, it is still important that materialism is, I say, a help, not a hindrance, to Christianity.

BOOTSTRAPPING

By *bootstrapping* I mean the way in which an inconclusive metaphysical argument for a position may be used to buttress what would initially seem quite circular. I apply this to Alvin Plantinga's claim that Christianity is warranted if true (Plantinga 2002). In his terminology, warrant plus truth equals knowledge. So he has argued that Christianity is known by Christians, provided it is in fact true. His case is based upon the way in which Christianity implies that the Holy Spirit guides humanity in its search for religious truth, either at an individual level or in a more collective fashion, as I would propose. He has also argued that evolutionary naturalism is not warranted even if it is true (Plantinga 2003). Now let us suppose that he is right on both counts. Then we might initially think that there is something horribly circular in trying to justify Christianity by showing that it is knowledge provided it is true. And as far as I know, Plantinga is not putting this forward as justification. But if evolutionary naturalism is somehow at a disadvantage because it is unwarranted if true, then we might expect the opposite for Christianity.

I propose that a fairly low probability of a non-deceiving God on grounds other than revelation or inspiration results in a quite high all-things-considered probability. Informally, the reasoning is that this fairly low probability provides some justification for relying upon revelation or inspiration. That provides additional support for the central message of revelation, which in turn provides additional support for the existence of a non-deceiving God, which then increases the probability that revelation or inspiration is warranted, and so on. The probability that is justified by going round the circle repeatedly in this way is that to which these iterations converge. If this probability is high enough, it, in its turn, justifies reliance upon revelation and inspiration. The further task of testing purported inspiration or revelation then depends on several further considerations, including what I called defensive apologetics: the showing of Christian doctrines as not silly. So the bootstrapping itself does not get us all the way to Christianity. But it does get us to a preliminary trust in revelation and inspiration.

Bootstrapping succeeds only given: (1) a high degree of confidence that inspiration or revelation is warranted on the supposition that there is a God conceived of in a certain way, namely as non-deceiving; and (2) a high degree of confidence that such a God exists on the supposition that inspiration or revelation are warranted. But assuming (1) and (2), it follows that belief in such a God is justified given that a fairly low, but not too low, probability arises from a purely metaphysical argument. This shows the importance of metaphysical speculations that give some support to the hypothesis of a non-deceiving God. Because of its apparent circularity, the case for bootstrapping is more persuasive given a formal, probability-theoretic analysis. This I have done elsewhere (Forrest 2006*a*).

DIGRESSION ON DECEPTION

I shall clarify what I mean by deception by using two, rather different, analogies. The first concerns the termination of a human life, where the Catholic tradition makes a distinction between killing, whether active or passive, and not officiously preserving life. There has been a tendency in secular thought on the termination of life to suppose that opponents of euthanasia are making a distinction between active and passive euthanasia, forbidding the former while permitting the latter, including such practices as killing a patient who is able to drink by withholding fluids. But the distinction between active and passive euthanasia is of secondary significance. Likewise when it comes to deception, there is a not very important distinction between actively misleading someone with either a lie ('Impure water does not conduct electricity') or a *suggestio falsi* ('H_2O does not conduct electricity well'), and passively misleading them by not telling them some truth they might reasonably expect to be told (saying, 'I don't know much chemistry' when the child asks, 'Does water conduct electricity?'). But all these cases of deception may in turn be distinguished from merely withholding the information that although pure water does not conduct electricity well, small quantities of dissolved salts ensure that it does; so, for most practical purposes, water is a good conductor, with dangerous consequences.

From examples such as these I draw the conclusion that a non-deceiving God might well allow human beings to reach false conclusions by withholding information, even when they live up to the very highest epistemic standards.

The other analogy is with scientific progress. Having noted the success of science, we might with hindsight see this as part of what God intended. But before that success had been achieved, there was no reason to believe that God wanted us to achieve an understanding of the nature of things. And for God to have just let us speculate in various ways never reaching the truth, would not have been deception, but merely a case of withholding information that we could not have reasonably been expected to be told. Given, however, the apparent success of science over the last few hundred years, it would be mischievous at best for God to have let this apparent progress occur if in fact the truth is totally otherwise. For example, for God to have created the universe a few thousand years ago with the fossil record in place, as Philip Gosse suggested in *Omphalos* (1857), would be indicative of a mischievous sense of humour or downright dishonest. Now God might well have a sense of humour, but to say that God is non-deceiving is to be committed to thinking it probable that the apparent success in science is real.

Applying this to the disturbing history of humanity's attempts to discover and to interact with the divine, I say that a non-deceptive God might well withhold information, and so would not necessarily be committed to revelation, but would not arrange matters so that a record of apparent revelations and apparent religious experiences was quite misleading. For that would be passive deception. There is a proviso, though: namely, that the history of these attempts is not so vice-ridden that God could say that it happened contrary to the divine intentions. But a not implausible way of approaching the history of religion is to see it as to all appearances a story of genuine but uneven progress, just as the history of science is to all appearances a history of genuine but uneven progress. The assumption that God is not deceiving does not by itself make it probable that there should be such a history of apparently progressive search for the divine, but it does make it probable that if there *is* such a history, then the progress is genuine.

SPECULATIVE THEODICY

The bootstrapping argument is based upon the assumption that the reliability of revelation or inspiration is high on the supposition of a non-deceiving God. Now it is widely supposed that God must be morally righteous and so non-deceiving, but what do we mean by moral righteousness? Here we should consider the possibility that there is metaphysical case, of not too low probability, for the existence of a God who is assumed to be only good in a consequentialist fashion. By *consequentialism* I mean any theory according to which one action is morally better than another just in case it has better overall consequences, and that an action is good if performing it is better than not performing it.

Even if a consequentialist God intended the process we call 'revelation', we should not assign a high probability to the reliability of apparent revelation. To be sure, God might be said to suffer on being aware of falsehood, but this divine suffering could easily be compensated for by divine joy in being aware of human beings engaging in a moral struggle and finally achieving, let us hope, a loving society. So it might well be for the overall good that we humans be deceived into thinking that there is a loving God. If bootstrapping is to ground a further inquiry based upon a general trust in revelation and inspiration, it requires, therefore, a metaphysical case for a non-deceiving God, one who is morally righteous in a way which implies that it is unlikely that God would set up a deceptive revelation.

I would like to stress the importance of having a case for a non-deceiving God, and a case that is, moreover, independent of revelation or inspiration or reliance upon the gift of faith. This is important even if we reject the bootstrapping argument. For there cannot be a rational inquiry into the claims of various religious traditions without some assessment of just how likely it is that there is a deceiving God. I say this even though I grant that someone distrustful of metaphysical arguments for and against there being a God might examine various religious traditions, including non-theist ones, and reflect upon religious and similar experiences. Such a metaphysical minimalist might well come to an informed conclusion. But even the minimalist must assign a rather low probability to the hypothesis that God deceives us for consequentialist reasons. The only argument I find at all persuasive for that low probability assignment is that a consequentialist often has good reasons to cease to be a consequentialist, and that God, in particular, has good reasons to become a loving God rather than a consequentialist one. And we may trust a loving God not to deceive us—at least not systematically. But I say that it is at least as probable that God is initially a consequentialist as that God is initially loving. Hence I make a serious plea for the sort of developmental theism that I am proposing, as a way of supporting the disjunction: either there is no God, or there is a God who does not deceive. For it is that disjunction that is the metaphysical minimum for inquiring into religion.

This brings me to the stubborn character of the problem of evil. Now I do not think that the evils around us provide much of a case against a God who is good only in a consequentialist fashion, maximizing the sum total of joy over suffering. One reason for this assessment of mine is that consequentialists are mindful not to omit their own joy and suffering in their calculations. Moreover, they usually grant that higher beings are capable of more joy than lower ones. Hence a consequentialist God would be motivated to sacrifice the joy of creatures for the sake of the divine joy if there is a clash, while being enormously generous to creatures if there is no clash. Now the divine joy in creating has, I shall argue, an aesthetic component. This implies that God will tend to create the most beautiful universe, not the one most congenial to creatures—what a bastard the God of the philosophers is! This unpalatable conclusion shows merely, I think, that this was not what the objector had in mind, which was a case against a loving God. And as I have already noted, relying upon revelation to show that God is not a consequentialist runs counter to the plausible enough suggestion that a false belief in a loving God might be just the sort of thing a consequentialist would promote, even if that consequentialist were God. And as I said above, this consideration jeopardizes the whole project of taking revelation and inspiration as genuine sources of religious knowledge, and accordingly seeking which, if any, is the correct revelation.

There is an extensive discussion in the literature of Stephen Wykstra's Noseum Defence, based upon the hypothesis that we should not expect to know, in this life, the divine purposes for which the evils are permitted (Wykstra 1984). That may well be so, especially when we get to details such as the point of the remaining half a billion or so years in which the Earth will probably remain suitable for life. But the Noseum Defence presupposes the consequentialist character of the divine goodness. For, not surprisingly, we judge whether God is loving in an intuitive and emotional fashion, and the intuitive emotional response is that a loving God would intervene and not sacrifice innocent individuals to some great unknown purpose, even if that has the best overall consequences.

The problem of evil is therefore a threat to any version of theism that asserts that the Creator loved what was to be created. Having created, God is, I submit, constrained by the laws of nature that were set in place. So, even though God subsequently loves what has been created, the scope for divine intervention is somewhat limited. My preferred theodicy is based upon the speculation that in the beginning God was not loving. An alternative is based upon the thesis that even a God with a loving disposition could not love what did not yet exist. Hence the thesis that God did not love what was to be created, but came to love it, does not require the sort of divine development that I am proposing. But the further thesis that God set up a universe with laws that largely prohibit further divine intervention is a genuinely kenotic thesis, one of God abandoning power for a good reason. It is precisely this piece of kenotic theodicy that, I say, enables us to reconcile the evils around us with the existence of a loving God.

In this regard I should respond to Plantinga's theodicy/defence distinction concerning the argument from evil. By a theodicy he means an account put forward as the correct explanation of why God permits, risks, or even brings about various evils. By a defence he means a hypothesis that shows that it is perfectly consistent with all we know, including the variety and abundance of evils, that God has permitted, risked, or brought about the world with these evils. There are, I submit, two ways in which a defence might fail to amount to a theodicy. The first is that we might have found an explanation of evil but have no reason to think that we have found the best explanation. The second is that even if the proposed defence was in fact the best explanation, it might be rather implausible. Consider, for example, the Free Will Defence: namely, that there are some very great goods for creatures that require that they not merely have acted freely but were free to act in ways that are wrong. In Plantinga's development of the Free Will Defence, the creatures with freedom include not only us, but also Satan. Let us suppose that there are no difficulties with the Free Will Defence except, perhaps, that it requires Satan as the source of natural evil. Then those who, like Plantinga and I, find the Satan hypothesis plausible would be able to say that this might be the correct theodicy. But even if it were the best available theodicy, how would we know that it was correct, since we have not a complete list of possible theodicies? For there may well be another, better one that no human being knows of. In that case the defence would be what I call a *speculative theodicy*. On the other hand, if, like many of our contemporaries, we judge the whole idea of Satan to be outmoded, then we will have to say that even if the Free Will Defence is the best explanation of various evils, it is just not good enough. In that case the Free Will Defence would be merely a device to establish consistency, and hence not a genuine objection to the probabilistic or, as it often called, evidential argument from evil (Howard-Snyder 1996).

One of my chief aims is to offer a speculative theodicy that explains the coexistence of a loving God with the many and varied evils around us. Its key feature is the dilemma that prior to creation God did not love what was to be created, and that when subsequently loving what had been created, God was constrained by the laws of nature. My preferred way of supporting this hypothesis is by means of an argument that a consequentialist God would choose to change into a loving one. So a co-rollary is that the reliability of revelation or inspiration is not threatened by the way in which a purely consequentialist God might deceive us. For even if God were once a consequentialist, God is not like that any more.

ARGUMENT-GENERATED COMPREHENSION

Consider John Henry Newman's distinction between a real and a notional assent (Newman 1870). As I understand it, the former is required for knowledge *of* something, while the latter might be a component of knowledge *that* something is the case. While this is an important difference, something like the real versus notional distinction can be made elsewhere, with real assent being emotionally rich, while notional assent is free of emotion. Those not in the tertiary education industry would call the notional *academic*. A diligent but uninterested mathematics student, for example, has many such notional beliefs. Thus the student might know perfectly well what it means to say that the square root of 2 is irrational and be able both to follow and to reproduce the proof, without it having the emotional impact that it might have on another student who was either better taught or just had a natural interest in mathematics, and who got excited and wanted to tell others. Newman rightly complains that traditional apologetics results in a merely notional assent. The same goes for much preaching, however eloquent. We are told, for instance, that Jonathan Edwards was astounded at how little impact his preaching about damnation had. It was not that his audience was full of Promethean defiance, but they granted the threat of Hell without mending their ways. I take it that those of the faithful who think philosophical speculation frivolous or even dangerous will nonetheless grant that a merely notional assent to a religious doctrine is second-rate.

What, then, is the diagnosis of a merely notional assent? In some cases it might be due to some mental disorder, such as depression, or due to an excessively busy life. In others, though, it is like the student who is curiously unmoved by the Greek discovery that 2 had no rational square root. In that case students may be helped to recapitulate the Greek experience by being asked to find the square root of 2 at a stage when they are innocent of irrational numbers. In the case of the Incarnation, the way to bring the dogmas to life is to play with philosophical ideas as to how to capture the early Church's tradition that Jesus was truly human but in some manner divine. Generally, I submit, too serious an attitude to religious teaching is the enemy of real assent—all prayer and no play makes Jack a dull believer.

DIALECTICS

It's fun playing with ideas, but this game serves a further purpose. For working through a speculation in some detail, and with as much clarity as you are able, can result in insights that would not otherwise occur. Thus the exercise of arguing against my position might help others clarify their own. In this connection I would like to make a plea for dialectics. It often happens that the case for and the case against a given position, although neither is conclusive, would both be strong enough to secure conviction if we ignored the rebuttal provided by the opposing case. If we adopt a static model of rationality, then the correct response is to compare the two cases and either suspend judgement or decide that one case is good enough to outweigh the other. But a faith that the real is rational (not that the real is the rational as Hegel had it) prompts me to seek a further position, the synthesis, which is supported by the positive arguments of both sides in the debate, but not subject to the criticisms.

In their different ways the scholastics and Hegel (or his Marxist heirs) have brought dialectics into disrepute among English-speaking philosophers. Nonetheless, dialectics is one way of making progress in philosophy, and I am guided by the need, as I see it, to complete a dialectic in which theism is the thesis and naturalism the antithesis, and also to complete a dialectic in which classical theism is the thesis and the idea of God-in-time the antithesis. Of these two dialectics *God without the Supernatural* (Forrest 1996*a*) was my attempt at the first synthesis. Kenotic theism is, among other things, an attempt at the second synthesis. Such dialectics are I submit, part of an ongoing historical process by which we hopefully will come to the truth.

PROVIDENTIAL AGNOSTICISM

Bootstrapping is an argument for a high probability of theism, all things considered, based upon metaphysical arguments that in them-selves would be judged as only fairly probable. Likewise a not-too-low probability of there being a God combined with a significantly lower probability that God would deceive provides the basis for the empirical confirmation of theism by means of an examination of religious traditions and religious experience. My overall judgement is that this results in a very high probability for theism and a fairly high probability for Christianity, indeed for generic Catholicism. But others might disagree and say that, all things considered, this leads to agnosticism. Well, so be it. If metaphysical speculation at the end of the day makes the difference between atheism and agnosticism, it has not been idle.

There is, however, a counter-move to this claim that metaphysical speculation would at least support agnosticism. It is the Argument from Divine Hiddenness expounded by John Schellenberg (1993), which relies on the premiss that a loving God would want us all to be theists, and that therefore the existence of rational and sincere non-theists is itself reason to believe that there is no such God. The force of this argument depends on whether the rational, sincere non-theist is the victim of circumstances that prevent reliable belief formation on the topic of theism, or whether the case for theism is itself inconclusive. In the former situation, which is the one I hold to be correct, agnosticism is not ideally rational, and my reply to Schellenberg is that the divine power to intervene is now limited in various ways, and that when it was not limited, God was not loving but good in a consequentialist manner only.

I am now, however, supposing the latter situation, in which I am suggesting that philosophical speculation might make the difference between being an atheist and being an agnostic. In that case the rational, sincere non-theist is not the victim of circumstances beyond God's control, but is making the correct assessment of the evidence, evidence that is itself the consequence of creation if there is a God. That is a more serious version of the argument. One response to Schellenberg is that God operates on a different time-scale from humans, and so is not impatient for the time when we can be together. Hence divine hiddenness affects the case for theism only as one source of suffering, being thus absorbed into the argument from evil. Moreover, my fall-back position is not mere agnosticism, but providential agnosticism. This states that a firm conviction of the truth of one of the major theistic religions is a moral hazard, and so, although God values our having true beliefs, it is on balance better if the evidence is inconclusive, which is therefore part of the initial divine plan. I anticipate the objection that, if correct, this would show that a providential God should have seen to it that we were all atheists, on the grounds that the best way to become fit for Heaven is to love others and do good with no hope whatever of a heavenly reward.

I assume, however, that God is reluctant to deceive, and so agnosticism is far more likely to be part of the divine plan than atheism.

The importance of providential agnosticism as a fall-back position precludes any joining together of agnosticism with atheism as non-theism, as if there were no important difference between the two. Providential agnosticism can form the basis of religious attitudes such as hope, as well as making prayer reasonable. An agnostic may even be a Christian in the sense of accepting the Christian teaching within the scope of the supposition that there is a God. Because even an inconclusive speculative case for a loving God is sufficient for providential agnosticism, such speculation is far from idle.

1

Overview

I shall be discussing the way in which God develops from Pure Will to Unbounded Love. Let me emphasize at the outset that this book is not about changing conceptions of God. It is about a God who changes.

1. THE NEW ORTHODOXY OF A CHANGING GOD

The orthodoxy used to be that God was unchanging, as in the words of Walter Smith's hymn: 'We blossom and flourish as leaves on the tree/And wither and perish but naught changeth Thee.' In recent times there have been several influential challenges to this traditional conception of God. I have in mind books such as *The Openness of God* anthology (Pinnock 1994) and *The God who Risks* by John Sanders (1998). Even among religiously conservative Christians, rather few defend the classical conception of God as necessary, necessarily simple, and necessarily eternal. Of course, all theists believe that God is everlasting, and most that God is *necessarily* everlasting, but to call God eternal is usually a way of saying that God is everlasting and undergoes no intrinsic change, but merely has changing relations with creation. Or it might mean that God is everlasting, but that there are no episodes or stages in the divine life that are before or after any events in the history of our universe. In either case, being eternal is inconsistent with being atemporal—that is, totally timeless.

No doubt there are other senses of 'eternal'. One that comes to mind is that for God past, present, and future are all part of the specious present: namely, that of which there is immediate awareness. In the human case the specious present lasts less than a second, so this would be quite a striking difference between the human and the divine. It is nonetheless compatible with a changing God, because the awareness of the future might well be an awareness only of future possibilities. And there is no reason for me to reject divine eternity provided that means only that God is everlasting and that the whole past as well as all future possibilities are included in what God is directly aware of.

There are religious reasons for this abandonment of the doctrine of divine eternity, and not only of the more extreme thesis of divine atemporality. For neither an atemporal nor an eternal being can be hurt or given joy by us or by any other creatures in our universe. Hence such a God cannot look down on the sufferings of the afflicted and suffer because they suffer. Such a God cannot see that what was created was good and rejoice, in that order, and cannot come to see that it has been corrupted and, as a consequence, save us, in that order. Nor can such a God respond to our prayers. This is all rather like an answering service, not like real religion!

Readers might wonder how I can complain like this on behalf of real religion while insisting that God cannot break the laws of nature. My answer is that I attach enormous significance to divine intervention, which I take to be constrained but not prevented by the laws of nature.

Classical theists used to hold the doctrine of divine impassibility: namely, that God cannot be affected by what creatures do or do not do. Maybe it is divine impassibility rather than eternity that is incompatible with contemporary religious sensibility. It might be suggested, then, that an eternal God could have a sequence of states, some temporally prior to others, but with none of them temporally comparable to ours. Or, even if God is atemporal, there could be a sequence of states some *logically prior* to others, where I take it that a state X is logically prior to state Y if Y or some feature of Y can be explained in terms of X, but not vice versa. In either case we could say that God's compassionate suffering is explained by the divine knowledge of creatures' suffering, and so God responds to their suffering. Likewise, God answers prayers in the sense that God's decision as to how the future unfolds, including the sense of being spoken to by God, is in part explained by the divine knowledge of creatures, including their prayers (Forrest 1998*a*).

Nonetheless, divine atemporality or eternity, even when combined with the rejection of divine passivity, has awkward consequences for human–divine relations. For if God suffers with our suffering and rejoices with our subsequent joy, we pass from suffering to joy, but God has the joy and suffering simultaneously, and so the former cancels out the latter, or vice versa. This inevitably devalues the sense of God sharing both our joys and our suffering. Of course, if that is a consequence of the divine nature, we can hardly complain that it fails to correspond to contemporary religious sensibility. All the same, to the extent that

16 *Overview*

this contemporary religious sensibility itself reflects the scriptural world-view, we should be reluctant to defend divine eternity on the grounds of tradition.

More pressing, perhaps, is the well-known philosophical problem concerning creaturely freedom. First, suppose that God knows, by observation rather than prediction, what happens as a result of creatures' choices. Could God both create and observe creation in the one eternal state? It seems not. For there is a causal or explanatory ordering of various states of affairs. God observes that, say, humans achieve perpetual peace in the year 2076. This is partially caused by human acts occurring in the twenty-first century, which in turn are partially caused by God's creative act. Next let us suppose, although this is controversial, that the difference between past and future is that on the whole causes are earlier than effects. In that case I draw the conclusion that wherever there is an overall causal ordering to events, there is thereby a temporal ordering. Hence God's creative act must be before creation, even if the universe is infinitely old, and God's observation of creatures' acts must be after their action. Therefore God is not eternal, and occupies at least two moments in Time comparable to ours—for instance, an alpha moment of Time prior to the universe and an omega moment after its end. It remains to be seen whether God occupies any moments of human history. If not, we could say that God was, God will be, but God is not, which no doubt bears on the Problem of Evil. But even that minimalist alpha/omega thesis is inconsistent with divine eternity, which requires us to deny the supposition that God knows creatures' acts in a way akin to observation.

There are three responses to this. One is to grant that God does not observe creatures' acts, but rather predicts them with certainty.[1] Another is the Thomist response that God knows creatures' acts by causing them, so they lack freedom in the libertarian sense. The third is by advocates of middle knowledge, who submit that God knows what creatures would freely do prior to creation. All three responses imply that God has some infallible belief as to what creatures will choose, which infallible belief can be said to coexist with the divine intention to create, either in the same timeless state or else prior in divine time to that

---

[1] Cf. 'On Ockham's Way Out' (Plantinga 1986). This is the position that divine knowledge about creatures' acts is not strictly speaking something occurring before the acts. I take this to imply that although the divine state of mind is unchanged, before creatures act, it is a warranted 100 per cent certain prediction, but not knowledge.

intention. This runs counter to the libertarian claim that at least some creatures some of the time (namely, we humans in this life) are free to do what is morally wrong or not to do it, and blameworthy if we do it. To be sure, much freedom is compatible with there being only one course of action that a reasonable agent would do, and so quite predictable assuming we know the agent is reasonable. But the libertarian position is that cases of blameworthy action are only of this kind if the agent already has a moral character as a result of earlier moral choices. Often our responsibility for our choices is obscured by the gradual decay of our moral character through many marginally blameworthy as well as blame-free wrong acts. Nonetheless, it is not fair for God to blame someone for acts the occurrence of which are believed by God in an infallible fashion, unless God's belief is dependent on the outcomes of at least some moral choices by that agent.

I assumed above a causal theory of temporal ordering. Instead, we may systematically talk of what is *causally prior* or *causally posterior* instead of what is before and after, and reach the conclusion that eternity would have to comprise at least two distinct states—one causally prior to and one causally posterior to the universe. In that case I wonder why we do not call them moments of Time. To do so does not require that we assign a duration lapsed between the divine state prior to creation and the beginning of the universe. For I take Time to be necessarily ordered by the before/after relation but not necessarily measurable using duration. If readers wish, they could say not that God is in our time, but that God is quasi-temporal, meaning that we may extend the temporal before/after relation to include cause/effect relations in so far as that is compatible. Instead, I shall stipulate that our concept of time is thus extended.

There is a further problem. Many philosophers hold that the present is ontologically privileged, either as the boundary between the real past and the not-yet-real future (Tooley 1997) or, according to presentists, as the only reality (Bigelow 1996; Zimmerman 1996; Craig 2000). In that case eternity, because it is real, has to be a *nunc stans* in the sense of being that which is shared by all the consecutive presents. As a consequence, *co-presence* is a symmetric relation but not transitive, and so is not, strictly speaking, the same as simultaneity.[2] Now there

---

[2] Eleonore Stump and Norman Kretzmann (1981) take ET simultaneity to hold between eternity and the present. So ET simultaneity entails co-presence, but not strict simultaneity, as I understand it.

is, as far as I can see, no contradiction between denying the reality of the future and holding that God is eternal.[3] Nonetheless, if the future is not real, then God cannot know what is in our future in a way akin to observation, because God cannot know what is not real—there is nothing to know (Geach 1977).

If God is unchanging, it would then seem to follow that God never knows what creatures freely choose to do in cases where there is a genuine libertarian moral choice. I suppose that Aristotle would have been happy enough with the conclusion that God is ignorant of such contingencies, but it is clearly a greater departure from the tradition of the Abrahamic religions than abandoning divine eternity. Defenders of divine eternity could respond that knowledge is a relation, and so an eternal God could have changing knowledge without any intrinsic change. The obvious rejoinder is that knowledge is not just a relation, but involves some kind of mental state, either a belief or a phenomenal state (a way things appear). This mental state would change with the changing objects of divine knowledge.

Even if divine knowledge were granted to be unlike human knowledge in lacking either a belief component or a phenomenal state, there is a further problem with the claim that divine knowledge is purely relational. For to call a divine relation with creation one of *knowledge* requires either that the relation be similar in nature to that of human knowledge or that it plays a similar causal role. Similarity in nature requires there to be an intrinsic component, as just discussed. But Thomists might respond that we say God knows creatures because this relation has similar effects to human knowledge. Now there seem to be four causal roles that human knowledge plays directly: to generate joy or suffering in the contemplation of what is known; to make further inferences; to motivate one's own action; and to communicate—that is, to inform others. Unless to acquire knowledge is to undergo an intrinsic change, the only causal role that divine knowledge could play is one of communication.

Suppose, then, that God knows that Herod has died and informs Joseph of this fact in a dream, as in Matthew 2. If this piece of divine

---

[3] As time passes, an eternal God comes to be co-present with more and more. Therefore, if we take it that we can refer to God at one time, we are referring to something else at a different time. Indeed, the God successfully referred to by Abraham may now be said never to have existed. This sounds alarming, but it is nothing more than a *Cambridge change*.

knowledge motivated the act of informing Joseph, then this is a motive that God could acquire only after Herod's death, assuming that Herod's way of life influenced the time of his death in one way or another, and assuming that the future is not yet real. Perhaps God had intended that whenever Herod dies, Joseph gets the dream. That makes sense even if God is unchanging, but in that case the knowledge of Herod's death does not cause the informing of Joseph. Instead, the death itself does, bypassing the knowledge. To make the knowledge the cause, we have to say that God has intended that whenever God comes to know of Herod's death, Joseph gets the dream. In that case if, *per impossibile*, it took time for God to get to know of Herod's death, then the dream would have to wait. Hence we would draw the conclusion that a certain kind of relation between God and creation deserves to be called knowledge because God has decided that others will, on occasion, be shown the truth, precisely because God stands in that relation to some event, whereas if God had decided that that others will, on occasion, be shown the truth, regardless of the relation, then that relation would not count as knowledge. Assuming that God knows that the truth and the divine knowledge of the truth are necessarily coextensive, it is hard to see how God could decide that the latter rather than the former cause the communication. Moreover, in saying that the relation may be called knowledge because it performs the right sort of causal role, we would be supposing that it performs this role as a result of the nature of the relation, perhaps unknown to us, not as a result of God's decision that it is this relation rather than the events themselves that cause the communication.

Complaints that my discussion of this issue is convoluted should be directed to those who suggest that divine knowledge is a relation without any correlated divine property. None of these complications occurs if we grant that divine knowledge requires an intrinsic divine mental state.

I conclude that either of two positions regarding time should motivate the theist to abandon divine eternity. One is the position that temporal ordering is just the overall causal ordering, so it is necessary that, for the most part, causes are no later than effects. The other is that the future is not real. If we abandon the thesis that there can be an eternal cause of that which is temporal, then these two positions are not independent, since if the future is unreal, there can be no backwards causation at all. But in the case being considered, they are alternative ways of arguing against divine eternity.

2. THE INTELLECTUAL APPEAL OF CLASSICAL THEISM

Is classical theism just a big mistake, then, a Greek eccentricity that we regret adopting—like the Olympic Games maybe? No, there are good reasons for believing in something like the classical position. For this is the God of the philosophers. I am going to assert something stronger, offensive even. No rational, well-informed person, I submit, should dismiss classical theism as completely erroneous. This is not a problem for agnostics, but it is a problem for atheists, and not merely for atheists, but also for those theists confident in their dismissal of classical theism. The position I am advocating allows that there is an important kernel of truth in classical theism.

What, then, are these reasons for classical theism? Precisely the awe-inspiring simplicity of the idea of unrestricted consciousness or Pure Will or, if we can make sense of this, a being whose essence is its existence—*subsistent existence* (Miller 2001). We may appeal to Occam's razor. Or if that is too swift, let us say that the goal of understanding might not be to understand everything, but it must be to seek a simple, unexplained explanation. Naturalists might hope to find this in some elegant simple laws of nature. But no one should *dismiss* the idea that there is something about us human beings, something in the general area of agency and consciousness, that defies understanding in physical terms, and which therefore establishes a precedent for a simple, fundamental, theocentric understanding of things. But this powerful idea is rendered quite useless if our theistic hypothesis gets too complicated. Likewise, the naturalists' goal of understanding fails if the fundamental laws are too complicated. In both cases we have to keep it simple. That is putting the point in terms of the goal of understanding. An alternative is to rely upon the principle that the simpler is significantly more probable than the more complicated. This principle is justified as implicit in our confidence in well-confirmed scientific theories. Hence, the God of the philosophers has much greater prior probability than the God of Abraham, Isaac, and Jacob.

For what it is worth, reports of mystical experiences seem to support something more like the God of the philosophers, but more ordinary sorts of religious experience confirm the God of Abraham, Isaac, and Jacob, the personal God with whom one can converse.

We have a problem, then. Religious tradition, individual religious sensibility, and the problem of reconciling eternal knowledge of creatures' acts with their freedom are serious considerations; but simplicity is, if anything, even more significant. Fortunately, there is a way out. If you like dialectics, think of classical theism as the thesis, and the God-in-Time of contemporary religion as the antithesis. Then we look for a synthesis. The result is not classical theism, but it is in many ways *like* classical theism, and it is like classical theism in just those respects in which that position is intellectually attractive. I shall refer to it, for reasons of pomposity, as the neoclassical theory of the Primordial God.

3. DEVELOPMENTAL THEISM

The synthesis is quite close to the process philosophy of Alfred North Whitehead, Charles Hartshorne, and, most recently, David Griffin (Griffin 2001). It might even cohere with the teachings of the Latter-day Saints. It is based upon the thesis that God is not merely in Time, but changes. Now the idea of a changing God could be restricted to God's changing knowledge and to God performing more than one act. But once we accept that God can change, we should take seriously the idea of a divine development, as in both Hegelian and process philosophy. Instead of thinking of the divine development as a Hegelian development towards something not unlike the God of classical theism, however, I take the neoclassical God as the starting-point. Only in that way do we retain the intellectual advantages of classical theism. For we understand by positing simple causes, not by positing simple effects. I shall argue that various stages in this divine development require a lessening of divine power, so this is a kenotic developmental theism.

Process philosophers obscure the issue by talking of *dipolarity*, the thesis that apparent opposites are often to be treated as differing aspects of the one thing. Thus their panpsychism treats all things as both parts of the causal network and as acting for ends, and the dipolarity of God amounts to saying that God has two aspects, one a temporal awareness of things and the other a timeless awareness. The problem, however, with any double aspect or dipolar theory is just how you combine the aspects or poles. This is a more general problem for anyone who, nodding sagely, says that there is some truth in both sides of an argument. Now there may be cases where we can do no more than nod, sagely or wearily as the case may be. Perhaps the physical and mental aspects of human beings provide an example. But in the case of God, there is no need for further mystery, and dipolarity is unnecessary. Take the Primordial God as the initial divine state, and note that this God could have been eternal had it not chosen to create a universe; but by choosing to create, it thereby becomes temporal, because the divine act of creation is then prior to the universe.

The Primordial God is not, then, eternal, but could have been so. This conception of the Primordial God has, I shall argue, all the appeal of classical theism. The resulting *developmental theism*, as I call it, provides the desired synthesis between an eternal and a changing God, between the God of the philosophers and the God of Abraham, Isaac, and Jacob.

Those who are alarmed at the mention of Hegel the Horrible will probably not be reassured by my enthusiasm for Whitehead, or even by my acknowledging a Spinozistic influence. But, for the record, much of what I say could have been derived from Baruch Spinoza if he had renounced determinism.

4. GOD, MATERIALISM, AND NECESSITY

Theism requires, I concede, that we do not find the case for reductive materialism persuasive. For the great intellectual advantage of theism lies in the explanation of the detailed structure of the physical universe as being the result of God's creative act. Hence theism requires consciousness and agency to exist prior to any actual complex physical structures such as, according to reductive materialism, explain consciousness and agency.

A first step towards rejecting reductive materialism is the admission that it is conceivable that some of us are *zombies*, that is, not really conscious, but only behaving as if we are.[4] It is also conceivable that some of us are what I call *wobblios*, that is, not genuine agents—the apparently free actions of wobblios are just random behaviour. If zombies and wobblios are not merely conceivable, but possible in the sense of compatible with the natural order, then either it is just a mystery who is a zombie, who is a wobblio, and who is a genuine person, with no assurance that even our nearest and dearest are genuine persons, or we

---

[4] *Positively* conceivable in David Chalmers' sense (Chalmers 1996).

suppose that God miraculously ensures that all of us are genuine. Or if we believe that God has middle knowledge—that is, knows what creatures will freely do before they are created—we could adopt the optimistic theory that God ensures that precisely those humans are genuine persons who will not freely choose to reject God for ever. Now mysteries should not be multiplied, and obviously those in need of persuasion of the truth of theism will not appeal to divine providence. So, at least for apologetic purposes, we do well to suppose that zombies and wobblios, although conceivable, are impossible. Is this impossibility a law of nature, due, theists say, to God's creative act, and perhaps one that God might miraculously break? Or is it the consequence of metaphysical necessity, by which I mean the sort of necessity which precedes creation and constrains even God, assuming there is a God? I take the latter to characterize moderate materialism, which is thus the hypothesis that the characteristically mental is correlated with the physical of metaphysical necessity.

One of my themes is that this sort of non-reductive or, as I call it, 'moderate' materialism is a help, not a hindrance, to philosophical theology. It has several advantages over dualism. The first is methodological: materialism, by restricting the range of possibilities, puts constraints on how we think of God and thus provides some discipline to speculations about the divine nature. I hope that this book illustrates this methodological advantage, which is not, of course, a reason for believing in materialism, so much as a reason for not fearing it.

The second advantage is that, by distinguishing possibility from conceivability, moderate materialism helps defend the thesis of divine non-contingency, which likewise distinguishes the genuine conceivability of there being no God from the spurious possibility. Putting the point the other way round: the chief case for dualism is the insistence that anything conceivable expresses a possibility, which is not compatible with the thesis of divine non-contingency.[5]

The third advantage is that the alternative is to posit psycho-physical laws connecting the physical state to the mental. We require these even if we think that it takes a special miraculous act to prevent a foetus from becoming a zombie or a wobblio. For otherwise we would have to assume *occasionalism*, the thesis that God directly causes the mental

---

[5] For a proposition to *express* a possibility is not the same as its being possibly true. The former takes the proposition to be expressed in the possible world in question, the latter takes the proposition to be expressed in the actual world.

states of individuals so as to correspond to the physical states. Few need an argument to judge this absurd; but if an argument is required, it suffices to note that it makes God, not us, the author of all wrong acts. Hence it both trivializes our moral life and renders the argument from evil almost conclusive. So even if it were neither nomologically nor metaphysically necessary that consciousness arises wherever the physical conditions are appropriate, anyone who rejects materialism must posit laws correlating anything mental that there might be with the physical. Now to posit laws that are themselves neither metaphysically necessary nor brought about by God is an arbitrary limitation on God's power, and as such makes theism less plausible. In addition such a denial is not acceptable to the theist who relies in part on the surprisingly, life-friendly character of the laws to argue for theism (perhaps also relying upon a subsequent bootstrapping). This then puts the theist who is not a reductive materialist but who relies on the life-friendly character of the laws in the position of denying that the laws governing the correlation of the mental and the physical hold for God, at least for the way God was before the laws were brought into being. Such a theist cannot then appeal to the analogy between human power to act and the divine power, because the former would, we are supposing, depend on divinely ordained laws. That we humans have the power to act is a mystery that we might well be prepared to accept without any further explanation; but if there is no analogy between divine and human power, then the divine power is a further mystery, and mysteries should not be multiplied. Hence theism would be vulnerable to John Mackie's (1982) critique, and we would have to abandon Richard Swinburne's project of treating agency causation as an ultimate way of explaining things, or else make that project implausible by taking the causation in question as unlike familiar agency causation.

In short, the third advantage is that non-reductive materialism enables us to provide ultimate agency-causation explanations, as Swinburne urges, without an unmotivated limitation on the power God had over that which is metaphysically contingent.

The fourth advantage is that moderate materialism implies something close enough to pantheism to help us understand how it is possible that human beings can come to know God, either in this life or the next.[6] We know other humans not *by* but *in* knowing their bodies and

---

[6] Close enough, because I think of human beings, and comparable extraterrestrials, as islands in the divine ocean, or as holes in God.

their deeds. Likewise, we can know God *in* knowing of creation and God's deeds. Just as we see happiness in the smile of a happy person, so we see God's glory in, rather than inferring it from, the wonders of creation. Traditionally, this has been thought to be analogical knowledge (knowing the cause by knowing the effects), but if moderate materialism is correct, then the connection between God and (most of) creation is too close to be causal, and is the same as the relation between a body and a person—namely, the relation between a thing abstracted from some of its most important properties and the thing in question. To be sure, this way of explaining how humans can know God is available to anyone who holds that God is a world-soul, or accepts panentheism, or even who emphasizes the immanence of God; but the advantage of moderate materialism is that it explains this immanence rather than either merely asserting it or watering it down, as in the analogical theory of knowledge of the divine.

An additional advantage of moderate materialism is that it may be used to explain why mystical experiences often seem to be of the God of classical theism. My, admittedly deflationary, explanation is that mystics have extraordinary experiences generated by their ordinary knowledge of God. Because God is known in creation, this knowledge is of the Creator, not of God subsequent to creation, who may be known in other ways, notably by revelation.

I have rejected reductive materialism. Should I also reject the thesis that the mental depends ontologically on the physical, much as surfaces, if there are such things, depend on the objects whose surfaces they are, so that we may say that objects are more fundamental than surfaces? Ontological dependence here means more than a necessary correlation. For the latter could be symmetric, but the former cannot be. The advantages of materialism for philosophical theology are compatible with, but do not require, the thesis that the mental depends ontologically on the physical. So I stipulate that what I mean by moderate materialism does not imply such ontological dependence, and is even compatible with the idealist thesis that the physical ultimately depends on the mental.

I have not explained what I mean by the physical. As Howard Robinson has pointed out to me, it would not affect my philosophical theology if I stipulated that anything with complex contingent structure counts as physical. I prefer, however, to think of the physical in narrower terms as anything describable in the vocabulary needed to describe inanimate things.

5. A SPECULATIVE HISTORY OF THE DIVINE DEVELOPMENT

Here is a brief history of God. There is a first moment of Time, at which God exists but nothing else, except any abstract entities such as universals, which necessarily exist. God has the power never to act. If God had never acted, that one moment would have been, as it were, the whole of Time. In that case, strictly speaking, there would have been no Time. For Time, I take it, is characterized by the before/after relation between its parts. As it is, there is a succession of other moments. Brian Leftow has pointed out that if you are the only person at the counter, you are not a queue, and that Time is like a queue in that respect. But as soon as someone else comes along, there is a queue, and you are at the head of it (Leftow 2002). Likewise, if there are no other moments because God chooses to do nothing, then that moment is timeless. Yet if God acts, there is then at least one other moment, and so there is Time. If God chooses to create this universe, then the creative act is before now, and so God is not eternal. In this respect my position is like that of William Craig (1979), who argues that without creation God would be timeless, but with creation God is in time.

What about the necessary existence of God? I have already suggested that what is metaphysically necessary is God's initial existence. I see no reason to hold that God necessarily continues to exist. That is, I hold God had the power to bring a universe into being and then cease to exist, while the universe went on. I do not believe that God has exercised that power, and if you hold that God never had it, so be it. It is not very important. Likewise, I hold that in the initial moment God was a *simple* being, in a sense I shall discuss.

Many classical theists are Christians, so they have the problem of how to reconcile divine simplicity with the doctrine of the Trinity. The problem is that if we grant that the Trinity has a relational structure, then the idea of simplicity seems to get watered down. The solution I favour is developmental. We obtain the intellectual advantages of simplicity by supposing that God was initially simple, but then became more complicated. In outline, then, I am following Swinburne (1994), who starts with the hypothesis of God who is the First Divine Person, and then suggests that the First Person generates the Second, and so on. I retain the idea of a necessarily simple God at the beginning, but, unlike Swinburne, I do not think of the Primordial God as the First Person. This God is, I shall argue, not a personal God at all. It is a self, not a person, rather like the Advaitin *nirguna* Brahman (Brahman without attributes) described as *sat-cit-ananda* (being-consciousness-bliss). I would call it agency-consciousness-bliss, but there is still a parallel. Personhood requires more than agency, consciousness, and bliss. For a divine agent could survey possible acts with the existence of many agents (some divine, others not) as the outcome, without having any sense of some of them but not others being the same as itself. Following Lynne Rudder Baker (2000), I say that being a person requires the *first-person perspective*, the distinction between self and other, both now and into the future. The Primordial God is, I shall thus argue, an it rather than a he or a she.

How, then, does the Trinity come about? First I should say that I am not committed to a Trinity, provided that God is more than one Person. Thomas Aquinas asks, rightly, why there might not be infinitely many Divine Persons. His answer uncharacteristically supposes that we know rather more about God than I would claim to. As I understand him, it is that once we have listed knowledge and love, we have run out of divine relations.[7] There is an argument here, but it is far from conclusive. So someone might speculate that there are more than three Divine Persons—maybe infinitely many—but that these extra Persons have not been revealed to us. Or, more radically, someone might insist that the Holy Spirit is the same Divine Person as the Christ. I can accommodate what I say to either of those speculations, but I shall proceed in an orthodox fashion, supposing that there are three Divine Persons. The impersonal God, precisely because it is not a person, has no difficulty in becoming many Persons. It undergoes fission. Alternatively, prior to becoming a community of Persons, it was not even the sort of thing to be one or many (Forrest 1998*c*). For perhaps we should say that there was divine consciousness rather than that there was one conscious being. But for the sake of exposition, I talk in terms of the fission of one being into three.

Now because personhood is conceptually tied to awareness of the possibility of having a future as the same person, I would say that for

[7] Aquinas states that there are four relations if we ignore identity and similarity. His count of four is based upon distinguishing each relation from its converse, so obtaining *paternity, filiation, spiration,* and *procession*. But putting it the way in which contemporary philosophers would, he is asserting that there are only two real relations. See *Summa Theologica*, Part I, questions 27, 28.

a person to undergo fission is for him or her to be annihilated; but an impersonal conscious agent, although aware of the possibility of the future, is not annihilated by fission. For the future is known impersonally as the possibility that such-and-such might happen to someone, not from the first-person perspective as the possibility that such-and-such might happen to me. I submit, therefore, that the impersonal Primordial God can decide to become one or more Persons without annihilation, and in fact chose to be three. Thereafter, altering the number of Divine Persons would require some to be annihilated, which we may safely assume does not occur.

At this stage, my account of the development of God becomes kenotic. There is a distinction between fighting with one hand *held* behind your back and fighting with one hand *tied* behind your back. I shall argue that God created the universe in such a way as to restrict, but not eliminate, the divine power. For I hold that God brought about *iron* laws (Armstrong 1983: 147), rather than *nihil obstat* ones. Iron laws have no exceptions, and constrain even God. I hold that God brought these about so as to give full responsibility to creatures. Otherwise, every act of ours would come about God willing. That God is thus bound by the natural order is, I say, the key to theodicy.

More tentative is the speculation that creating non-divine persons requires not merely a self-sustaining universe, but a temporary contraction of divine consciousness. This I call the Swiss Cheese Theory of persons. If there were no non-divine persons, then panentheism, such as I have previously advocated, would be correct (Forrest 1996*a*). God would be immanent in all things. We are, however, the holes or the bubbles of the non-divine.[8] The price we pay for full personhood is alienation from God, the potential for evil. If you like to put it this way, the evolution of full personhood was the loss of innocence we call the Fall. The price God pays for creating us is not merely an abdication of power, but the abdication of divine presence.

My kenotic theism is inspired by Gottfried Thomasius and Charles Gore, although my position is closer to that of the former (Welch 1965; Gore 1922). I am referring to their different developments of St Paul's hint concerning the kenotic account of the Incarnation. The Second Person of the Trinity did not cease to be God, but rather ceased to have, for a while, divine power and knowledge. I endorse this idea of kenosis,

---

[8] But the holes are not empty; we have consciousness and agency. The metaphor of the hole concerns selfhood, individuality. Cf. Sorensen, forthcoming.

but extend it. To create non-divine persons is itself an act of divine kenosis. And to create a self-sustaining universe operating in accordance with iron laws is a prior act of kenosis.

You may be thinking that I have crossed over from the radical to the insane, and that I should not be heard. Bear with me, please. I am a sheep in wolf's clothing. Once all the bits are in place, you will understand why I have colleagues who think I might have been a philosopher if only I could have got the Pope off my back.

6. AN OBJECTION THAT CANNOT WAIT

All the details are to come, but there is an objection that is so obvious that it cannot wait. By giving an account of divine development, I am surely complicating my overall hypothesis, abandoning, it could be objected, all the intellectual advantage of the God of classical theism. To that I reply, 'Yes, I am complicating my overall hypothesis; but no, I am not abandoning all the intellectual advantage of classical theism.' Why not? First, the neoclassical Primordial God is, I shall argue, simpler than the God of classical theism, so it starts off ahead. More important, though, I shall endeavour to explain *why* the Primordial God develops in a certain way, by understanding God's motives for development. Hence I am not merely hypothesizing that it develops as it does. This keeps the probability of the total theory not too much less than that of the Primordial God.

7. A QUALIFICATION BASED UPON PROBABILITY THEORY

There is a qualification that applies to all of metaphysics. Either explicitly or implicitly, we appeal to considerations of simplicity. Simpler theories are more probable than more complicated ones. It does not follow, however, that the simplest theory is more probable than not. Typically, the only way to arrive at an account which is more probable than not is to note that there is empirical evidence which forces a choice between a rather simple theory and one which is much more complicated. That is, I say, what experimental science achieves, but alas, metaphysics does not.

I am supposing that we are reflecting upon religious traditions and forming various hypotheses about the divine, including of course the error hypothesis that there is nothing divine. In that case, our accounts are likely to be speculative in the sense that we put one forward as more probable than its rivals, without any confidence of its being more probable than not. For example, John Leslie has recently defended a form of many universes polytheism in which no two gods have power over the same universe (Leslie 2001). He has his reasons, based upon his extreme axiarchism (Leslie 1979). Supposing, though, we reject Leslie's reason for holding his theory, I think most of us would judge that many universes created by many different gods is a somewhat extravagant hypothesis. It is less probable than one or more universes created by the one God. But it does not follow that the latter is more probable than not. For there are other hypotheses, notably no God at all. Clearly, if we assigned probabilities 45 per cent to monotheism, 35 per cent to atheism, and 20 per cent to polytheism, we would have indeed treated monotheism as the *most* probable, but not as more probable than not.

I have much the same probabilistic response to the pessimistic induction. That fine phrase is due to Newton-Smith, and although he was thinking of science, his pessimistic induction applies with a vengeance to philosophy (Newton-Smith 1981: 14). Philosophers keep on finding the position of their predecessors quaint. So we should, it seems, extrapolate and conclude that our own positions will come to be seen as quaint. This should make us blush. Likewise, replacing history by geography, I wish I could give a talk on philosophy of religion without someone informing me, as if I did not know, that there is a country called India. This proliferation of historical and geographical points of view results, and may be intended to result, in intellectual giddiness. Take a deep breath, I say, examine the widest range of positions, historically and geographically, and assign probabilities to them all. Most metaphysics is, I suspect, the pursuit of the fairly probable, not the highly probable. My response to this dismal assessment of metaphysics has already been discussed in the Introduction.

8. THE DEMARCATION DISPUTE

I am a philosopher meddling in theology. How can we make a principled demarcation between philosophy and theology? Aquinas would say that theology takes as its starting-point revelation, and then reflects upon that in ways that these days we would call philosophical. I am happy enough with that demarcation. According to it, most of what I am doing is philosophy proper, but when I discuss what we Christians believe, what I am doing is theology. It is, of course, philosophical theology: namely, theology done by philosophers, as opposed, say, to theology done by Scripture scholars.

Now although I have not met them, I hear rumours of people who brazenly assert that there is no place for philosophical theology. That assertion must be based upon the thesis that some kinds of reasoning that are suited to philosophy generally are not valid when applied to theology. In particular, there is a kind of reasoning that Charles Peirce calls abduction, that Gilbert Harman calls inference to the best explanation (Harman 1986: 67), or which follows, as Swinburne urges, from the standard principles of probability together with prior assignments of significantly higher probabilities to simpler theories (Swinburne 2001: 83–99). Or more crudely, but often more appealing, there is Occam's razor. Let us call this *theory-choice reasoning*, for it is the way we choose between competing theories when they are on a par empirically. It may be contrasted with deductive reasoning, as in pure mathematics, with statistical reasoning, of the sort used by pollsters, and, significantly, with our ordinary trust in experience and testimony. Deductive reasoning is almost universally considered applicable in theology, which is concerned to be consistent. Experience and testimony are quite central to religion. Statistical reasoning would in principle be applicable, but I know of no actual instances of its use. Here is a far-fetched example. You argue that God would create billions of angels, but would create them only if God knew that at most one in three would rebel. An angel appears to you and tells you to do something that seems ethically neutral, as, it might be, starting the Lord's Day rest at dusk rather than midnight. Is this a good angel or one of the rebellious minority? Statistical reasoning would tell you that it is more probable that not that this is one of the good ones. A silly example, but I think it shows that a principled theology/philosophy demarcation would not be along the deductive reasoning/probable reasoning divide, but would instead exclude from theology just one aspect of probable reasoning, and the most problematic aspect at that, theory choice.

A good example of the way this demarcation has worked in practice concerns the infamous condemnation of Galileo. That most reasonable theologian Cardinal Bellarmine was willing to treat scriptural references to the stationary Earth as instances of the accommodation to our ordinary ways of thinking, provided there was a need for this accommodation (Feldhay 1995: 35). He assumed, as was traditional, that the resort to accommodation should apply only in cases of the conclusive refutation of Scripture, and, rightly, he saw the reasoning of Copernicus and Galileo as inconclusive. My suspicion is that something like this demarcation survives among our contemporaries, even though they are less inclined to treat isolated passages of Scripture as authoritative.

Against such a demarcation there lies nothing more, but also nothing less, than the intuitive universality of our reasoning practices. Unless that is undermined in some way, the demarcation should be rejected. Instead, we might distinguish between different sorts of scholarship that can be brought to bear on revelation: history, literary criticism, and philosophy, jointly resulting in theology.

I allow, though, that the intuitive universality of our reasoning practices might perhaps be undermined. For theory-choice reasoning is not self-evident in the way deduction is. In terms of probabilities, we can prove that the simpler must on the whole be more probable than the more complicated, but that argument does not tell us that the simpler is significantly more probable, as theory choice requires. We know that we do reason in a theory-choice fashion. And usually there is no alternative but scepticism. But theory-choice reasoning invites the question, Why should we be so lucky that the way things are corresponds to the way we tend to think? Here Einstein's famous remark is as good an answer as any: 'God is subtle but . . . not malicious.' Assuming that God is non-deceiving, we should say that either God would not leave these clues lying around to enable science to make apparent progress or the apparent progress is genuine. Our ability to do science can be explained by God's ensuring that the universe is not too complicated and that we have an innate, and presumably God-intended, preference for simplicity. So there is a theological way of understanding our collective ability to do science. Likewise, we might well suppose that God wants us to know about theological truths. But here there is a complication. God has the power to ensure that the correct scientific theories may be arrived at using our innate preference for simplicity. God can do that by making the universe simple enough—but how can God ensure that theology is knowable? For example, we might ask how God could help human beings come to know of the Trinity. In the case of our knowledge of science, God, we are here supposing, created the universe with a certain structure and created us, using evolution, to have various intellectual practices, and so could arrange that the two correspond. But it is not plausible that God chose to become a Trinity just so that we could come to know it using ordinary theory-choice reasoning, rather than choosing to become something else quite incomprehensible to us. We may infer that God would want us to know as much about the divine nature as we can comprehend, but might have to, rely on revelation instead of theory-choice reasoning. Therefore our usual reasoning practices would not be universal.

This style of explanation thus uses a theistic explanation of the success of ordinary theory-choice reasoning in science to undermine its applicability to theology. And here we may note that many people, including many without religious convictions, hold that our ordinary reasoning does not apply to theological questions. As a philosophical imperialist, I would try to explain away their opinion as an internalization of the convention not to argue about religion with others. But if my philosophical imperialism is undermined, then it is undermined in just the place that we would expect God providentially to ensure that it would be: namely, by not using ordinary theory-choice reasoning when reflecting upon what is granted as prima facie authoritative in religion, whether it be Scripture or tradition.

Notice that the inference by which we come to this explanation is itself theory-choice reasoning. But that is not self-refuting. For we may reason thus: either, as is being argued, theory-choice reasoning is inapplicable to theology, or, relying on that kind of reasoning, we arrive at an account which undermines theory-choice reasoning in the case of theology. So in either case we conclude that theory-choice reasoning is inapplicable to theology.

I take this to be a serious objection to my case for neoclassical theism, a case I develop over the next four chapters. My reply is that revelation is no substitute for theory-choice reasoning, because there is a plurality of competing claims of revelation. This reply might at first seem incompatible with my position that the history of religions is on the whole a progress towards the truth. But they are compatible, because the progress requires a choice between competing claims as part of the process. The same goes for the progress of science. Without a wise choice between theories, we could still be defending geocentrism.

If there was only a single tradition or a single Scripture that was prima facie authoritative, we might reasonably refrain from theory-choice reasoning, and hope that God is not a deceiving God. But there are many prima facie authoritative traditions and Scriptures. Either we cannot decide between competing claims of revelation, or we decide between them in the way we usually assess testimony, or we have to supplement revelation by theory-choice reasoning. The standard ways of assessing testimony rely in part on how probable we think the story attested to. For instance, how we treat reports of alien abductions will depend very much on how likely it is that aliens might be visiting Earth on a regular basis. Therefore testimony is not a genuine alternative to theory-choice reasoning. Applying this to religious revelation, I would say that the belief that Jesus was divine as well as human and the belief that this Divine Person was one of three Divine Persons constituting but a single God should be rejected as implausible except for some philosophical account. Hence I claim that either (1) we cannot decide between competing claims of divine revelation; or (2) we should reject Christianity as implausible; or (3) we decide between them using a combination of theory-choice reasoning with other ways of assessing testimony, such as historians use in those cases where there is nothing especially implausible being attested to—as, for instance, in the near universal agreement that Jesus was a historical figure who was executed by the Romans.

9. A SUMMARY OF MY AIMS

I aim to provide an account of the kenotic development of God from the neoclassical Primordial God to one that is more in tune with various religious traditions, notably Christianity. A subsidiary aim is to exhibit the utility of supposing the moderate materialist thesis that agency and consciousness follow of metaphysical necessity from the purely physical description of things.

2

Theism, Simplicity, and Properly Anthropocentric Metaphysics

1. THE NEOCLASSICAL VERSUS THE CLASSICAL CONCEPTION OF GOD

The central claim of classical theism is that God is a necessary being that is necessarily without structure and necessarily unchanging. To this are added the claims that God is necessarily omnipotent, necessarily omniscient, and necessarily good. Such a God is simple in the sense of lacking structure, although we are left wondering how it is possible for a being without structure to have apparently distinct attributes, such as omnipotence and goodness. Moreover, if we inferred that the hypothesis of a simple being was a simple hypothesis, we would be equivocating on the word 'simple'. Classical theism stresses divine simplicity, but it is not an especially simple hypothesis, where, roughly speaking, we measure the complexity of a hypothesis in terms of how long it takes to state it. For if we abandon some of the claims such as that God is necessarily unchanging and necessarily good, we obtain a simpler hypothesis. Or so I say. Scholastic philosophers and their sympathizers might disagree, saying that their fundamental theistic claim concerns pure being or, as they sometimes say, subsistent existence, and that the details follow from this. (See Miller 2001.)

There are three difficulties as I see it with this scholastic approach. The first is in grasping the concept of subsistent existence, pure being, or pure act. What does it mean? The second, which is an *ad hominem* one, is that if classical theists believe in the Trinity, then to establish the consistency of that doctrine with the simplicity of God requires intellectual contortionism. Third, and more generally applicable, is that the reasons given for believing that there is a necessary and simple being are only reasons for holding that, necessarily, at some time, there exists such a being. There is nothing incoherent in the idea that there was a first moment of Time, and that everything that was the case then was necessarily the case, including the existence of a simple being. That leaves open the possibility that this being might change or even cease to exist, contrary to classical theism.

Which, then, is the intellectually attractive position, belief in a simple being or belief in a simple hypothesis? Both in different ways. We love to understand, and are frustrated when an increase in knowledge does not lead to understanding. But we also, I hope, fear falsehood, and hence respect the often pedestrian rules that govern rational belief and so constrain our quest for understanding. One of these rules is that, other things being equal, simpler hypotheses are significantly more probable than more complicated ones. Using that rule we should prune the hypothesis of classical theism, rejecting the thesis of immutability and bracketing off for the moment the thesis of divine goodness. By bracketing it off, I mean that we should not hypothesize divine goodness as something additional to the attributes of a simple Primordial God. But of course, if it follows as a result of further argument, then we are not guilty of hypothesizing it. Much the same goes for the hypothesis that the Primordial God was loving. Theism rests upon a simpler hypothesis if we do not assume that this is so.

For the most part, what enables us to understand is more probable than what leaves us puzzled. So, for the most part, the quest for understanding and the respect for the rules governing rational belief are in harmony. An interesting exception occurs in the case of some mathematical proofs that proceed in a roundabout fashion introducing an apparently irrelevant topic but eventually establishing the required result as a corollary. These provide conviction, but not understanding. An example, drawn to my attention by John Bigelow, concerns the fact that π is irrational, a geometric truth presumably believed in, but not proved, by the Greeks. There are various proofs, but one of them is a corollary of the proof that the number e, of no obvious connection with geometry and unknown to the Greeks, is a so-called transcendental number. Because of its roundabout character, this does not help us understand why π is irrational. Mathematical understanding seems to be largely a matter of elegance, of not using a sledge-hammer to crack a nut. Quite generally I would argue that understanding has an aesthetic dimension: to understand is to see the beauty or fittingness in things. This holds for a scientific theory of everything or an account of the divine. Here I am, to my immense surprise, following Jonathan Edwards (Smith 1992).

Another place where the goal of understanding and considerations of probability diverge is the notorious question of why there is something rather than nothing. As a request for understanding, the only sensible answer is going to be that there is some necessary being, something that could not have not existed. And if necessity requires simplicity in the sense of being structure-free, then we would need to believe in a simple being. But the hypothesis of a necessary being is no simpler as a hypothesis than that of a contingent being. Arguing using the complexity criterion for hypotheses, we might think that there being nothing was more probable a priori than there being something. Given that we know that there is something, we can ignore the totally a priori probabilities and consider instead the relatively a priori probabilities of various hypotheses on the supposition that there is something, thus deliberately not answering the question 'Why there is something rather than nothing?'.

I do not want to arbitrate between an aesthetically based goal of understanding and an austere theory of probability if these are in conflict. We should try to combine the two, and so prefer the simpler, other things being equal. If on some occasion the simpler is uglier, well then, perhaps other things are not equal. But on the whole, this is not the case. Now the hypothesis of a simple being in the structure-free sense is not automatically a simple hypothesis. Hence I seek a neoclassical account according to which both the existence of God is a very simple hypothesis and the Primordial God is a simple being. On one of two equivalent ways of describing the Primordial God, it is indeed a simple being. According to my developmental theism, God becomes complex.

I summarize the comparison of the classical with my neoclassical conception of God, as follows.

1. The classical conception is of God as necessarily existing *at all times,* whereas the neoclassical is of God as necessarily existing *initially.*
2. Both can make the claim to divine simplicity.
3. Neoclassical theism is the simplest conceivable theistic hypothesis, but the classical is fairly simple.
4. The God of classical theism is necessarily eternal and hence immutable, but the neoclassical God can choose to change, but would otherwise be eternal.

2. IMPROPERLY ANTHROPOMORPHIC VERSUS PROPERLY ANTHROPOCENTRIC METAPHYSICS

The simplicity of the hypothesis of a Primordial God is enough to establish that it has a non-negligible probability even prior to looking at the evidence, *provided* we start with suitable metaphysics. For if we started with reductive materialism, then by hypothesizing the Primordial God we would have complicated our overall metaphysics. In this section I introduce my starting-point for philosophical theology, which I call *properly anthropocentric metaphysics*.

There are those who think of God as like Santa Claus after a diet. The tendency to anthropomorphize the divine is more general than that, though. And it is easy enough to suggest that any belief in a personal God is such an anthropomorphism. But that is lazy philosophy. Instead, I distinguish a proper anthropocentricism from an improper anthropomorphism. We know, I say, that we, like many other kinds of animals, are conscious agents. We know that, like few other kinds of animals, we have a first-person perspective, distinguishing self from others, and thus are capable of reflecting upon our beliefs and our actions, and that we have a sense of our persistence over time. We know that we have emotions, imagination, and aesthetic sensibility. The position I call properly anthropocentric metaphysics takes all these things, together with the sciences, as the starting-point for reflection on the nature of things. Some call this position humanism, but humanism is usually taken as an anti-religious and anti-Christian tradition. Well, I am a Christian, and my attitude towards religions is ambivalent rather than downright hostile, so I prefer not to be called a humanist.

Properly anthropocentric metaphysics provides the basis for reasonable thought about God, assigning some of our characteristics that cannot adequately be understood in purely scientific terms. You might think that this is the God of the gaps fated to dwindle to nothing as scientific understanding becomes ever more complete. Better to call it a God of the *ultimate* gaps. The characteristics that cannot be understood in scientific terms are not details, such as that we are living organisms. For perhaps life was just a fluke that in a large enough universe was likely to occur somewhere. Rather, they are ones that are not of the right kind to be understood in scientific terms, such as the mysteries of consciousness and agency. Here it is worth noting a tendency for naturalists not to explain but to deny these characteristics, especially agency. This is evidence that they grant that they are not of a kind to be understood scientifically.

Improper anthropomorphism occurs when we assign to God details of our nature that depend on our physical constitution. So ascribing agency to God is part of properly anthropocentric metaphysics, but it is improper anthropomorphism to think of God at creation as a very able mathematician working out detailed solutions of differential equations so as to plan the future history of our universe. For we believe that our capacity to make complicated inferences, and our intelligence generally, has to do with the detailed structure of our brains. God is not brainy like that. Much the same can be said for belief/desire psychology, which requires that the agent have two states, a desire (e.g. for coffee) and a matching belief (e.g. that the liquid in the cup is coffee). Agency at its simplest would be motivated by single act of awareness of something as good. In the human case, this is the positive motivation provided by the awareness of an enjoyable feeling the person might have or a negative one based on the awareness of possible suffering. More sophisticated motivations involve imagination of the outcome, but they too are based ultimately on an awareness of possible joy or possible suffering.

I have yet to explain why I draw the distinction between proper anthropocentricism and improper anthropomorphism along these lines. The reason is that belief in God is partly justified in terms of the explanatory power of creation. God creates the physical world either out of nothing or out of something rather formless. To say otherwise is to forfeit the theocentric understanding of the existence of our complex physical universe. But if we ascribe to God the sort of detailed characteristics that we know in our own case depend on physical details, then we cannot answer the old question of who designed the designer. The answer to that question is that God created the physical universe without designing it, and that the attributes required to be a creator do not themselves require actual physical complexity.

We know in advance that any metaphysical system will leave a handful of mysteries, and a good metaphysician has a nose for where the mysteries might be located. The occurrence of agency is the right sort of mystery to have. Simple laws of nature are also, I concede, the right sort of thing to be accepted as a mystery, as is a simple initial condition for the universe. I concede this, even though as a theist I shall not be treating them as mysteries. Other things being equal, explaining the physical universe in terms of creation, on the one hand, and explaining it in terms of simple initial conditions and simple laws, on the other, are roughly on a par. It is reasonable to believe in creation only because other things are not equal. But the important point here is that it would be silly to jettison the capacity of an act of creation to explain the existence of the complex physical universe by believing, quite unnecessarily, in a God who has many detailed characteristics that we can explain, in our own case, by appeal to the physical sciences.

A straightforward, but in my view mistaken, way of developing properly anthropocentric metaphysics is available to extreme dualists who hold that we have a thinking, willing, non-physical part, the soul that affects and is affected by the body. It is worth suspending any disbelief about souls for a while and thinking about the account of God that flows from belief in a non-physical soul. For it is then a simple hypothesis to think of God as a super-soul, like our souls, but not limited by association with limited bodies. There is an interesting hypothesis due to Ramanuja that God is the soul of all our souls, but perhaps a more straightforward idea is that God is the World Soul—that is, the soul of the whole physical universe. Who knows how souls come to exist? Maybe they have always existed. Maybe God creates them. But the power of a super-soul to create a new soul is not something we have precedent for in the human case. So dualists should say that there are souls we know not how. In that case, the existence of the super-soul God or of many super-souls, the gods, would simply be another instance of an already accepted mystery, and so of little intellectual cost. Dualism gives us little idea of where matter comes from. But it does commit us to an ability of souls to control their allotted bodies.

Given the acceptance of all these mysteries in the human case, we have an economical enough hypothesis about the divine. Perhaps God does not create *ex nihilo* but is a world-soul with power over the universes, including the power to organize the matter in those universes to make bodies suitable for other lesser souls. For other universes separate from ours, there might be other gods. On this super-soul account, improper anthropomorphism would largely be the result of attributing to the divine features that derive from the human body, such as sexuality.

This was intended only as an example of how properly anthropocentric metaphysics works. As I have already said, and for reasons I give in the next chapter, I reject dualism in favour of a moderate—that is, non-reductive—materialism.

3. FROM ANTHROPOCENTRIC PHILOSOPHY TO PHILOSOPHICAL ANTHROPOLOGY

One of the many great nineteenth-century intellectual achievements was the unification of the theory of electricity with the theory of magnetism. What were previously two distinct branches of scientific inquiry became a single branch concerning a single set of laws, whose discovery was completed by Maxwell. What has that to do with theism, or even with properly anthropocentric metaphysics? It is a paradigm of the unification of two branches of inquiry without the reduction of one to the other. Something like that is required to provide a satisfactory metaphysics of human beings. The scientific understanding and the other, anthropocentric bits need to be integrated into a single coherent account. To that end we should first note the aspects of human beings that defy a purely physical explanation. Some of these are such as we might expect to be able to explain with more research. There is a lot we do not understand about the way memory is stored, for instance. Two features of human beings stand out, however: consciousness and agency. They are connected, in that the idea of an unconscious agent is incoherent. It is worth noting why Charles Darwin thought that certain plants had rudimentary mental life (Darwin 1875). He was impressed by the apparently purposive behaviour of climbers. Agency presupposes consciousness, so it sums up what it is about us humans that most clearly defies physical explanation. From the lack of physical explanation it does not follow that there is some non-physical explanation of these features of humans. Instead, agency and consciousness might be brute mysteries.

I follow Swinburne in holding that one of the fundamental ways of understanding is in terms of an agent who has the power to bring about a situation of a certain kind, who has a motive to do so, and so does it. If I understand him correctly, one of the central ideas of Swinburne's impressive natural theology is that theism is reasonable because it enables us to use agency to explain what would otherwise be improbable.

Consciousness is often either joyful or suffering, rather than neutral. This *hedonic tone*, as I call it, is presupposed by agency, for without it there is no motive for action. And, like consciousness itself, it cannot be understood in physical terms. Positive and negative hedonic tone are expressed by the unreflective assertions 'That's good' and 'That's bad', or the more cautious 'Bracketing off consequences, that is good' and

'Bracketing off consequences, that is bad', or the, to my mind excessively cautious, 'That seems good to me' and 'That seems bad to me'. These assertions have a conceptual complexity that in the human case derives, I am supposing, from brain structure. But the tone itself, as opposed to the behaviour it helps to explain, cannot, I claim, be understood in purely physical terms.

This clue, then, to an adequate unified account of human nature suggests that agency is central to human nature, and our nature includes our being limited agents. Or to put it in a way that might remind us of Arthur Schopenhauer and Friedrich Nietzsche, our nature is to be a limited will, with the presupposed consciousness.

A further feature of persons, a feature not presupposed by agency, is that persons *persist* from one time to another. I claim that the concept of a person is of a conscious agent whose motives concern the same being in the future and, typically, refer back to the same being in the past, where sameness here is understood as contrasted with others. Persons might conceivably be in error about their persistence, and that we are in error in this way is an important Buddhist theme, especially for Theravadins. But I am assuming that we are not in error. Whether our persistence can be understood in purely physical terms—for instance, as the persistence of the animals that we are—is a controversial question about which I shall be neutral.

We have, then, several features of human beings that are not explained in purely physical terms and that we may, therefore, use to describe God prior to creation. These features include consciousness, agency, and hedonic tone. My neoclassical conception of the Primordial God is that of an unrestricted agent with all that this agency presupposes, including consciousness and hedonic tone. The Primordial God is, I am supposing, impersonal, so the question of persistence does not yet arise. Nor is it supposed that the Primordial God has any thoughts of I or other.

Agency does not just presuppose consciousness of what is actual; it also presupposes awareness of the possibilities that the act would directly bring about. As indicated above, a person acting has in addition a sense of what she or he already is, and what she or he has already done. These are important as a component of characteristically personal motives. But agency as such could be purely forward-looking: the awareness of various possibilities and of the action that would directly brings about some of these. I take the Primordial God to be an agent of just that sort.

4. WHICH THINGS ARE CONSCIOUS AGENTS?

Darwin thought that climbing plants might be conscious and that earthworms had some rudimentary affection for each other (Darwin 1875, 1883). How quaint!, we think. But why? Granted that consciousness and agency are the fundamental metaphysical categories about which properly anthropocentric metaphysics revolves, the question of just what things are conscious agents is a crucial one. Moreover, we humans have an innate tendency to see agency everywhere: anyone who cannot see the appeal of Greek, Norse, or Vedic polytheism is lacking in imagination. Just what sorts of thing, then, are conscious agents? One basic principle here is that of harmony between agency and behaviour. We could call this the harmony between efficient and so-called final causes, and suggest it as a charitable interpretation of process philosophy's dipolarity.

This harmony holds because neurocentric organisms that survive and reproduce must have neural processes that results in adapted behaviour. If they are conscious, and if they act, then this behaviour must be compatible with their motives for acting, in the simplest case avoiding pain. Hence a necessary condition for positing conscious agency is that the thing in question behaves in such a way as could be understood in terms of agency.

So how widely should we ascribe consciousness and agency? I have already stated a necessary condition, but that is only half the answer. If we do not require a systematic answer, then we should ascribe agency and consciousness as widely as we need to in order to understand. We should not be niggardly, ascribing consciousness and agency only as little as we can get away with. For given that we are conscious agents, this niggardly approach is an abuse of Occam's razor. Hence, I say, we should take seriously the pan(en)theistic hypothesis that the system of all that is real, the actual and the possible, will, provided it counts as a single system, correspond to a divine agent. As I indicated in the first chapter I shall qualify this, submitting that the physical correlate of God is not so much everything as everything except those sub-systems that constitute created persons.

Initially, there is no actual physical universe like ours. So, given my moderate materialism, what is there? The obvious answer is that there would be nothing at all except perhaps a moment of Time. I think we should reject this answer, because we should require some *truth-makers* or, if you prefer, *grounds*, for the truths about what was and was not possible. As far as I know, the only alternative to grounding possible truths in reality is to ground them in our ways of thinking about reality, by assimilating the possible to the conceivable. That is not available to moderate materialists. For, as David Chalmers and others have pointed out, there is no inconceivability in supposing that some, physically quite normal, human beings totally lack consciousness. Or, if you find that controversial, you should at least grant the conceivability of autarchs, beings like us with libertarian free will (that is the sort of free will that is incompatible with causal determinism), as well as the conceivability of wobblios, beings with exactly the same physical composition, which act in ways that are random. Because there would be no physical difference between autarchs and wobblios, materialists are committed to distinguishing the metaphysically possible from the conceivable but impossible, assigning the latter status either to autarchs or, as I would urge, to wobblios.

There are several hypotheses about just what distinguishes the metaphysically possible from the consistent but impossible (see Divers 2002). My claim is that whatever the correct hypothesis, there are some necessary features of the initial situation grounding the metaphysical possibilities. According to the moderate materialist, these features should be correlated with the initial mental state, if there is any. One good theistic speculation is that the grounds for metaphysical possibility just are the ideas in the mind of God. In that case there is nothing physical initially, except a moment of Time, and necessarily correlated with this moment is God who has the ideas of all possible universes. This is not in the spirit of materialism, because there is no detailed correlation of the divine structure on the (structureless) moment of Time. Nonetheless, we could postulate that God has these ideas as a matter of metaphysical necessity, thus satisfying the letter of moderate materialism.

Another speculation, and one that is probably the most popular among philosophers, is that initially there were some abstract entities such as propositions, and that these in some way or other ground the possibilities. For instance, maybe p is possible if and only if p belongs to a maximal consistent sets of propositions (Divers 2002: 178–80). Or perhaps possibilities are grounded in (as yet) uninstantiated universals (Divers 2002: 177–8). Whatever the details, we may say that there are abstract entities representing the possible ways a physical universe might be.

Less popular is modal realism, which in the present context we may restrict to the physical, saying that the possibilities are all grounded in an array of real concrete physical universes.[1] David Lewis then proposes that the actual is not different in kind from the merely possible. This feature of his metaphysics has been widely criticized, and even more widely rejected. Elsewhere I have proposed a variant according to which we think of the possible physical universes as overlapping so as to form a tree (Forrest 2002*a*; see also Davis 1991; McCall 1994)). That is, universes that are physically indiscernible up to a certain time are identical up to that time, but once discernible, never thereafter overlap. It is then up to agents, human or divine, to decide just which branches have consciousness on them. So to be actual on this account is just to belong to the same branch as a conscious being. A branch without any consciousness is a mere might-have-been. On this account, not merely zombies but universes that never develop life are real but not actual, which is, I grant, peculiar.

Finally, we might think that the possible depends on the actual, and so for there to be various possibilities in the initial situation we might posit some initial chaotic actual state, which contains processes that, if prolonged and combined, would generate all possible universes. This is a difficult hypothesis to state clearly, and I record it without seeking to defend it.

Let us suppose that we refrain from postulating some fundamental principle governing the occurrence of consciousness and agency. Then theism may be treated as the hypothesis that there is an agent conscious of and with power to actualize any (all?) of the range of possibilities for physical universes, either because these are ideas in the mind of God or because there are abstract entities that ground this range of possibilities. What this actualization requires depends on just how the possibilities are grounded, but in all cases we may say that God has the same sort of power as humans but without our restrictions. Now I grant that this is speculative, but what I am trying to do here is: (1) show that the idea of a Primordial God of unrestricted power is not so improbable that it cannot be raised to a fairly high probability by further considerations such as the suitability of the universe for life; and (2) investigate what the Primordial God might be like.

What if we do decide to postulate some fundamental principle governing the occurrence of consciousness and agency? Here there are only two principles I can think of: panpsychism and idealism. I reject

---

[1] David Lewis called himself a materialist, but I consider him a dualist, for he believed in worlds with non-physical components. But I am ignoring these.

panpsychism, for either it posits genuine consciousness to electrons and positrons, which is explanatorily redundant assuming they are not agents, or, as in process philosophy, it requires something more primitive than consciousness out of which they arise. The trouble with the latter is its lack of economy. Consciousness is said to arise out of prehension, which is a something otherwise unknown, which we posit in an *ad hoc* fashion. Likewise, agency somehow arises from final causes. This might seem sensible enough except that final causes have, I believe, been rendered quite redundant as explanations by the last few centuries of science. If we might otherwise still need them in biology—something I doubt—then theism offers a way of assimilating the so-called final causes to agency, which is a kind of efficient causation. As far as I can see, it is only anti-Darwinian atheists who need to posit final causes as explanations. This is just the converse of the way in which Darwinian evolution theory undermined the Paley-type design argument, which may be reconstructed as offering a choice between genuine final causes and theism, a choice obscured somewhat by anthropomorphic talk of Nature as acting like an agent when, strictly speaking, final causes are being appealed to, not agency. Thus, if someone says that Nature ensures that stressed plants produce seed early, he or she must be interpreted either as saying something about evolution or as saying something about God or as saying that the way in which plants grow and flower is to be explained in terms of their final cause, which is to reproduce. But it is not a statement about Nature as an efficient cause.

Panpsychism, then, either assigns consciousness and agency too widely or is an uneconomic hypothesis, requiring *prehension* and final causes. This leaves the idealist thesis, that every physical situation has the property of there being consciousness of it. Or better, I say, that every physical *universal* has a way in which it appears.[2] Initially the physical situation consists entirely of whatever represents possible physical universes: abstract entities maybe, together perhaps with Time. We may then ask how this consciousness gets divided up into distinct minds. The answer must be that initially it does not. In that case absolute idealism is correct as the description of the initial situation, so the Primordial God becomes highly probable even without any further considerations. It is worth

---

[2] It cannot be that simple, however. One complication is that brain processes of a certain kind must appear like the situations they represent. Another is that there must be a way in which instantiated universals appear, another way in which universals appear as they are being instantiated, and a third way in which as-yet-uninstantiated universals appear.

noting that absolute idealists tended to distance themselves from the personal conception of God, and that 'The Absolute' is as good a translation of 'Brahman' as 'God'. Merely to say that there is consciousness of all things does not, therefore, require Berkeley's subjective idealism; for we may say that there is awareness or consciousness of all things without attributing that awareness to one or more minds or souls or selves.

As already mentioned, I refrain from building into the definition of materialism that the mental is ontologically dependent on the physical. Conversely, I refrain from building into the definition of idealism dependence the other way round. What we should not hold is that the mental depends on the physical, and vice versa. But even if we are materialists who hold that the mental depends on the physical, we may still entertain the hypothesis that all things appear, and use this to give a systematic account of how the mental arises.

I submit, therefore, that even without a systematic approach to deciding what things are conscious agents, we should take the idea of a Primordial God seriously, and, moreover, that the most plausible systematic approach leads directly to a Primordial God that could be identified with the Absolute.

5. OBJECTIONS TO THE PRIMORDIAL GOD

The idea of a super-soul required an untenable version of dualism. Instead, I submit that conscious agency is a mystery, which we have to accept in the human case, and hence we may, without multiplying mysteries, posit a God who is Pure Will: that is, a God which is aware of the whole range of possibilities for universes, with the power to select some to be actual.

There are several objections to this hypothesis of a Primordial God which is Pure Will. Before answering them, I note that it is the work this hypothesis does in explaining various data which raises it from the not-too-improbable to the highly probable. What I am here defending is its not being too improbable to be taken seriously even before that work is done.

The first objection is that what I dismissed as niggardly is merely proper intellectual caution. We should extrapolate from the human situation, and hence, it is objected, we have no reason to ascribe conscious agency except to similar beings such as apes. That objection would be in order if we thought of conscious agency as a mere detail. For instance, there is the question of whether the colours other animals see are like those that humans see. It is reasonable to extrapolate to other primates but not, say, to marsupials, even though marsupials enjoy colour vision as rich as primates. But we are dealing here with an important metaphysical category, conscious agency. To limit this to one kind of physical system is parochial.

This leads to the second objection, based on that question beloved by atheists, 'Who designed the designer?'. The objection is that for the Primordial God to have the power to create a universe or several universes, it would have to have some brain analogue, which would turn out, therefore, to be a more complicated thing to posit unexplained than the laws and initial conditions left unexplained on a naturalistic account. This would be a devastating objection if we thought of the Primordial God as intelligent or as seeking means to a good end, but not if we adopt a simpler hypothesis. The possible ways a physical universe might be are, I submit, themselves necessary. This is the orthodoxy that anything possible is necessarily possible. I do not think that this orthodoxy is to be accepted as obvious. All I am doing is assuming that it is a priori as likely as its negation and asserting my right to a hypothesis that is in fact the orthodoxy, but not because it is an orthodoxy. It is then the simplest hypothesis concerning agency that there was a primordial act of a being directly aware of the whole range of possibilities and choosing to actualize some rather than others. That requires no hidden structure. We humans need brains to imagine—that is, to represent what is possible. We need brains to think about how to achieve an end. We need brains so as to be influenced appropriately by our environment, and so on. More fundamentally, we need brains to be separate from the rest of consciousness. But God has no such need. God is directly aware of all the possibilities. Those who believe that the God they worship is wise and providential, perhaps even liking the image of God as the perfect cosmic Go-player, might be scandalized by my idea of a God who just sees what is good and acts spontaneously to create it. If so, that is a further reason to hold that God develops, and that part of what the Primordial God sees to be good is a situation in which God is indeed wise and providential.

Here we have a choice of description. Either we take the possibilities as necessary beings distinct from God, or we treat them as parts of God. Given the first description, the complexity is in the system of all possibilities of which the Primordial God is aware. In that case God is a simple being. Alternatively, we might re-describe the Primordial God by saying that there are entities that represent all possibilities, universals maybe, and that they make up the divine brain analogue or body analogue. In that case, although God is immensely complicated, to posit God adds little to the intellectual cost already incurred in positing the abstract entities, universals, or whatever, so the hypothesis of theism is very simple.

Perhaps you are a nominalist in the strict sense and reject all abstract entities. In that case I commend an alternative in which the possibilities do not really exist even as ideas in the mind of God, but somehow sneak in as the intentional objects of imagination and deliberation. I fail to understand how calling them intentional objects explains anything, but this, I suspect, is what nominalists are committed to, and if you are a nominalist, so be it. In that case the very real intellectual pressures towards believing in a realm of possibilities should make you take seriously the idea of a Primordial God for whom all these possibilities are intentional objects of imagining. Among other pressures I would mention the provision of an adequate philosophy of mathematics.

I doubt whether it makes much difference to the overall metaphysics to take possibilities as ideas in the mind of God, to take them as represented by abstract entities, or to take them as concrete or as mere intentional objects of divine awareness. In all cases the supposition of the Primordial God is a very simple hypothesis—given that we are already committed to some ontology or other for the possibilities, a commitment that follows from the moderate materialist refusal to assimilate the possible to the conceivable.

This leads in turn to the third objection. In the human case our awareness of both actual and possible situations is correlated with actual concrete physical entities: namely, brain processes. Yet I am postulating a Primordial God that is directly aware of as yet non-actual universes without any concrete actual physical correlate. For the correlate, if there *is* one, is some sort of abstract entity such as a universal or a proposition. Hence, the objection goes, human consciousness and agency are no precedent for the Primordial God. My response is that even in the human case the awareness of actual and possible situations should be analysed in terms of such abstract entities. The difference between the divine and the human cases lies, I speculate, in the difference between a vast system with its possibilities for change and a much smaller one. Given the unexplained assumption that there is conscious agency, we may explain the existence of sub-systems of the awareness of all possibilities by means of the functional roles that brain processes play, which restrict the changes to those sub-systems. So our actual brain processes are what keep us from being a part of God. An actual brain analogue is not, therefore, needed for the initial system comprising all possibilities.

The final objection is that it is just too easy to postulate a consciousness of all things with power to bring about any of the possibilities that it is aware of. Contrast this with the hard work required to understand how the human brain works. We should, the objection goes, be wary of easy explanations. While this objection lacks precision, I think it is a common one among those who take religion to be intellectually shallow. My reply to those who find positing God too easy an explanation is that the hard intellectual work has to be done elsewhere. Suppose we grant, as we should, that it is not too improbable that there existed a Primordial God understood as the awareness of all possibilities and the power to choose some of them to become actual. Then the hard work is in understanding how there can be creatures who are agents, and whose wills do not necessarily coincide with God's will. Continuing my reply to the previous objection, I note that brain processes result in a restricted set of possibilities for the future of a human animal, which, as it were, carves out those possible futures from the possible futures of the rest of the universe. To understand how brain processes do this is to understand the functional roles they play.

I should add that, if it turns out that folk psychology is not as good a guide to the functional roles played by brain processes as we might have hoped, then we might have to replace folk psychology by something else. But this will affect only the ways in which human beings are unlike God. For the basic facts of consciousness, hedonic tone, and agency are not, I say, understood by the details of brain processes, and it is these that are the precedents for the divine, not the details of folk psychology.

Conclusion

I have argued that properly anthropocentric metaphysics provides an intellectual niche for a Primordial God, which is in many ways like the God of classical theism. This God is conscious and has power, but with no detailed structure other than awareness of and ability to actualize the possible physical universes. By treating the realm of possible physical universes as external to the Primordial God, we obtain something like divine simplicity. If we think of that realm of possibilities as like the body of the Primordial God, then we do not have genuine divine simplicity, but we still have an economic hypothetical beginning of everything.

3

Materialism and Dualism

I hope that my position of moderate materialism is clear enough: the mental is correlated of metaphysical necessity with the physical. I am rejecting, however, the thesis that the mental may be understood in terms of the physical, insisting instead that various rather basic features of human beings resist understanding in physical terms. These features provide the precedent for a properly anthropocentric understanding of God. I do not, however, reject the thesis that the mental depends ontologically on the physical. Thus, nothing I say is incompatible with the thesis that the mental consists of properties instantiated by the physical and that, contrary to what I believe, properties cannot exist uninstantiated, and so depend on the things that instantiate them, in much the way the surface of an object is widely thought to depend on the object. If that should be the case, then the Primordial God is something physical, a moment of Time perhaps, which has various mental properties. Although I am not assuming that such a dependency thesis is false, I am not assuming that it is true either. For the necessary correlation between the mental and the physical does not imply that one depends on the other.

In this chapter I shall say a little more about why I reject reductive materialism, why I reject various kinds of dualism, in what way I think the mental is correlated with the physical, and something about the qualia problem, which seems to support dualism. All this amounts to my positive case for moderate materialism. Even if it is rejected, a philosophical theology based upon it remains of interest because of the current popularity of materialism.

1. AGAINST REDUCTIVE MATERIALISM

In Frank Jackson's famous example, Mary the brilliant scientist knows everything about the optics and the neurophysiology of colour vision, as well as anything else there might be to know about the physical explanation of colour vision, but she has not experienced colour (Jackson 1982, 1986). When she does eventually experience it, she comes to know something new, which must, therefore, be non-physical. At the time, Jackson took this as a counterexample to materialism. Although this example is initially appealing, I accept David Lewis's response: namely, that what Mary comes to have is a new way of knowing colour, not something she did not previously know, so it does not show that colour vision involves something non-physical (Lewis 1983). I would describe the situation thus: previously Mary knew all about colours; now she knows them by acquaintance; but knowledge by acquaintance is not a matter of knowing *more* than knowing about something.

Let us modify the example and consider Mary's daughter, Mary II, who, like some human beings, has no sense of pain. She studies pain and is often annoyed at the Animal Experimentation Ethics Committee for insisting that she pay volunteers rather large sums of money to inflict pain on them instead of letting her use rats as subjects. The Committee keeps saying to her, 'If you only knew what pain was like you would not dream of inflicting that on rats.' But she does not understand. To her, pain is an interesting neurological phenomenon that explains, in a neurological way, pain-avoidance behaviour. Then one day she has a brain tumour removed, and suddenly she can feel pain for the first time. Her reaction is one of dismay at the pain she had been causing the rats when she ran out of money to pay humans, and so disobeyed the Ethics Committee. This variant adds something to the story about colour. To have experienced pain is to have a prima facie reason to avoid pain in yourself and others, although not necessarily an all-things-considered reason. In fact, the subjects whom Mary II had paid to undergo pain had an all-things-considered reason not to avoid the pain. And as she gradually reduced the sum paid, there must have been a point at which some subjects would have been quite undecided as to whether the gain was worth the pain. Now, after she has experienced pain, she understands the way the reasons are balanced. Before that she must surely have thought that the subjects had an aversion to pain that interfered with their rational desire for money (as a means to some end such as going on a holiday). She understands this aversion, for it is quite clear to her that the subjects' neural activity (corresponding to the memory of pain) produces in them a tendency not to sign on. But she does not understand how it could be rational to be indecisive, or rational to refuse to be the subject of a pain experiment for a significantly lesser sum.

This modified example exhibits what Joseph Levine (2001) calls *the explanatory gap*. It shows how the neurophysiological understanding of human beings does not enable us to understand conscious experience as a reason for acting. Hence we should reject reductive materialism. Moreover, it is the anticipated hedonic tone, in this case one of suffering, of that conscious experience that provides the motive for acting. It is precisely these features of human beings, the ones that are not understood physically, that provide the precedents for the divine mind.

The reductive materialist might be tempted to modify Lewis's response to Jackson and say that being in pain is just a different way of knowing a certain kind of neural process. Indeed that might be so, but this way of knowing enables us to understand why certain behaviour is rational rather than a comprehensible irrationality, and so exhibits rather than closes the explanatory gap. At this point the reductive materialist might say that Mary II just made a mistake in saying that it was irrational for her subjects to say the gain was not worth the pain. For the reductive materialist might say that rational action is itself just behaviour with a certain kind of neural cause, which kind happens to play the role that common sense describes as rationality. And Mary II should have known that it did play this role. My rejoinder is to modify the example. Perhaps she did not judge the subjects irrational. She could have accepted that they were in fact rational without understanding why they were rational. Indeed, I do not need to mention rationality at all if that gives offence. Instead I could point out that Mary II lacked a certain way of understanding behaviour, and that after she had experienced pain, she had that way of understanding behaviour.

Hence the objection to reductive materialism amounts to this: there is an anthropocentric way of understanding human behaviour, *verstehen*. For X to understand Y's behaviour in this way is for X to interpret it as an action motivated by Y's anticipation of experience, relevantly similar to one that X has had. Examples such as Mary II show that such understanding would not be provided by a neurophysiological explanation of behaviour, however detailed. But—and this is stipulative—I take reductive materialism to be the thesis that nothing can be understood that cannot just as well be understood in purely physical terms. It follows that either we reject *verstehen* as merely an illusion of understanding, or we reject reductive materialism. That we are faced with this choice should at the very least throw considerable doubt on reductive materialism.

My case against reductive materialism depends on the way of understanding behaviour as *action*, either done for a reason, or where there is lack of an explicit belief about the consequences of the act, at least being motivated by what is anticipated. I reinforce this case by considering the wobblio, whose behaviour is the result of some random process, so that in the case where a normal person would have to decide between balanced reasons the wobblio just has a fifty–fifty chance of deciding one way or the other. (Someone who decides to toss a coin, or even decides to imagine tossing a coin, is not, however, a wobblio.) The wobblio lacks something. Just what the wobblio lacks is a matter for further debate, and I would go so far as to say that a neurophysiologically normal human who was a wobblio would have to be a zombie. But let us put that further debate to one side.

We would not hold the wobblio morally responsible for the choice made, whereas the normal human being, the autarch, who in cases where the reasons are balanced makes a genuine decision, *is* morally responsible. This anti-compatibilist account of moral responsibility reinforces my rejection of reductive materialism, which cannot distinguish wobblio from autarch. And I trace such popularity as reductive materialism has to the corrupting influence of David Hume on generations of philosophers who come to think of compatibilism as a sensible position. The great divide between a properly anthropocentric metaphysics and naturalism occurs at this very point, I say.

An interesting response to the explanatory gap is that of Max Deutscher, in conversation, and, more widely known, that of Galen Strawson (1994). The way Deutscher put it was that he rejected physics-alism but not physic-alism, meaning that there was far more to the material world than physics teaches. Strawson has argued that we think that there is an explanatory gap because we think, incorrectly, that we understand the physical (Strawson 1994). I interpret Deutscher and Strawson as being moderate materialists, who in fact acknowledge the explanatory gap but relocate it by using the terms 'physical' and 'material' in ways that correspond perhaps to ordinary usage, but not to that of philosophers. Within the scope of the supposition that such common inorganic stuffs as rocks, metals, water, and so on are lacking in consciousness, we may characterize reductive materialism as saying that the science required to understand rocks, metals, water, etc. is sufficient to understand living organisms and, moreover, human beings. To say there is an explanatory gap at the onset of consciousness is to deny this, as it would also be if we were to say that there was an explanatory gap at the onset of life.

2. THE THREAT OF EPIPHENOMENALISM

Familiar philosophical arguments, as presented above, provide a prima facie case for rejecting reductive materialism. Many materialists, including the lapsed dualist Jackson, would concede the prima facie case, but are persuaded by the threat of epiphenomenalism. For the sake of exposition, let us grant substance dualism. Then the mental consists of extra items, a special entity, the *self*, related by awareness to other special entities, the qualia, and related by intention to yet other entities that represent the intended action. So, the objection goes, all these things are epiphenomenal, they do not influence the physical. Or, strictly speaking, they do not influence the physical to do anything other than what it would do anyway. Consider, for instance, the memory of dreams. Although the dreams figure in our ordinary explanation of the memory of the dreams, presumably there is a perfectly adequate explanation in terms of brain functioning. So dreams turn out to be redundant in our explanation of the memory of dreaming. If all of the mental is explanatorily redundant in this way, then we should embrace reductive materialism.

The threat of epiphenomenalism arises, I submit, only if we have already rejected irreducible agency accounts of human responsibility. For consciousness is of explanatory power when, and only when, combined with agency. It is because we act as a result of being consciously aware of what difference acting would make that the mental is not redundant and that epiphenomenalism is incorrect. Moreover, in cases where a genuine choice is made by the agent, the purely physical description would, if complete, imply that the agent was just a wobblio, making a decision at random corresponding to a random weighing up of reasons.

3. THE CASE AGAINST EXTREME DUALISM

What is it like to be deep-frozen in liquid nitrogen? Most of us would answer that there is nothing it is like, even if there remains the possibility of being successfully thawed out at a later date and resuming life as the same person as was frozen. For we tend to assume that total brain inactivity must result in there being no mental states and no consciousness. But that is not, it seems, what Socrates held. Even without the possibility of recovery from an overdose of hemlock, he looked forward with some equanimity to an altered state, one in which, to be sure, he would have no sensations and would no longer be able to converse with others, but in which various intellectual activities would still be possible, which assumes the retention of memory. This raises the question 'Do we need brains (or some brain analogues) in order to think in complex ways, such as in sentences, and to remember, or is the brain instead a device by which an immaterial being, the soul, affects and is affected by the physical so as to communicate with other souls?' Let us call the latter position extreme dualism.

The rejection of extreme dualism is one of the presuppositions of contemporary Western culture, but that does not make this rejection obvious, merely seemingly so. What explicit argument can be provided? The following argument, which I first heard clearly stated by David Londey, is, I think, representative.

4. GENETICS AND BRAIN DAMAGE

The way in which brains differ is partly the result of genetics. In addition, some unfortunate people have brains that are different from others as a result of damage. Such differences apparently affect the way the person's mind works, not just by slowing it down or speeding it up, or by subjecting it to confusing stimuli. The most impressive but also distressing instance of this is character-altering damage to the brain. Dementia is an all too common example. Extreme dualists are forced to deny this, insisting that the sufferer from dementia is confused and so responds to others inadequately, but has not been altered in character. Likewise, the extreme dualist has to interpret disinhibition, whether due to frontal lobe damage or alcohol, as a matter of finding oneself doing something inappropriate, such as taking off one's clothes at an office party, without intending to, rather than as the result of inappropriate intentions. Such an interpretation is contrary to the usual folk-psychological explanations of behaviour. Again, it is clear that character and various abilities are partly genetic. (Studies of identical twins separated at birth and adopted into different families show this.) How are the genes meant to affect the non-physical soul? Suppose, for instance, that the ability to compose music was a property of a non-physical soul quite independent of the brain. Then we should expect it to develop to the same degree in all children with normal hearing who are given the same musical education from an early age. But it does not.

There are three much better explanations for dementia and disinhibition, and for the genetic origin of differing abilities. But all three are based upon a necessary correlation of mental attributes with brain structure. One is that materialism of some sort is correct, and that the mental is correlated of metaphysical necessity with the physical. The second is that there is such a correlation, but it is merely nomological, as in David Chalmers's version of dualism (Chalmers 1996).

The third is that there is some immaterial self, but that this lacks any intrinsic personality or character. Such a self is like the atman of much Hindu thought, or Kant's transcendental ego. It is posited because it is assumed that nothing can appear without appearing to something. My response to this is that we can mistake a non-relational attribute for a relational one, and that there could be a property of *appearing* without any need for something that is appeared to. Nonetheless, adjoining such an atman-esque self to moderate materialism makes little difference to the uses I make of it, and I am prepared to accept it as a dualist amendment, if the reader insists. I shall call this position *quasi-materialism*. Apart from this, dualists are driven, I conclude, to something like Chalmers's position. In any case, they should reject extreme dualism on the grounds that there are better explanations of various distressing phenomena due to brain damage and better explanations of the genetic variability of character.

5. SOME CONTEMPORARY DUALISTS

It might be helpful to note just where some contemporary dualists stand on this issue. I have chosen those whose work on dualism I am familiar with. Hopefully they are representative. I have already mentioned Chalmers as a nomological dualist (Chalmers 1996). Here I shall respond to his case for rejecting the sort of metaphysically necessary links between the physical and the mental that I am proposing. His case is that all the uncontroversial cases of the conceivable but impossible may be understood as Kripkean examples, cases in which what is conceivable is that something of a given appearance turns out to be necessarily other than that which we believe it is (Kripke 1977). So, to use the standard example, water is, we believe, necessarily H_2O; but it is conceivable, although most unlikely, that what appears waterish might turn out to have a different composition, because the whole of chemistry rests upon a stupendous error. In that case water would not be H_2O. I agree with Chalmers that no such appearance/reality distinction could be made for the appearances as such, and therefore that this way of understanding the conceivable but impossible is not applicable to the mental. Chalmers's case therefore rests upon a supposed lack of what he calls *strong necessities,* whose negations are non-Kripkean examples of the conceivable but impossible.

I have two responses. The first is that this rejection of strong necessities begs the question against theism, and, as an aside, that our concept of necessity may well have arisen in the theistic context. For the distinction between the nomologically or physically impossible, on the one hand, and the metaphysically impossible, on the other, corresponds, modulo a few technicalities, to the distinction between (1) what God can or could have brought about even though it is impossible for us and (2) what not even God could ever have brought about. With that characterization of the distinction, it follows that some things are conceivable but impossible, such as that God never have existed, which are not Kripkean examples. Maybe Chalmers could reply that I have merely made a distinction between two grades of nomological necessity. So be it; I am not attached to the label 'materialist', which I find misleading, and if Chalmers considers my position dualist, that is fine by me, so long as I can rely on a stronger necessity than the ordinary nomological necessity.

My second response is that, in any case, there are heaps of plausible non-Kripkean examples of that which is conceivable but impossible. Some examples are provided by analytic ontology. Consider, for instance, the following claim. If there are two disjoint objects of the same mass, they share a universal. Pure mathematics provides other examples, such as the Axiom of Choice or the Continuum Hypothesis. Those are examples where we hold the claim in question to be either necessary or impossible, without being sure which it is. An example of a truth which almost all of us believe to be necessary but which is conceivably false is the Principle of Ontological Uniformity. This states that if an analytic ontology is adequate, say, on planet Earth, then it is also adequate elsewhere. So we should not, for instance, hold that on Earth there are only particulars, but elsewhere there are no particulars without universals instantiated by them. Likewise, we hold the necessity of the temporal uniformity of ontology. It is presumably impossible for

God to ensure that there are universals in this life, but there are just particulars after Judgement Day.

Richard Swinburne is reluctant to posit psycho-physical laws. That reluctance stems from his claim of the lack of system in the correlations between brain process and mental states. On my classification, he is, however, not an extreme dualist, for he holds that a soul could exist disembodied but would have no mental life in that state. He is certainly neither a moderate materialist nor a quasi-materialist, being quite explicit that the correlation of the mental with the physical is not a matter of metaphysical necessity. To the extent that he relies upon the principle that what is conceivable is either possible or a Kripkean example, he is open to the same responses as Chalmers.

In addition, Swinburne relies quite heavily on our intuitions of personal identity, using thought experiments to argue that fission is inconceivable, but that anything physical could split into exact duplicates without ceasing to exist. His example is a more realistic version of Roderick Chisholm's (1976: 104–13), and is based upon an only slightly idealized possibility of transplanting both halves of the brain into different brainless bodies (Swinburne and Shoemaker 1984). Assuming that we could survive as at least one person, it seems to follow that there is a non-physical indivisible component, a *self*, or else a non-repeatable property, a *haecceity*. Now I have no objection to the argument from inconceivability to impossibility, but the mere conceivability of my surviving bodily fission as the same person does not convince me of its possibility, especially since the only case that convinces me of its conceivability is a Kripkean example in which I can conceive of the nature of personhood being other than I believe it is. This case is that in which the whole universe undergoes fission many times a second into daughter universes. If this were so, then we, the paradigm persons, survive fission somehow or other. In that case being a person is necessarily other than we think it necessarily is. Presumably, in that case the required self/other distinction is relative to a single branch of the resulting tree of sub-universes.

There is, however, a different, and familiar, argument for the possibility of surviving bodily fission, one that does not depend directly on its conceivability: namely, that because someone would survive a failed attempt at fission in which one half ceased to exist, surely someone should survive successful fission (Swinburne and Shoemaker 1984; Swinburne 1986). Thus suppose your brain could be divided into two and each half placed in a brainless body. Then we are asked to compare (1) the case in which one of the bodies dies under the anaesthetic, in which case you survive as the other body plus half your original brain, with (2) the case in which both bodies survive, in which, I say, you fail to survive. What is the relevant difference? My answer is that to be a person requires having an objectively grounded self/other distinction, and that this distinction has to extend over time, rather than just occurring at an instant. Hence the fission of one sentient being into two, although possible, destroys the person by removing all grounds for a self/other distinction around the time of the fission. If, by chance, only one half survives, then this half has such grounds. The intuition that you survive, but only once, strikes me as a confusion of the intuition that you can survive fission as the same sentient being combined with the intuition that you cannot survive as two persons.

Another important contemporary dualist is Howard Robinson. He has presented a case for there being mental properties that cannot be identified with physical properties, and he has also argued that a person cannot be identified with any physical system (Robinson 2003). His case for not identifying mental with physical properties is interesting, and I find it persuasive; but it does not undermine the sort of moderate materialism that I am relying upon. Provided the correlations between the physical and the mental are metaphysically necessary, the resulting account is materialist, in my sense. Perhaps that makes me a crypto-dualist, not a real materialist. The label does not matter.

A more serious threat is Robinson's case for substance dualism, based on the premiss that if the mind has structure (that is, it is not simple), then it would be vague as to whether you would still be you in some counterfactual situations. For instance, if your brain was gradually replaced by bits of someone else's, at what point would you cease to be you, and so cease to exist? According to Robinson, there must be a precise answer; yet, if the mind is just the brain, or some other physical system, there can be no precision. As far as I can see, this is merely an argument for what I have called quasi-materialism, which would not greatly threaten kenotic theism.

Nonetheless, it is worth defending moderate materialism from Robinson's argument. It belongs to a family of continuity arguments in which our common-sense intuitions tell us that an individual (or a kind) has a precise essence, and yet the scientific account tells us there is continuity. Another example is Derek Parfit's case that if persons persist at all, they do so by enduring as the very same things—the Simple View of Chisholm (1976) and Swinburne (Swinburne and Shoemaker

1984). Parfit then infers by *modus tollens* that we do not persist, but my interest is in his continuity argument. He considers the gradual replacement of parts of him by parts of Greta Garbo (Parfit 1984: 236–9). So he is considering being the same person as we change over time, whereas Robinson is considering being the same person as we vary the counterfactual circumstances. He invites us to deny that there could be a gradual change of him into Garbo, and draws the conclusion that our concept of personal identity over time is one of strict identity—the Simple View or, in the Johnston–Lewis terminology *endurance* rather than *perdurance* (Lewis 1986: 202).

   The difficulty with such arguments is that we have no reason to pick and choose, yet a wholesale reliance on common sense against the scientific image would result in similar arguments against, say, the identification of rocks with sums of rock-parts such as fundamental particles, or, more accurately, the identification of a rock with the sum of rock-stages that are the sums of rock-part-stages. The argument here is that there is no precise limit on how extensive rock-parts can be replaced while the rock remains the same. Not merely is a dualism of objects and object-parts implausible, but it invites the materialist rejoinder that in such a metaphysics we could be material things that are not identified with the sum of our parts. Quite how we should respond to these continuity arguments is not my present concern, which is merely to resist their misleading application to the case of persons, whether by Parfit or by Robinson.

6. HOW SERIOUSLY SHOULD WE TAKE ZOMBIES AND WOBBLIOS?

Although I reject the principle that *all* conceivable impossibilities are Kripkean, I nonetheless endorse the principle that necessities are not to be multiplied more than is necessary. Yet I reject the metaphysical possibility of zombies and wobblios, even though a case for their possibility could be based on reluctance to multiply necessities. This case can be undermined somewhat by the intuitive plausibility of the metaphysically necessary dependence of hedonic tone on the (non-hedonic) content of mental states. Could an otherwise relaxed awareness of a calm blue sea be one of suffering? I think not. Again, although many philosophers suspect that we are all wobblios, I claim to know better, and many dualists would agree that actually there are no wobblios.

Here I suggest that there is a necessary connection: any wobblio would be a zombie, although wobblios who are not zombies are conceivable. These examples are not intended to *prove* that zombies and wobblios are impossible. Instead, they are meant to set some standard for the sort of gain that is worth the pain of positing conceivable impossibilities, thus undermining the great reluctance of dualists to do so.

Even more bizarre examples come to mind. There are the *week-enders*—that is, molecule-for-molecule replicas of normal human beings who are zombies on weekdays, conscious at the weekend. And then there are the *westies*, whose conscious episodes occur when, and only when, listening to Country and Western music. These two examples are spurious, but in an instructive fashion. They are spurious because the dualist may reasonably claim that their implausibility derives not from impossibility but from their low probability relative to the du-alists' overall metaphysics. What is instructive about these examples is that they require no hypothesis to exclude them as unreal: either they are impossible, or they are highly improbable. By contrast, some of the other examples, such as wobblios who are not zombies, have to be hypothesized not to occur, either by declaring them impossible or by declaring them possible but non-occurring. Although I grant the presumption in favour of possibility, the cost of not overcoming it in the case of zombies and wobblios is to be committed to hypotheses about their non-existence, even though these are said to be possible and even though the physical origin of human beings provides no reason for denying that there are zombies or wobblios.

Initially, therefore, we have a stand-off: either side has to hypothesize that there are neither zombies nor wobblios, and it does not make a great deal of difference whether this is hypothesized as necessarily or merely actually the case. To this initial stand-off, theists might well respond that it would be wrong and unloving of God to create some zombies alongside ordinary humans: unloving because of the risk that those we humans love are zombies, wrong because it is a presupposition of all morality not to treat your neighbour as a zombie, and God would act wrongly in allowing the presupposition of all morality to be, unknown to us, false. Moreover, this providential solution to the threat of infiltration of humanity by hordes of zombies is consistent with the developmental theism that I am proposing. For, if it requires a special act of creation of the soul for God to ensure that a human being is neither a zombie nor a wobblio, then these acts will occur after creation and hence, I assume, after the development from Pure Will to Unbounded Love.

Because of the presumption against positing necessities, I would say initially that atheists should suspend judgement between nomological dualism and moderate materialism, while theists should incline towards the version of dualism in which souls are created but their states are providentially correlated of nomological necessity with physical states. In the next two sections I present some arguments that should make us all incline towards moderate materialism, regardless of belief in God. As this talk of inclinations shows, I doubt if any of these considerations are conclusive.

7. WHY NOMOLOGICAL DUALISM IS NOT GOOD NEWS FOR THEISTS

Theists should say that the laws of nature are the result of the divine choice to create a life-friendly universe. Otherwise they take as mysterious something with a perfectly good theistic explanation: namely, the astounding fact that the universe has life-friendly laws of nature. And theists should say this even if, perversely in my opinion, they do not use this explanation as a reason for believing in God. For even if you believe in God on grounds other than explanatory power, you are still under an intellectual obligation to use theism as an explanation where appropriate. So all theists, including those who are dualists, should understand the laws of nature as due to divine choice. In addition, there is the question of what distinguishes metaphysical from nomological necessity. Again, theists should avail themselves of a perfectly good way of making the distinction: the difference between nomological and metaphysical necessity is precisely that God ordains the former while at all times being constrained by the latter. Theists who are nomological dualists should therefore take the laws governing the interaction of the mental with the physical to be caused by a divine decision. But, as Mackie (1982) points out, this divine ordaining of the laws would itself be an instance of the laws governing the interaction of the mental with the physical. Or if not, then divine agency is supposed to operate in a way unlike human agency, preventing the latter being a precedent for the former, and so greatly increasing the intellectual cost of theism.

There is, then, a serious dilemma for dualists who are theists: either the psycho-physical laws are exceptions to the way in which the laws of nature are the result of God's choice; or these laws undermine the precedent that human agency sets for the postulate of divine agency. Suppose the attempt is made to go between the horns of the dilemma by abandoning nomological dualism and saying that souls are to be understood as substances with irreducible powers and capacities, rather than as substances with mental states constrained by the combination of laws of nature and brain processes, on which their powers and capacities depend. It then becomes puzzling as to why, in the human case, genetics and brain damage affect these powers and capacities.

I draw the conclusion that the advantage of a unified hypothesis concerning God and human beings outweighs the disadvantage required in hypothesizing the metaphysical impossibility of zombies and wobblios. If there is a non-physical self, it lacks all intrinsic character and personality and serves only the, to my mind unnecessary, theoretical purpose of being the relatum of the appearing relation. Hence theists should be either moderate materialists or quasi-materialists.

8. WHY NOMOLOGICAL DUALISM SHOULD NOT BE COMBINED WITH EVOLUTIONARY NATURALISM

The previous section might perhaps be taken by some dualists as an objection to theism. I shall now argue that, on the contrary, it is an objection to nomological dualism of the sort espoused by David Chalmers. For the chief alternative to theism is evolutionary naturalism, which cannot adequately explain why we have the psycho-physical laws we do have.

I say that we do not need to explain the correlations between the mental states and the functional roles they play, roles that are instantiated by physical processes. These correlations are, I say, perfectly comprehensible and known a priori. For the phenomenal character of mental states must be such that they provide reasons for acting in ways that correspond to the behaviour that our brains tend to cause. The alternative would be an absurd world which we can begin to imagine by extrapolating from the milder abnormality of behaviour that does not correspond to how we feel, like Patricia Smith Churchland's example of incontinent grief, where the patient sobs and exhibits other characteristic grief behaviour while reporting feeling no grief (Churchland 1986: 222–3). But the cases that we are to imagine are ones in which, in spite of feeling joy, the sufferers assure us they do feel grief, and, moreover, they have what we would take as good reason for grief. Such emotional inverts are, I grant, conceivable, but if the psycho-physical laws were metaphysically contingent, these laws might have systematically correlated feelings of joy with grief behaviour, even when there were good reasons to grieve. This is, I say, absurd—meaning that we know it a priori not to be the case. That does not *entail* that it is metaphysically impossible. But I take it that having a priori knowledge of something is *evidence* for its metaphysical necessity. So we obtain the Principle of Harmony: the phenomenal character of a mental state must be such as to provide some reasons for acting in ways that result in the behaviour that the physical processes tend to cause. Or at the very least, I would say that there is a metaphysically necessary conditional principle: if there is any awareness of this state, then that awareness is appropriate to the functional role that state performs. In that case we might go on to posit an atman-esque self as the conscious thing, but we would not have nomological dualism.

The nomological dualist must reject this apparently a priori and obvious character of the harmony between the functional role and the phenomenal state as merely the result of our being accustomed to the correlation. (Shades of David Hume!) Now we theists can give a providential explanation for the harmony in question, on the assumption of nomological dualism. But how could the naturalists explain it? The only explanation would be that as agents we have some control over what is merely a tendency or propensity to behave a certain way, and so if the phenomenal character was inappropriate, we would act differently, with disastrous consequences for our survival. Thus, if we felt an enormous revulsion at the thought of eating when our brain state was one of hunger, we might, it could be suggested, refrain from eating and so starve. So there is a survival-of-the-fittest story to be told about why we have psycho-physical harmony. But survival of the fittest is only half the story: evolution also requires the genetic inheritance of traits with occasional mutations. And there is just no mechanism for the inheritance of or mutation in a psycho-physical law of nature. Consequently, the evolutionary explanation amounts to something like this: a vast array of possible neural architectures could have evolved, but unfortunately most of these, although functioning at the physical level, result in disharmony between the phenomenal character and functional role. So organisms with these kinds of neural architecture die out, leaving only those for which harmony holds.

The difficulty with this naturalistic explanation is the role it assigns to agency. At what stage in the course of evolution does agency arise? Suppose, as might seem plausible, that it requires a rather high degree of mental sophistication reached only by some mammals. All these have the same basic neural structures, and the chance that this is one that results in psycho-physical harmony would be low. So the explanation would require an unwarranted appeal to good luck. At the other extreme, if we posited agency at a time when various phyla were evolving from worms, we could easily suppose such a variety of neural architecture that only those survived which satisfied psycho-physical harmony. But such an early date for agency is not plausible. Perhaps the best that naturalists can do is to compromise, and say that there were three groups of organisms with fairly advanced neural architecture: cephalopods, dinosaurs/birds, and mammals, all three of which were at the threshold of agency. In that case naturalists could speculate that only mammals had, by chance, the required psycho-physical harmony to allow the evolution of agency. Does three or even, say, six different neural architectures provide enough opportunities for psycho-physical harmony to avoid the appeal to good luck? It would if all we had to consider was the way pain feels, but mammals are motivated not just by the desire to avoid pain; there are other stimuli which, although not painful when mild, are avoided, notably itchiness, hunger, thirst, cold, and heat. And mammals are motivated positively by the desire for sex and status. With such an array of motivating phenomenal states, psycho-physical harmony would still seem too much like good luck. I conclude that if nomological dualism is correct, then the best explanation for psycho-physical harmony would have to be providential. So naturalists as well as theists should take the correlations between the mental and the physical to hold of metaphysical rather than nomological necessity.

9. DUALIST VARIANTS ON MODERATE MATERIALISM

I have already noted one reason that could be given for rejecting even moderate materialism. It is evident that mental states *appear*. If these states are physical, then some, maybe all, physical states *appear*. Common sense would tell us that there can be nothing that appears without it appearing to something, a *self.* I myself see no reason to follow common sense in this regard, being quite happy to say that we mistake a non-relational property of appearing for a relational one. (See Forrest 1996*a*: ch 5.) But if we do follow common sense, it would seem that there must be a self to which things appear. This might be an individual self, but many Indian thinkers, notably Sankara, have held that there is just the one self, not a different self for each human being. In Western philosophy, Aristotle's active intellect and, for all we are supposed to know, Kant's transcendental ego would likewise be the same for all of us.

Somewhat more persuasive is the argument that the unity of the mind at one time is incompatible with materialism, because, it is said, any complex physical system may be analysed as a collection of interacting parts. This unity is, I suspect, revealed not, in introspection so much as in reflection upon agency. Whereas mere behaviour could be analysed in terms of the causal interactions between various parts of the brain and the rest of the body, there is no physical part of a human being smaller than the cerebral cortex which may be identified as the agent.

Although this is not the same as Robinson's continuity argument, it might be used to reach a similar conclusion: namely, the identification of an agent with a non-physical self. I disagree. Although I grant that unity is a necessary, but not sufficient, condition for something to be an agent, I claim that a *holistic* physical system satisfies this condition. A holistic physical system may be characterized negatively as one that is not completely decomposable, where by a complete decomposition of a system I mean: (1) a way of correlating the state of the whole with the states of and relations between the parts; together with (2) an associated dynamics, whereby changes to the whole state, whether determined or governed by probabilistic laws, is specified by the behaviour of the parts and the ways in which the relations changes. The holistic character of quantum theory is supported by the well-known violation of Bell's Inequality; but since this is beyond the scope of this work, it suffices to challenge anyone to argue that the empirical evidence currently available supports the complete decomposition of even finite isolated physical systems. If this challenge cannot be met, then there is no good argument against materialism from the unity required for agency. The holistic character of quantum theory does not explain either consciousness or agency, but it does remove the obstacle to the idea that a complex physical system might be an agent, acting, temporarily at least, as one.

It might be objected that the brain is a classical, deterministic system, rather than one that requires quantum theory to understand it. I take it that the work of Roger Penrose (1987), Michael Lockwood (1989: ch. 14), and others in trying to discover the scientific basis of consciousness has in fact shown how quantum-theoretic phenomena might occur in the brain, even though it is too early to decide this.

This use of holism to defend materialism may be seen in its historical context—history of the only kind I know, sweeping and idealized. Regardless of the state of science, the unity required for agency sets up a disjunction: either dualism or holism. Modern science began as mechanistic, and hence non-holistic. And that was no accident, for completely decomposable systems, such as idealized pendulums, springs, and solar systems are the easiest to investigate. The correlation of dualism with mechanism is therefore not a quirk of Descartes. Given the background assumption of a deterministic and completely decomposable physics, a proper appreciation of agency must lead to a dualism in which, from time to time, agents break the laws of nature. This is ugly metaphysics, however elegant the physics. Thank God for quantum theory!

Yet other reasons for believing in a non-physical self or soul might be provided by the unity of consciousness at a time and by the identity of a person over time. I have already considered and rejected these reasons when discussing Robinson and Swinburne.

While I think the case for a non-physical self or soul is unconvincing, I am prepared to accommodate it in one of two ways. The first is a version of dualism according to which the soul is something non-physical and there is a metaphysically necessary Conditional Principle of Harmony: namely, that if there is a soul, then the way things appear to it must harmonize with the functional role. This is a version of what I have called quasi-materialism. The second is a modification of moderate materialism that asserts that, as a matter of metaphysical necessity, whenever there is a suitable physical system, there must be a self or soul as just described.

Another modification occurs if we grant, as many do, that the qualia are under-determined by their functional roles. In other words, it is suggested that the phenomenal character of sensory states, especially of sight, hearing, and smell, could have been different without any difference in the way in which these states interact with other mental states to affect behaviour. The most familiar example in the literature is red/green colour reversal, where the sensation that one person gets when looking at a colour chip labelled 'green' is just like the sensation the other person gets when looking at a chip labelled 'red', and vice versa (Byrne 2005). The functional role of colour vision is to discriminate between colours. Hence the reversal would not, it seems, affect the functional role. This example can lead to rather inconclusive discussions of the lack of any perfectly symmetrical colour reversal. In addition, we might note the aesthetic difference between a non-representative painting and its red/green reverse. Perhaps, therefore, a better example concerns scents. Many flowers are pleasant to smell—for instance, roses, violets, sweet peas, and gardenias—and their fragrances differ. Differences in scent do play some functional role, but for a human being the variety of scents far exceeds the variety of functional roles. If roses always smelt to you just like gardenias smell to me, and vice versa, what difference would it make?

Assuming that it is metaphysically necessary that physical states appear in ways appropriate to their functional role, we might well allow that there is nothing whatever determining the precise qualia from among a range all equally appropriate for the functional role. This does not mean the qualia could change, for constancy in the qualia plays a functional role. (In some cases the difference is noticed. For instance, those who acquire perfect pitch in childhood notice a gradual change in music resulting from the ageing process.) So perhaps we should modify the weak materialist position: the metaphysically necessary truth that the phenomenal qualities be appropriate to the functional role fails to determine just what the phenomenal qualities are like. This does not, however, require a return to nomological dualism. What is not constrained of metaphysical necessity need not, in this case, be constrained at all.

Of these modifications, the only one to affect anything I have to say in this book is that in which there is a non-physical soul and the psycho-physical correlations, although metaphysically necessary, are conditional upon the existence of a suitable soul. That position would prevent me from saying that various physical changes automatically have various mental consequences, for God and for creatures. Instead, I would say that these physical changes are pre-conditions for the corresponding mental change, leaving the decision as to whether the mental change occurs to divine choice. For example, instead of thinking of the evolution of organisms as proceeding to a point where the individual organisms (human beings) become persons distinct from God, I would have to say that evolution proceeds to the point where God may ordain that those organisms be non-divine persons. Readers who are not persuaded of the correctness of moderate materialism may well prefer that account.

4

The Power, Knowledge, and Motives of the Primordial God

In Chapter 2 I argued that there was an intellectual niche for the hypothesis of a Primordial God. That is, even before we consider what theism explains, this hypothesis is not too improbable to be entertained. In this chapter I consider the power, knowledge, and motives of the Primordial God, and the important question of whether this God is morally good.

1. THE MIND OF THE PRIMORDIAL GOD

As a preliminary, I shall now summarize my hypothesis about the Primordial God, as presented in Chapter 2. In the human case there is a limited awareness of future possibilities and the ability to reject some and so choose others. I take it, then, that in the beginning there was an unlimited awareness of future possibilities with an unlimited capacity to reject some and choose others. All these possibilities supervene on the material or, more accurately, the non-mental, in that there is no difference between them without a non-mental difference. This is the hypothesis of the Primordial God. But there are three further points of clarification. The first is that, as far as we know, we can replace 'non-mental' by 'physical', but we do not know that there are no alien possibilities with humanly incomprehensible properties that are neither physical nor mental.

The second point of clarification concerns the divine self-knowledge. In animals, including us, personhood develops with self-knowledge. For there can be no sense of self that is at all accurate without a sense of what is other than self. But because for the Primordial God there is no other, it is possible for that God to know itself in the sense of being aware of the unity of all that appears to it (namely, the possibilities for the future) without any sense of the other. Hence the Primordial God could be a self with self-knowledge but without personhood. I am supposing that this unity is required for agency, for without it there would either be many agents or just a parcel of vain strivings. But to say that the Primordial God is a self does not imply self-awareness. Nonetheless, the simplest hypothesis about the Primordial God is that it is aware of all there is, and hence aware of the unity of the system of possibilities of which there is awareness. Hence we should think of the Primordial God as self-aware if and only if we identify it with all there was at the beginning.

The third point is that we may stipulate whether we include the grounds for the possibilities—abstract entities, maybe—as parts of the Primordial God, or whether we treat them as something external of which It is aware. If we want to retain the tradition of divine simplicity, we shall make the latter stipulation. If we identify the Primordial God with all there is initially, we shall make the former one, and so think of the initial awareness of the unity of all there is as self-knowledge. Now there is a difficulty in making an abstract/concrete distinction among necessary beings, but we do have some relevant intuitions. Suppose, first, that, as I am inclined to believe, the self is constituted by the unity of the appearances. In that case a self without the things that directly appear to it would be abstract, and we should therefore stipulate that the Primordial God is all there is, and so has genuine self-knowledge. On the other hand, suppose that there is a self distinct from appearance, and not ontologically dependent on anything else. Then, intuitively, this would seem a concrete entity even if it is one among many necessary beings. In that case we should identify the initial self with the Primordial God, in distinction from the possibilities. We should then be agnostic about whether the Primordial God was self-aware, because it is not clear that the human case provides any precedent for knowledge of a self distinct from appearances. Hume famously denies being able to find one (Book I, Part 4, Section 6, of *A Treatise of Human Nature*).

2. THE POWER OF THE PRIMORDIAL GOD

The Primordial God is not constrained by anything external to it. It has the whole realm of possible universes to choose from. Moderate materialism implies, however, a limitation of the possibilities to physical universes. Hence the Primordial God could not create a non-physical realm, even though this is conceivable, and so, although almighty, it is not omnipotent, in the sense of being able to do all that it is conceivable that a unique God might do. Thus God could not create angels if these are bodiless souls. Instead, I suggest that speculations about angels be interpreted as about beings whose physical embodiment is not matter in the ordinary states of solid, liquid, and gas. I am not denying that God could, and perhaps has, created such beings either in our or some other universe.

In the human case our power to act directly is only the power to cause various bodily movements or various mental events. Although this is extremely limited, it is, I submit, the precedent for divine power. Our limited power is future-directed, in that we imagine a way things might become in the immediate future and, if we are able directly to bring it about, do so. So if we consider the Primordial God as having unlimited power, then we may reasonably suppose that this power extends to the whole future of a universe, so that what God is choosing is that there be a (not necessarily determinate) type of universe with its history—a history that is all in the future at the time of the Primordial God's choice. Now I grant that it is plausible that whenever an agent acts, something happens immediately. In the case in which God chooses what will happen in the future, this something would be, I submit, a law of nature. But there is a rival account of what constitutes the natural order, involving kinds of being having as essential properties various powers and capacities. If this rival account is correct, then God brings about some persisting entity, plausibly a whole universe, with various essential properties (Bigelow, Ellis, and Lierse 2004). But in either case, although God brings about something immediately, the intention of the act is to affect the future in a way that is not mediated by any other intention. Thus God is not limited to choosing an initial condition. Here the Boethian image of God looking out on the universe, past, present, and future, all at once holds, but not for the actual world so much as for the possible ones. God could have chosen to create one or more determinate universes complete in every detail at all times, in which case the Boethian image would have held of the actual universe. In that case there would have been no room for any further agency, whether divine or creaturely. But, as it is, there are other agents, including human ones.

A corollary of this account of God's power is that, even if the universe is infinitely old, we must say that the creative act precedes the universe. For otherwise we would have to say that the laws of nature are repeatedly brought about by God. And by that I do not mean that God keeps on ensuring that the laws hold for the next moment. For in that case they would not be genuine laws, and I shall argue in Chapter 5 that God would bring about genuine laws rather than mere regularities. The case being considered is that God would repeatedly have to cause the very same laws. But this is paradoxical, because at every time the divine act would be pointless, the laws in question already existing, and yet if God therefore were never to bring the law about, there would be no law. Because of this paradoxical consequence, we do better to insist that God would precede an infinitely old universe.[1]

Within the scope of the supposition that the universe is infinitely old, I need to defend the prior existence of God from the charge of absurdity. But I am not worried by William Craig's arguments (1979: 65–110) against the coherence of an infinite past. For if these arguments hold, then the universe cannot be infinitely old, God or no God. My concern is with the additional problems that arise if there is an infinite duration between God's creative act and the present. I suspect that part of the problem is the thought that there is no number minus infinity, and hence no date minus infinity BC. But there is no problem with the mathematics of plus and minus infinity, and the relevant infinity in this case is the smallest infinite ordinal.

Here is a genuine problem. If we suppose that there is an infinity of stages to the history of the universe, each of which causes and hence explains the next, then we require any two stages in the causal/explanatory chain to be connected by intermediaries. This connectedness requirement is satisfied by an infinite regress of causes or explanations, but not for the system consisting of an initial stage, then an infinity of intermediate stages, and then the present stage. This problem would be insoluble if God's creative activity directly affected only that which was in the immediate future. But I have already argued against that restriction. Because in the one creative act God can directly affect a whole infinite sequence of events, there is no failure of connection between the initial divine act and our present state. If the universe is infinitely old, I hypothesize that in the one creative act God brings about the whole history of the universe up to a certain stage, which stage is a finite number of years ago.

Maybe there is another problem. It may well be incoherent to think of a sentient being that has undergone an infinite sequence of distinct experiences. If this is a genuine problem, then we may think of God's act of creation occurring at an alpha moment with the next divine mental

---

[1] I am indebted to a referee for the Press for pointing out that this is a version of the Assassin Paradox. The first assassin will kill if the victim is still alive at, say, 11 p.m.; the second will kill if the victim is still alive at 10.45 p.m.; the third if the victim is still alive at 10.37.30 p.m.; and so on for an infinity of assassins. So no one kills the victim. But in that case they all do! It is worth noting that this paradox is more than a conundrum in the theological context. It becomes a genuine problem.

state occurring at a beta moment, an infinity of time later, whenever the initially predestined sequence of events terminates. This would cohere well with the hypothesis that our universe has undergone an infinity of cycles, with only the most recent one being suited to life. For then the beta moment might coincide with the beginning of this cycle. It coheres somewhat less well with the hypothesis that non-divine persons have arisen in an infinity of previous cycles. For then the infinitely many that lived before the beta moment would have had their acts predestined by God. If there were well-confirmed scientific theory that implies an infinity of life-friendly cycles, I would be somewhat disturbed and forced to admit that even divinely predestined lives are worth living.

3. THE KNOWLEDGE OF THE PRIMORDIAL GOD

My hypothesis implies that the Primordial God is aware of the possible physical universes, but it does not yet tell us in what ways God is aware of them. It does not answer the question of what it is like to be God. In the human case we have some, albeit limited, capacity to imagine what it would be like if such-and-such occurred, and we can imagine this to some extent for other persons. So we might say that God is aware of possible worlds only in the sense of imagining what it would be like to be every sentient being in every possible world. Suppose that there is nothing it is like for a creature to perceive a quark. It would then be rash to assume that, nonetheless, there is something it is like to be God seeing or maybe smelling the quark.

An alternative, which I used to hold, is that God knows what a quark is like from every point of view relative to a quark and in every possible sense modality (Forrest 1996*a*: 210–12.) These two accounts might coincide, but if, for instance, it is not possible for a creature to perceive a quark, then my new account is weaker than the old one, and so I am not, strictly speaking, hypothesizing a Primordial God of greatest conceivable knowledge of the physical. Nonetheless, the hypothesis of a God who knows what it would be like to be any possible creature is of a knower who is perfect in the sense of having knowledge complete of its kind, without external limitations.

I submit, then, that the Primordial God is aware of all possible physical universes, and knows what they would be like, at least in the sense of knowing what it would be like to be any sentient creature in them. What about hedonic tone? Sentient beings are aware of things, and sometimes this is mere awareness; but often the awareness is modified, in that it is either joyful or suffering awareness. Now to provide a motive for creation, some such understanding of joy and/or suffering is required. If God were aware only of suffering, it is hard to see how God could derive joy from being aware of the lives of sentient creatures that would not be derived from the awareness of non-sentient ones, which are just as pleasing. This leaves two hypotheses: that the Primordial God is aware of joy and suffering, or is aware of joy only. The latter is tempting, because it offers us a way of dealing with the Problem of Evil. For, without saying that evil is the privation of good, we could say that the only evils God knows of are privations. Thus God would not be aware of any difference between someone who is joyless without much, if any, suffering—your average non-acute depressee—and someone who is joyless because of immense suffering. God would be aware only of the lack of the joy that this sort of being has the capacity to experience. Nevertheless, I appeal to the principle that an arbitrary limitation on God is implausible. So if God is aware of joy, I think that God should be supposed to be aware of suffering too. And God is, I am supposing, aware from the inside, as it were, knowing what it would be like to be each creature.

'How do I know all this?', you might well ask. Of course I do not know it, but I am developing the idea that a being without the sort of complex brain processes we have would have to be aware in a way that involved no thought or belief or reasoning, and being aware of possibilities in this way amounts to imaging how things might be.

4. THE CHARACTER AND MOTIVES OF THE PRIMORDIAL GOD

What do I mean by saying that God might have character? The idea of character is, I think, best explained by saying that to have character is for it to be appropriate to say that you act in character or act out of character. So character is something that motivates an agent to act in some ways but not others, where the other ways are such that another being of the same kind in the same situation might be just as motivated to perform.

We may therefore say that God has character if God is motivated to perform some acts but not others from among the range that we might expect a God to perform. Consequently, rationality is a character trait for human beings, but would not be for God if God is not the sort of being that could act irrationally.

We have, then, a dilemma: should we hypothesize that the Primordial God has a certain character? If we do, for instance by saying that the Primordial God is loving, then we have complicated theism considerably. For we may suppose that in the human case character is largely a matter of habit or else innate, but in either case presumably something to do with the neural architecture we have acquired. We know, sadly, that dementia does not just result in confusion, but also all too often in a deterioration of character. There are exceptions such as St John, who it is said in old age answered every question by saying 'Love one another'. But most dementia is not so benign. Because of its dependence on neural architecture in the human case, it would be improper anthropomorphism to ascribe character to the Primordial God. That leaves us with the other horn of the dilemma. Without ascribing character to the Primordial God, we must find a motive for acting that derives solely from the kind of being it is, Pure Will or unrestricted agency, and it is hard to see how such a kind of being would have a motive to do anything, even though it could do an enormous variety of things.

My aim will be to blunt the second horn by finding motives that require no character, and hence adopt the simpler hypothesis that the Primordial God has none, although if having character is a good thing, no doubt God acquires it later. And I suspect that this is precisely what does happen and the divine character is loving, although, at least for the First Person, it also manifests itself in a rather stern sense of justice, a love of obedience, a sense of humour that finds the downfall of the proud amusing, and in a loyalty that demands reciprocation. These are all character traits, and I do not ascribe them to the Primordial God.

To be an agent requires having a motive for acting, and we are seeking a motive that does not depend on character. In the human case things are complicated by our limited capacity to imagine outcomes and our limited power to bring them about. In the interests of metaphysical simplicity, we should posit a God not limited in these ways. So what we say about means to ends in the human case will not be relevant. It is the ends themselves that are the precedent for the divine motives. Here I recall my favourite passage from Hume's *Dialogues* (Part III):

All the sentiments of the human mind, gratitude, resentment, love, friendship, approbation, blame, pity, emulation, envy, have a plain reference to the state and situation of man, and are calculated for preserving the existence and promoting the activity of such a being in such circumstances. It seems, therefore, unreasonable to transfer such sentiments to a supreme existence, or to suppose him actuated by them.

I am inclined to agree that these sentiments are not such as we would expect the Primordial God to feel. But Hume is looking at detailed motives, and, characteristically, the detailed motives can be analysed as the application of more generic motives to the human situation. For instance, in so far as anger is a motive for action, as opposed to a mere cause of behaviour, the motive is surely the suffering caused by restraining the anger and the anticipated joy at the result of the expression of anger.

Even if we did not have to meet Hume's objection, we should be looking for rather basic or generic motives. For human motives are complicated, so complicated that moral psychology, which examines them in detail, should be studied not by philosophers, who are too impatient, but in literature departments—after sending all the post-modernists into early retirement. But my purpose is to extract from the wonderful confusion of human motives those we might ascribe to a Primordial God, without character or personality. And I am committed to simplicity as a guide to theory choice.

Let us begin, then, with some rather basic motives, ones that do not obviously concern the human situation. Much attention has been paid to moral motivation. It is asked whether awareness of the moral required-ness, or even the supererogatory goodness, of an act is an adequate motive for acting. Again, there is a similar question concerning value motivation in the broader sense: namely, that awareness of value, perhaps aesthetic value, is taken as a motive for acting. At the other end of the spectrum, there is the thesis of ethical egoism, according to which the basic motive is always the expected state of the individual concerned. Against this we have the occurrence of acts of compassion, whose paradigm, the Good Samaritan, is indeed fictitious but nonetheless true to life. And all these discussions are intertwined with discussion of the adequacy of belief/desire theories of motivation. Hopefully, I can cut through a great deal of this detail, in the highly simplified case of the Primordial God.

First, what is the difference between a reason and a motive? Well, as I understand it, a reason is a belief, and beliefs involve a way of symbolically representing the possible futures. Motives I take to include reasons, but also to include something that I think is rather important in both the hu-man and the divine case: imagining what it is like to be in a certain kind of situation. We might, for instance, think of the Good Samaritan as be-ing moved by a capacity to imagine what it would be like to be wounded and abandoned by the side of the road, without putting it into words.

Now there is an ongoing discussion of whether motives have to include a component of desire (Gaus 1990). But desires, like beliefs, involve representation, and it would seem that something more immediate is possible, while still motivating an action rather than merely causing behaviour. Motives involve a hedonic tone, which is either positive (of the joyful kind) or negative (of the suffering kind). To call this a 'tone' is to suggest that it is adverbial—that is, it qualifies some other mental state. So there can be joyful awareness of something, perhaps even joyful self-consciousness as in the state of bliss. But I doubt that there can be joy just by itself. Likewise, I doubt whether there can be pure suffering without content.

One motive for acting, then, is the imagination of the joy of being in a certain situation. Another, of the opposing kind, is imagination of the suffering of being in a certain situation. Taken together, I call these the hedonic motive. Why not call it eudaemonic? My answer is that eudaemonism treats flourishing as the greatest good, and it is not the same to say that people flourish and that they have joy. For a drug-induced euphoria is not typically a state of flourishing. Moreover, things that are not persons may be said to flourish. The connection between flourishing and joy is that the awareness that things and especially people are flourishing typically gives joy to those aware of it. So typically, a person's awareness of her or his own flourishing is a source of joy. Hence the hedonic motive for creation should result in a great deal of flourishing, which gives joy to God and others who are aware of it.

The advantage of postulating the hedonic motive for the Primordial God is that the motivating power of anticipated joy and suffering is obvious. To be sure, in the human case there is the contest between my joy and the suffering of others, and between my suffering and the joy of others. If, as I claim, there is no self/other distinction for the Primordial God, then we are left with an entirely comprehensible motivation without such contests.

This raises the question of just what kinds of situations give joy when there is consciousness of them, and which give suffering. To say that *anything* could, for all we know, give joy, and *anything* give suffering implies the possibility of the sado-masochist of holy will who so loves painful sensations as to inflict them upon others out of sheer goodness of heart. But to deny variations in what gives joy is to remove all impact of character on hedonic motivation. When asked what studying nature had shown him about God, Haldane quipped that God had 'an inordinate fondness for beetles'. Let us take this reply with a seriousness that was not intended. Might joy at the wonderful variety of beetles be the chief reason for creation, with us being a mere by-product? That seems odd, very odd. But might we say that God does derive more joy from the variety of beetles than most humans do? That is less odd. Who are we to assume that God is just like us? This suggests the following compromise position. First I stipulate that by a *source* of joy or suffering I mean that which directly occasions joy or suffering, respectively, to someone. Then I submit that there are some metaphysically necessary constraints on sources of joy and suffering, but it is a matter of the character of the agent concerned as to which possible sources actually give joy or suffering. Thus I suggest that pure malice is impossible. That is, it is not possible *directly* to enjoy the suffering of others, and malice arises from envying others their joy, and so indirectly reducing your own suffering of envy by inflicting suffering of others. On the other hand, it is possible to enjoy sharing what gives you joy, but it is not inevitable that this be so. A plausible general principle here is that no possible source of joy is a possible source of suffering.

Assuming that the Primordial God lacks character, we would expect it to be motivated positively by all possible sources of joy and negatively by all possible sources of suffering. Now I am not supposing the Primordial God to be simple, if we include as parts of its description everything it is aware of. So there is a place for joy in the awareness of some rather complicated situations. Quite why such an awareness should be a possible source of joy is a mystery, but it is one we are familiar with in the human case, where we call it aesthetic. Again, it is mysterious why others having false beliefs should be a source of suffering, but we know that this is a possibility from the human case. The hedonic motive, then, covers an enormous variety of situations that the Primordial God would find joy in being aware of, including aesthetic pleasure and sharing that pleasure, as well as situations that it would find suffering in being aware of, including false beliefs and malice. The difficulty in deciding what the Primordial God would do, and perhaps the cause of some arbitrariness in its action, is in weighing up these sources of joy and suffering. And it is here that we should be careful before saying that the Primordial God is benevolent. For a benevolent person has a character that results in the sacrificing of some other sources of joy—for instance, the aesthetic appreciation of things—for the sake of the well-being of others. And I see no reason to assume that the Primordial God is benevolent in that sense.

Implicit in the above is an account of the qualified objectivity of aesthetics. For I am claiming that the *possible* sources of joy and of suffering are fewer than the *conceivable* sources, and that no possible direct source of joy is also a possible direct source of suffering. Applying this to those complex sources of joy we call aesthetic, I arrive at the position that beauty is objective, in the modal sense that it is a possible source of joy but not a possible source of suffering. The aesthetic remains subjective, in that actual conscious beings, excepting God, typically have a limited number of experiences that are actual direct sources of joy. It also remains the case that a given object might appear differently to different sentient beings, resulting in quite different experiences, one a source of joy, the other of suffering. For instance, beings that see a different range of light frequencies might experience something as horribly garish that we find pleasing. Notice also that this qualified objectivism about the aesthetic is available only because I distinguish the possible from the conceivable. Even though it is quite conceivable, I deny that exactly similar experiences could be direct sources of joy to one and suffering to another.

It is so widely assumed that beauty is in the eye of the beholder that even my qualified objectivism about aesthetics might seem implausible. But the qualified objectivism that I propose coheres much better with the experience people have of growing, rather than merely changing, as they come to appreciate what they had been unable to previously.

I claim that the hedonic motive is not just one motive, but that it is the only motive that we should ascribe to the Primordial God, and that it is based upon a capacity to know what it would be like to be in various circumstances. This further suggestion is supported by an elimination of other motives. Some of these are based upon character, character such as God might later acquire—perhaps even before creation. Other general motives such as the love of truth or beauty may be reduced to the hedonic. Thus the love of beauty just is the anticipation of the joy of being aware of the beautiful. The love of truth, I would suggest, is in fact better described as the hatred of falsehood: a system of beliefs, however useful, is a source of suffering for those who judge it false.

I anticipate the objection that this reductive account of the love of truth and beauty disregards what I take to be Plato's thesis that to be aware of the good automatically motivates a person to act rightly, regardless of joy or suffering. The objection, then, is that, however complicated such values as truth, beauty, and goodness are, they are real features of the possible universes, and hence the Primordial God is aware of them, and to be aware of them is to be motivated to create only the good-and-beautiful universes.

This objection threatens me with what David Stove used to call the 'spaghetti effect'—you attempt to fork up a little and find you have the lot. An adequate reply might cover the whole of meta-ethics. Instead,

I merely state a parsimonious account of values. Beauty and moral obligation are such as must indeed motivate any normal person who is aware of them, but their capacity to motivate should be understood as a constraint on potential analyses of these properties rather than as an unanalysable feature of them. For treating them as primitive complicates our hypothesis about ethics. Furthermore, in the human case I assert that this motivation proceeds either via habit or via hedonic tone. Thus beauty motivates lingering with the beautiful thing or person, but the answer to the question of why you linger should not in normal circumstances be 'Because it's beautiful', but 'It gives me joy to see it'. Likewise, moral obligations motivate either because of habit (a righteous character) or because of the suffering involved in doing what is prohibited. A possible exception would be an innate character trait which functions like a habit. So an innately virtuous person might act as if habitually righteous. All this is too complicated for the Primordial God. I conclude, then, that the sole motive for this God is imagination of hedonic tone.

5. THE IMPORTANCE OF THE AESTHETIC COMPONENT OF THE DIVINE MOTIVE

Ours is a universe of great beauty, which is perhaps the chief reason for preferring the theistic over the naturalistic way of understanding, provided part of the motive for creation is taken to be aesthetic. There is no problem with holding that the aesthetic is a source of divine joy. The problem is that God could achieve this joy, we might think, simply by imagining beautiful universes, and imagining the drama of creatures endowed with freedom engaged in the battle between good and evil. Why would God need to behold actual beauty to derive aesthetic joy?[2] There are, I hold, three answers. The first is that there is joy in performing beautifully as well as joy in beholding beauty. Perhaps we should think of creation as like a dance. To be sure, it could be retorted that God could derive the joy of performance just by imagining it, but that is not as clear as in the case of the joy of beholding the beautiful. The second answer is that we humans can attend to some things rather than others, but God, or at least the Primordial God, cannot be selective in this fashion: it was

---

[2] Previously I made the mistake of extrapolating from the human situation and assuming that no one capable of appreciating drama could fail to be moved by the suffering of the participants (Forrest 1996a: 159–62).

burdened with an awareness of all possibilities. Hence there is no way the Primordial God could attend only to the beautiful possibilities while ignoring the ugly ones. And who is to say that the beautiful ones outweigh the ugly? Instead, by creating only one, or only some, of the universes, God may cease attending to the others, which become mere might-have-beens. Therefore, while we humans may to some extent decide what we will attend to, God can do this only by deciding what to create. Or else God creates by choosing which possibilities to attend to. In either case, the divine joy is increased by creation. The third answer is that even if the divine aesthetic joy is achieved by imagination, rather than creation, God would derive further joy by sharing this aesthetic joy with creatures that can come to have the joy of beholding the beauty of creation.

This last motive might seem fantastic. Does God really create this sort of universe with all its suffering just to give us creatures the joy of beholding its beauty? Would not the majority of creatures just prefer either that their basic needs are satisfied or to derive joy from loving relationships with each other? And in an afterlife, would they not derive joy from perfected loving relationships with each other and with God? Isn't aesthetic joy just an optional extra? By no means, I reply. Love does not operate in a vacuum. It requires there to be something enjoyed by those who love: something given, something received. Now the events of salvation provide quite an exceptional basis for love between God and human beings. But the beauty of creation may be taken as a basis for a loving relationship between God and humans that exists alongside the basis due to salvation. One motive, then, to create a beautiful universe is as a gift to creatures, for creatures to enjoy not merely as beautiful but as a beautiful gift from one who loves us, and for the joy this gives God and the joy that in turn this gives creatures, and so on. This motive is compatible with my hypothesis that the Primordial God was not loving. For it has good reason to become loving, and as part of this becoming loving to create for the sake of love between God and creatures. Moreover, if we may think of the universe (apart from creatures with freedom) as the body of God, then this gift is the beauty of God itself.

6. MODERATE MATERIALISM AND DIVINE MOTIVATION

There are, I consider, two central problems that theists must solve. The first is how a God without any structure would be able to design a complex universe suited to life. The second is what motive God could have to create. My solution to the first problem was that God is not simple if we include as part of God the array of all possible physical universes, one or more of which God could create. Or if we treat this array as external to God, then we may say that God is simple, but we can appeal to the divine awareness of the necessarily existing array of possibilities. A common solution to the second problem is to posit divine moral goodness as an extra, and thus complicating aspect of theism. This is, I believe, a mistake, for three reasons. The first is that, in view of the manifold evils afflicted upon us and upon non-human animals, there is a prima facie inference to the conclusion that the motivating goodness is of a consequentialist kind, and not what most of us take moral goodness to amount to. But in that case we should say that God creates in a certain way not because it is right to do so, but rather because to do so has intrinsically good consequences. However, we multiply mysteries unnecessarily if we do other than identify the intrinsically good with that which occasions joy and the intrinsically bad with that which occasions suffering. Hence the consequentialist motivation is tantamount to the hedonic one.

The second reason why I think that it is a mistake to posit divine moral goodness as a complicating factor is that the question 'Why should I be morally good?' is a sensible one in the way that 'Why should I seek joy for myself and others?' is not. One, partial answer is that a bad conscience is a source of suffering. Another answer might be the fear of divine displeasure or the desire to please God. As a rule utilitarian, I would say that in a calm reflective mood we can see that sticking to the moral rules on the whole helps ourselves and others flourish, and therefore we have good reason to inculcate these rules in ourselves and others and to be wary of breaking them in moments of passion, even when to break them would seem to have good consequences. If asked why these rules then present themselves as unconditional, I would say that this extra unconditional aspect of the rules results from a further rule to obey God, who has commanded the other rules, and that there is a good utilitarian justification for the further rule of obeying God. (Compare Forrest 1996a: 121–33.) Maybe readers have their own answers to the question, of why they should be morally good, but my point is that it seems a rather sensible question, and that any answer to it will involve hedonic reasons. I fail, then, to see why the moral motivation should be a mystery in the divine case when we are so reluctant to accept it as a mystery in the human case.

The third reason for not positing moral goodness as an independent divine motive is that the hedonic motive is so obvious as a motive that it would in any case have to be adjoined to the moral one. Hence there is a genuine complication to the hypothesis in positing two distinct sources of divine motivation, the hedonic and that of moral goodness.

This appeal to the hedonic motive to explain the first act of God is, however, one that moderate materialists should be far more comfortable with than nomological dualists. For it is conceivable that there be agents who act as a consequence of their own anticipated joy or suffering but take neither further joy in being aware of joy, their own or that of others, nor further suffering in being aware of suffering, their own or that of others. Moreover, it is conceivable that God be like that, and so motivated purely by the aesthetic joy of creation, including perhaps the joy of the human drama. Again, it is conceivable that there be a God who is positively motivated by joy at the joy of others but quite unmoved by their suffering. Both these alternatives seem as good an explanation of the divine act of creation as the good-in-a-consequentialist-fashion hedonic motive that I am attributing to the Primordial God. So those who restrict the impossible to the inconceivable have to postulate a quite contingent attribute of God: namely, a character of some sort to explain creation, and they have no reason, other than subsequent revelation, to believe in one rather than another character. Unless God has a morally positive character, it is not clear why revelation that was genuine in the sense of inspired by God should be genuine in the sense of truthful. Hence the appeal to revelation would be dubious.

There is a further problem for those dualists who restrict the impossible to the inconceivable. Consider the hypothesis of a malicious God who derives aesthetic joy from creation, including the human drama, but would derive suffering rather than further joy, from sharing this aesthetic joy with creatures. The only reason I can think of for rejecting that hypothesis is that reflection upon human motives gives us insight into the metaphysically necessary constraints on sources of joy and suffering. These insights tell us, among other things, that sharing joy may directly occasion further joy, but never directly occasions suffering. And even God is bound by metaphysically necessary constraints. It remains conceivable, however, that God have a malicious character, as hypothesized above.

Now dualists might decide not to reject such disturbing hypotheses about the divine nature. The supposed possibilities they exemplify are, however, counter-intuitive, and it might be preferable to reject instead the dualist restriction of the impossible to the inconceivable. Moderate materialists, on the other hand, are entitled to hold that the hedonic tone of a mental state is necessarily correlated with its phenomenal content—how it seems—in much the way that the phenomenal content is necessarily correlated with the functional role of that state. We are then entitled to extrapolate from the human sources of joy and suffering to the divine, explaining human malice as a disorder due to envy and taking the sources of joy as the pleasurable, the beautiful, and the awareness of the joy of others, with the sources of suffering being pain, the ugly, including falsehood and injustice, and the suffering of others. Thus one of the great advantages of moderate materialism is its ability to give an answer to the question of what motivates God, an answer which is neither adds to the hypothesis about the divine, nor leads to such disturbing possibilities as a thoroughly malicious God.

7. THE REJECTION OF AXIARCHISM, INCLUDING PERFECT BEING THEOLOGY

In rejecting such motives as the love of truth, of beauty, and of moral goodness, except in so far as they may be taken as hedonic, I am implicitly rejecting an alternative approach to philosophical theology, that of Perfect Being theologians such as Thomas Morris (1987) and Katherin Rogers (2000), who rely upon St Anselm's definition of God as that than which no greater can be conceived, taking greatness to include being valuable. They argue that a Perfect Being in this sense should have such good-making characteristics as loving truth, beauty, and moral goodness. The obvious problem with this is to ask why we should believe in a Perfect Being. Here I assume the failure of St Anselm's Ontological Argument, interpreted, perhaps incorrectly, as an argument for a Perfect Being. I shall come to axiarchism soon. The other answers I can think of concern either trust in the tradition of a worship-worthy being, which presupposes that there is one; individual experience; a *sensus divinitatis*; or divine revelation. But these show at most that God is now a Perfect Being, not that God always was such. And although I think that tradition, experience, and purported revelation must all negotiate with, rather than overrule philosophical reasoning, I have no quarrel with the thesis that God is now a Perfect Being. If that is so, it is because God made itself a Perfect Being, for there is joy in excellence.

The version of Perfect Being Theology that is a rival to my developmental theism is one that takes the thesis of the existence of the very best as fundamental in the sense of not requiring further explanation. Let us call this sort of Perfect Being Theology 'moderate axiarchism', so as to remind ourselves of John Leslie's extreme axiarchism (Leslie 1979): namely, that we can explain the existence of the very best because it is the best, or on Leslie's own version because it is morally required. Hugh Rice has also proposed a similar extreme axiarchistic metaphysics (Rice 2000), as did Alfred Ewing (1973).

The position I am rejecting, then, is not that there is a Perfect Being, but that the existence of perfection is a suitable starting-point for philosophical theology. My starting-point, recall, was properly anthropocentric metaphysics.

So why should we reject the seemingly quite simple metaphysical hypothesis of axiarchism, that the ultimate explanations are in terms of values, or, more moderately, the hypothesis that what is most valuable exists? My answer is that these hypotheses are more complicated than they initially seem. Familiarity can easily hide from us the sheer complexity of values, which makes them ill-suited to appear in a fundamental account of anything. Thus John Mackie in his case against moral realism talked of the *queerness* of moral values (Mackie 1977). The belief that some possible act has the supposed property of moral requiredness automatically provides a prima facie reason for performing the act in question. Now whatever account we give of human motivation, we shall be able to describe complex, relational properties that do provide prima facie reasons for performing the act. For instance, I would say that being such that it increases joy is just such a property. What would be *queer* would be a simple, unanalysable property of moral requiredness. Hence Mackie's argument shows not that there are no such properties, but that these properties are not simple. Similar peculiarities show that truth and beauty are not simple, as we might have supposed. Hence, I say, the hypothesis of a Primordial God whose first act is governed by the hedonic motive alone wins on grounds of simplicity. To be sure, hedonic tone is mysterious too, but it is not as complicated as such values as truth, beauty, and goodness.

8. IS THE PRIMORDIAL GOD MORALLY GOOD?

My reason for rejecting the hypothesis that the Primordial God was motivated by the love of truth, beauty, and goodness (except in so far as these lead to joy or remove suffering) amounts, then, to the greater simplicity of the hedonic motive. And this is in spite of the spurious apparent simplicity of Perfect Being Theology or of Axiarchism. Likewise, I am rejecting as unnecessarily complicated any positing of divine moral goodness. But this leaves open the possibility of deriving moral goodness without positing it. This is what I shall now explore.

The Primordial God has the hedonic motive. Therefore it is good in the sense of having the joy of creatures as a positive motivation and their suffering as a negative one. Therefore we may take it to behave as a consequentialist says it ought to: maximizing the good and minimizing the bad. But I suspect that this is not what most people mean by moral righteousness. For the Primordial God, like any good consequentialist, would deceive and break promises for the sake of a good end. Again, some may have an ideal of altruism which the Primordial God as portrayed lacks. I am not even supposing that the Primordial God is unselfish. The question of self-regarding versus other-regarding appetites arises only for a person. For the Primordial God there is no self/other distinction.

9. DOES DIVINE CONSEQUENTIALISM HAVE COUNTER-INTUITIVE IMPLICATIONS?

I have reached the conclusion that the Primordial God is a good consequentialist, while denying that it is morally good in a more robust sense. It might be thought that this has implications contrary to either our experience or our intuitions. First, there are the implications of the emphasis on hedonic tone. Would not such a God just see to it that creatures were flooded with pleasure, contrary to what we experience, and contrary to what we might expect? Although we need our little pleasures, such a life would, we think, be trivial. So something must have gone wrong with the thesis that implies that God would create in this way. Or again, why not create a fools' paradise in which the creatures think their crude theories are true, their inept artistic creations beautiful, and their wretched environment sublime? Even more disturbing is the suggestion that God might create a universe inhabited only by a sadist subject to the illusion of torturing others.

My response to these objections is that God suffers as a result of being aware of the sadist and even of a fools' paradise. So the consequences of creating such universes are not as joyful, all things considered, as some other choices of what to create. For 'all things considered' must include the divine state of mind. This response, in turn, depends on the thesis that the hedonic tone of awareness is not independent of the content of awareness. The divine joy is based upon awareness of certain kinds of situation rather than others. I think of it as having two main components: aesthetic joy and joy in the awareness of joy. But, however we think of the divine joy, the important point is that it is beyond God's power to decide what kinds of situation will give joy to the beholder. We may say, therefore, that even the Primordial God is *just*, in the sense that awareness of certain kinds of situation causes God suffering, as they do us, because they are morally ugly. Likewise, falsehood occasions suffering in us and hence, presumably, in the Primordial God, which may therefore be said to hate falsehood.

A second family of objections to a consequentialist God concern the supposed crass Benthamite implication of a utilitarian calculus with God maximizing the sum total utility, sacrificing some for the sake of others. My response is that several of the supposedly crass features of utilitarianism concern the attempt to compare the joys and sufferings of different creatures, and there might be some arbitrariness in how we decide what is the best overall outcome. Or maybe there is no best in the case of God's acts. Those are the reasons why I prefer to say that the Primordial God was a consequentialist rather than a utilitarian. But if, in fact, there is a best or equal best utilitarian outcome, then I accept the Benthamite implication that God will create a universe or universes with the best or equal best outcome, including, of course, the outcome for the divine awareness of the resulting universe or universes. I myself think that complaints in this regard betray anthropomorphism. For I hold on consequentialist grounds that human beings need to follow rules—for the most part anyway—rather than be act utilitarians. This is because we are rather better at judging general tendencies (for example, deceiving others tends to undermine trust) than at estimating the consequences of particular acts (deceiving another in this case will be harmful). God has no such limitations. But assuming that being a crass utilitarian is incon-sistent with moral righteousness, I would accept the conclusion that the Primordial God was a crass utilitarian, and not morally righteous.

Another objection, drawn to my attention by a reader for Oxford University Press, is that I am supposing that the divine joy or suffering depends in rather complicated ways on what God is aware of. This raises the question of whether I am violating the principle that the simpler is more probable. My response is that the joy or suffering of any being, whether God or a creature, depends of metaphysical necessity on that of which the being is aware. The nature of this dependence is not part of my hypothesis about the Primordial God. If it is in fact rather complicated, that is something I find puzzling, but it does not complicate the hypothesis about God.

10. ON THE ACQUISITION OF A DIVINE MORAL CHARACTER

In pursuit of a parsimonious philosophical theology and, for that matter, a parsimonious ethics, I have arrived at an account of the motivation of the Primordial God as consequentialist, in the sense that the Primordial God will act for the sake of the hedonic tone of both divine and created beings. A complication is that even prior to creating our universe God might have chosen to come to have a certain kind of character, and this might interfere with my claim that creation was performed by a consequentialist Creator. Given the speculative character of my thought about the Primordial God, I cannot ignore this possibility.

You might think that creation is bound to be part of the first divine act, for God could have no reason to wait before creating. Perhaps, though, God acquires character at the same time as creating first-generation universes, and as a result of this character, creates second-generation universes, ones that a consequentialist God would consider not worth creating. Thus our universe could have been a second-generation universe created after and as a result of various events occurring in a universe made for angelic beings. All we can say here is that we have no reason to deny the hypothesis that our universe was created by a consequentialist God, a hypothesis that will help understand the evils we, and other animals, suffer from. In addition, in Chapter 1, Section 4, I sketched an explanation of why mystics so often experience a classical-type God. This explanation required that creation was by the Primordial God, which is, then, further support for the thesis of a consequentialist creator.

Should we be concerned that God might derive joy from having a cruel or malevolent character? Or from an art-for-art's-sake indifference to creatures' well-being? Assuming that such character traits as justice would result in vastly greater hedonic tone for creatures than cruelty or even indifference, and assuming that there is joy to be had for God to have a character of some kind, then the Primordial God would choose to be just rather than cruel or indifferent unless there was greater joy to be had in a cruel or indifferent character rather than a just or kind character. And that is not plausible. For the joy of having character is independent of whether it is a virtuous or a vicious character. The joy involved derives, I suggest, from the joy of being a person rather than a mere self. In so far as humans ever deliberately choose to have a vicious character, that is because in the circumstances this seems the only way to be an individual, to stick out from the crowd. Hence, even if there was some arbitrariness in a divine choice of character, the consequentialist righteousness of the Primordial God would ensure that any character chosen was virtuous, not vicious.

What is fairly plausible is the thought that there is enough divine joy to be had in justice and moral righteousness to make God become the somewhat stern God of the Abrahamic tradition rather than a morally lax God concerned only that a good time be had by all.

11. SOME CONCLUSIONS

Considerations of simplicity support the thesis that the Primordial God acts in a consequentialist fashion, motivated not, however, by a virtuous character, but by an awareness of the hedonic tone of all beings subsequent to any possible act of creation. In that rather restricted sense we may say that the Primordial God is good. We might also say that the Primordial God is just, in the sense of finding certain acts morally ugly. It is a mistake, however, to think of the Primordial God as altruistic. Indeed, the hedonic tone of the divine consciousness is likely to be the dominant motive for its act.

5
The Existence of the Primordial God

In the previous chapters I have been discussing the neoclassical conception of the Primordial God, a being of unlimited power to act and aware of all possibilities, but not yet personal, not yet loving, not yet a worthy object of devotion. The key chapter is the next one, in which I explain how this God changes. But in this chapter I argue for the existence, in the beginning, of the Primordial God. This is familiar territory, but there are some topics that need clarification, especially concerning fine tuning and the argument from our knowledge of morality and rationality.

The chief difficulty in arguing for the existence of God is the weight of history. And in particular, if in the past the attempt has been made at conclusive proof, then probabilistic considerations seem, by contrast, unconvincing. If only we could come at the issue fresh, not having thought about it before! Then we would see just how strong the case is.

1. GOD AND PHILOSOPHICAL ANTHROPOLOGY

This is a topic already discussed in Chapters 2 and 3, but here I emphasize that what we decide about human beings is the key to whether or not we can make a convincing case for theism of some sort, and for the Primordial God in particular.

There is a spectrum of positions on what we human beings are. First, there is the position that consciousness and agency are quite redundant, in that human beings can be understood in purely physical terms. This I call reductive materialism. Then there is moderate materialism, the position that I incline towards: namely, that although the mental is non-redundant, it is correlated with the physical in a metaphysically necessary fashion. This is compatible with its mirror image, moderate idealism, the thesis that although the physical is non-redundant, it is correlated with the mental in a metaphysically necessary fashion.

Contrast this with reductive idealism, the position that the physical is strictly speaking redundant in understanding the seemingly material world around us. In addition there is the explicitly dualist position that the mental and the physical are correlated only contingently by laws of nature.

If you are convinced of the redundancy of the mental when it comes to human beings, then you will presumably find the idea of God implausible. So any case for theism will require at least the casting of doubt on the thesis of the redundancy of mental. Consider, next, my preferred thesis that the mental is necessarily correlated with the physical, but is not explanatorily redundant. This prompts the question 'Whence consciousness and agency?'. Once we postulate consciousness and agency in the human case, we will presumably think that they occur quite widely among animals, very probably in chimpanzees, probably in dogs, perhaps even among cephalopods. In Chapter 2 I argued that even without a systematic approach to deciding what things are conscious agents, we should take the idea of a Primordial God seriously. For note that Occam's razor as usually stated (entities are not to be multiplied more than is necessary) is better formulated as a warning against postulating excessively many *kinds* of entity. The warning should be more severe if we postulate a radically different kind, as opposed to a new species of a familiar genus. Hence the more vigorous the pious protestations about God being totally other, and quite unlike us, the less probable theism is initially—that is, prior to the evidence. It is not a crass anthropomorphism but an application of Occam's Razor to conceive of the Primordial God as like us in being a conscious agent necessarily correlated with whatever was there in the beginning: a moment of time, maybe, together with whatever abstract entities such as uninstantiated universals, numbers, or propositions that we are forced to treat as necessary beings. Unless we invoke a further metaphysical thesis such as panpsychism or idealism, the only guidance we have as to just which things are conscious is that we should posit consciousness only where to do so helps us understand behaviour as action. Theism satisfies that criterion, because it is based upon the agency understanding of the origin of the physical universe with its laws of nature.

Of the two systematic answers, I rejected panpsychism not because we have some trustworthy intuition that only animals could be conscious, but for the obvious reason that we should not posit consciousness unless to do so explains behaviour as action. The behaviour of many things is explained physically by applying simple laws to moderately complex systems. In such cases it is hard to see why we need to appeal to consciousness and agency. The reason why animals are a somewhat special case is that even if the physical explanation succeeds in their case, a properly anthropocentric metaphysics, by ascribing consciousness agency to us, also strongly supports agency for many animals, precisely because they are similar to us.

The other systematic answer is idealism, in the form that states that necessarily everything, or, as I prefer, every universal, *appears*.[1] In that case an initial moment of Time necessarily appears a certain way. Even if we think of particulars appearing, we may also suppose that the abstract entities such as uninstantiated universals or whatever we posit, also appear some way. It is then plausible that either there is a mind to which the initial situation appears, or these appearances constitute some sort of mind. So once again the Primordial God is at least fairly plausible.

What about an explicitly dualist position? In that case it is going to be an additional hypothesis to decide just which physical systems are associated with minds or souls or whatever we call the non-physical bit. What probability should we assign, then, to some kind of world-soul with the characteristics of the Primordial God? It is hard to say. Anyway, in Chapter 3 I explained why I rejected most sorts of dualism. The sorts I did not reject with any confidence were minor modifications of moderate materialism and do not affect the case stated above. Nomological dualism is in the awkward position that, on the one hand, the harmony between the way a mental state appears and the behaviour it causes cannot be explained naturalistically and cries out for an explanation in terms of divine providence, but, on the other hand, the capacity of God to bring into existence and to affect the physical universe seems to presuppose psycho-physical laws. For that reason I rejected nomological dualism. Although I believe that the remaining varieties of dualism are outmoded, if we hold them, they would provide a clear precedent for God as a super-soul.

Therefore the probability of theism prior to examining detailed evidence is negligible only if we are almost certain of reductive materialism, a position that, along with nomological dualism, I have argued against in Chapter 3.

---

[1] Universals have different ways of appearing, depending on whether they are instantiated, are becoming instantiated, or are not (yet) instantiated.

2. NATURALISM

Having rejected the threat of epiphenomenalism in Chapter 3, I submit that the only rational grounds for the confidence which many philosophers have that the mental is redundant is their prior adherence to naturalism, understood as the thesis that all explanations are replaceable in principle by scientific ones.[2] Naturalism is also associated with the thesis that the physical is a complete system, a *closed shop*, to use David Armstrong's phrase. It is naturalism understood in this way as a comprehensive metaphysical system that sets up resistance to arguments for the incompleteness of the physical description of human beings and other animals. Again, it is naturalism understood in this way that sets up an antecedent rejection of agency accounts of responsibility and hence gives some plausibility to the threat of epiphenomenalism.

The appeal of naturalism is that of a systematic metaphysics. Now theism and idealism also have just this appeal, and are rivals to naturalism, but not to each other. Because idealism is compatible with theism, and because we are considering naturalism here, we may concentrate on the clash between naturalism and theism. And, as Richard Swinburne has pointed out, we may simplify our metaphysics either by reducing personal explanation to physical explanation, or vice versa. Theism is a coherent, simple, metaphysical scheme that reduces physical explanation to personal explanation by giving agency explanations of the laws invoked in physical explanations, of the initial conditions of the universe, and of its evolving one way (towards a life-filled universe) rather than another (a lifeless universe) if the laws fail to imply a high probability of the way it actually evolves.

Because naturalism and theism are rival systematic metaphysics, any commitment to naturalism as a metaphysical system is premature. It has to come, if at all, after the case for theism has been evaluated, but on it depends any confidence in the redundancy of agency and consciousness.

Naturalists might invoke the slogan 'Only one way of being'.[3] Naturalism by being allied with materialism has, it is said, all the

---

[2] Elsewhere (Forrest 1996*a*) I have been at pains to distinguish naturalism from anti-supernaturalism and defend the compatibility of the latter with theism.

[3] The Australian-Scottish philosopher John Anderson was rather keen on this slogan and thought he could argue for it by pointing out that if there is not one way of being, then the different ways could not interact. So, for instance, psycho-physical laws are neither purely physical nor purely mental in character. As far as I can see, this

advantages of there being a single fundamental kind, the physical. Theists could retort that idealism too results in just one way of being. Moreover, I have already given reasons for rejecting reductive materialism, and if moderate materialism implies one way of being, then, as I am at pains to argue, moderate materialism coheres better with theism than does its chief rival, nomological dualism. So, that there is only one way of being is either untenable or coherent with theism.

3. UNDERMINING THE APPEAL OF NATURALISM

Not only are theism and idealism serious alternatives to naturalism, but we may undermine the appeal of naturalism itself. It appeals initially because it is a world-view that is broadly speaking mechanistic, with events causing other events in accordance with strict laws of nature. But I say that naturalists have no right to help themselves to such causal explanations. Naturalists should treat causation as thoroughly anthropocentric. For, following Robin Collingwood (1940), Douglas Gasking (1955), and Georg von Wright (1971), I would say that our ordinary concept of causation is that an X causes a Y if an agent could have brought about a Y by bringing about an X. We may then extend the concept of causation to cover other cases. Nonetheless, it is rooted in agency as a way of explaining. Moreover, fundamental physics can be stated without any reference to causation or even the asymmetry between past and future. As Huw Price (1996), has argued, it is hard to see how physics provides us with any reason for saying that the past explains the future, not vice versa, or that the past is now necessary, while the future is still contingent.

Naturalists may well say that they obtain a better metaphysics by adjoining causation to the austere account depicted by physics and by making a significant distinction between past and future. And they may be motivated by a laudable desire to integrate biology into naturalism. All this seems sensible enough; but once the austere, supposedly complete metaphysics has been added to, it is hard to see why there should be opposition to further additions concerning consciousness and agency. Although not naturalistic in the narrow sense, they are part of the natural world also. There is nothing spooky about them. Further, once we have

argument merely shows that if there is not one way of being, there must be at least three.

adjoined agency and consciousness, then we have the wherewithal to explain the physical in terms of theism.

I suggest a dilemma, then. Either naturalists stick with an austere world-view in which causation and the significant difference between past and future are treated as mere anthropocentrisms, or they grant that various additions can be made to the naturalistic picture, so it is not a closed shop after all. The former is unattractive and, more important, inadequate to our experience. The latter is a piece of anthropocentric metaphysics, albeit a small one, showing that the difference here between the naturalist and the advocate of properly anthropocentric metaphysics concerns just how much it is worth adjoining to the austere picture of a pure naturalism in order to understand the world.

4. A VERSION OF THE COSMOLOGICAL ARGUMENT

What I have been arguing so far is not that we should be confident theists, but rather that we should not be confident atheists. For reductive materialism is rationally grounded, if at all, only in naturalism, and naturalism is not all that it's cracked up to be, with theism being prima facie at least as good a way of providing a systematic metaphysics. Subsequently, we may confirm theism in the usual ways, provided we grant that the prevalence of evil does not disconfirm the theism in question.

The moderate materialism that I favour enables us to explain why there is anything contingent at all. The explanation takes for granted the necessarily existing realm of possibilities. It is, then, a plausible metaphysical hypothesis that necessarily there is some consciousness and some agency related to the realm of possibilities in the same way that a human being's consciousness and agency are related to the much more limited realm of possibilities within her or his control. So using the necessarily existing realm of possibilities, we arrive at the fairly probable hypothesis of the necessity of the Primordial God, which is then used to explain the existence of our universe.

It should be noted that although I am putting forward a non-contingent metaphysical hypothesis, this version of the Cosmological Argument is not intended as conclusive. How much support does it give to theism? The answer depends on our attitudes towards inference to the best explanation, and to simplicity, topics already mentioned in Chapter 1. Should we come to have the beliefs that enable us to understand, so as to achieve the goal of understanding? Or should we instead rely on the principle that the simpler is more probable, so as to arrive at the truth, and then treat understanding as a welcome by-product? I am inclined towards the latter answer, in which case the understanding of things in terms of a metaphysically necessary being, although a source of intellectual joy, should not be a goal of intellectual inquiry. Hence I have a rather low estimate of the degree of support given by the version of the Cosmological Argument that I have just stated.[4] It is nonetheless important as one half of an overall argument for theism in the form of a constructive dilemma: we should either believe in such a way as to understand, or adopt the more austere probabilistic framework. In either case, I shall argue, we have good reason to be theists.

5. FINE TUNING VERSUS COARSE TUNING

The familiar argument from fine tuning states that there are various fundamental constants which, had they varied ever so slightly, would have given rise to a universe unsuited to life. The equally familiar reply is that there could be many universes or many domains of the one universe, with varying values for these constants, which explains why we are in one of those rare universes, or domains, suited to life (Leslie 1989). I would put it this way. Call the constant in question $k(u)$, where u is the universe in which the constant has that value. Then the hypothesis that there is some special value c for which there is some universe u such that $k(u) = c$ is not significantly simpler than the hypothesis that for every x there is a universe u for which $k(u) = x$.

A minor difficulty with the many universes response to fine tuning occurs if there is over-tuning. Huw Price, developing a point of Roger Penrose's, argues that the Big Bang is far smoother than required for life, because a less smooth universe could still provide us with one galactic cluster in which life could evolve even if elsewhere in the visible universe there is just gas and dust (Price 1996: 58). Theists could perhaps take this as evidence that God intends there to be many kinds of

---

[4] For a discussion of the versions of the Cosmological Argument that aim at a deductively valid argument with the Principle of Sufficient Reason as a premiss, see Gale 1991: ch. 7.

created persons, able eventually to communicate. The many universes hypothesis would, however, fail. For, given all values for the constant in question, there will be far more universes in which conditions for life arise only once or twice in a region the size of the visible universe (because there is only one suitable galactic cluster) than ones in which it arises many times (because the region is full of suitable galactic clusters). Moreover, the many times at which life could arise in a universe like ours in no way compensates for the improbability of a visible universe as smooth as ours. So, on the many universes hypothesis, we should, it seems, say that it is far more likely that we live in a privileged position in the one suitable galactic cluster in the visible universe than that there are galactic clusters suitable for life everywhere. But the astronomical evidence suggests that we are not thus privileged. This is, however, only a minor difficulty, unless we do make contact with extraterrestrial life in or near our galaxy. For unless we make contact, we may say that it is so unlikely that advanced life forms like ours occur in any one galactic cluster that a region the size of the visible universe must be suitable for life to make advanced life forms likely somewhere. Hence, although if SETI does make contact with extraterrestrials unrelated to us, no doubt it will be heralded by many as a serious set-back for theism, in fact it will have re-energized the problem of over-tuning. Over-tuning is, then, a potential threat to the many universes approach, but not at present a serious difficulty.

The argument from what I call *coarse tuning* is less spectacular than that from fine tuning, but more robust, in two ways. First, it would survive the shift to a theory that had no tuneable constants. Second, it resists the many worlds reply to fine tuning. Coarse tuning goes like this. Think of the theories obtained by fiddling with constants (or initial conditions) as species of one genus of universe. Regardless of the precise values of the tuneable constants, we have to have the right genus of universe for there to be life. Most genera of universe are hostile to life no matter how we tune them. The simplest, and hence most probable, universe is nothing at all. Among other simple ones, are a universe made of homogeneous stuff and one in which there is never anything but random fluctuation of field strengths. And so it goes on. In principle, we can rank theories in order of increasing complexity by expressing them in a canonical language. But I doubt if we need such a Procrustean procedure. My conjecture is that ours is one, perhaps fine-tuned, species of the simplest genus of universe that is suited to life. But ours is by no means the simplest of all the genera, including the ones hostile to life. Even if I am wrong about ours being the simplest genus suited to life, it is still plausible that the very simplest universes are inhospitable to life. The probability of a universe suited to life, even ignoring the fine tuning of constants, is, then, fairly small, which, given the usual considerations of probability theory, provides significant confirmation of theism. Notice that the sort of probability of life without theism that we might be thinking of here could be, say, 1 in 1,000, not the 1 in some astronomical figure of fine tuning. And that is why this argument requires us not to be antecedently a confident naturalists. But given, say, an initial estimate of the probability of theism as 1 in 20, a 1 in 1,000 probability of life given atheism, and a 1 in 5 probability of life given theism, we get to a posterior probability of theism of about 90 percent. And that is before any further arguments or boot-strapping.

Is there a many universes response to coarse tuning? Recall that the many universes response to fine tuning is to posit universes of different species belonging to the one genus. The many universes response to coarse tuning would be to posit universes of different genera. But this requires there to be more of the simpler genera in order to cohere with the principle that simpler is more probable. The reasoning here is that provided by John Leslie, Robert Adams, Jack Smart, and myself, on different occasions, as an objection to David Lewis's theory of real possible worlds (Lewis 1986; Forrest 2001*b*). If there are as many of the more complicated as of the simpler universes, then only a small proportion of all sentient beings capable of epistemological reflection will be in simple universes. So unless we have some *special reason* to believe that we are in one of the simpler ones, we should believe that we are in one of the more complicated, contrary to our usual theory-choice reasoning, which prefers the simplest hypothesis compatible with the empirical data. By a special reason here I mean one that would not be available to the sentient beings capable of epistemic reflection that live in more complicated universes. I suppose there is the remote possibility that God creates the more complicated universes as well, but sees to it that the sentient beings in those universes are metaphysics-averse. But, of course, this is not a rejoinder available to atheists. So they have to assume that there are more of the simpler genera of universes.

That there are more universes of the simpler genera of universes implies that there are fewer and fewer universes of a genus as the genera get more complicated. That in turn requires there to be some infinite decreasing sequence of cardinal numbers N_m, where N_m is the number of universes belonging to the mth simplest genus. Or if there are several genera of the same simplicity, then N_m is the cardinality of the union of all the mth simplest genera. Suppose for some m—call it m^*—the number N_{m^*} was finite. Let $k = m^* + N_{m^*} + 1$. Then, because the sequence is decreasing, N_k would be negative, which is absurd. So all the N_m are infinite. Now if $m < n$, $N_m > N_n$. But because they are infinite cardinal numbers, if $N_m > N_n$, the ratio of N_m to N_n must be infinite. Hence, if the mth genus of universe is the simplest compatible with our current empirical evidence, we should be certain that ours is of that genus or one of equal simplicity, and not even seek further evidence. For if the next simplest genus compatible with the evidence is the nth simplest, then the ratio of N_n to N_m is infinitesimal, and so we may be certain that we are in a universe of the mth simplest genus rather than of the nth simplest genus. Even if we had all the possible evidence, that result would be startling; but it holds even if we have very little evidence, which is absurd. And in any case we should worry about postulating infinitely many universes of each genus.

Naturalists could hypothesize that there is some upper bound to the complexity of the universe and declare that only ones that are simpler than this bound occur. Because we do not know what this bound is, that hypothesis coheres without assignment of probabilities, with the more complicated less probable. Positing this upper bound to complexity is, however, itself a rather complicated, because *ad hoc*, hypothesis, and hence not the simplest theory compatible with there being life in the universe.

6. THE BEAUTY OF THINGS

The undoubted beauty of the universe is often taken to confirm theism, as in Mark Wynn's recent treatment (1999), but it threatens to undermine the argument from coarse tuning as follows. To understand is, I submit, to experience the fittingness of things, and so is ultimately aesthetic (Forrest 1991). Hence beautiful universes satisfy our urge for understanding, even if they are more complicated than simpler ones. Life is conducive to beauty, so even if rather complicated, the most beautiful universe must be suited to life, and so requires no further explanation. Other things being equal, fundamental simplicity is conducive to beauty, hence the appeal to the beauty of things coheres with our theory-choice rule of preferring simplicity in theories, provided we have enough complexity for life.

Perhaps you judge my aesthetic approach to understanding to be somewhere between eccentric and insane. But if it undermines the argument from coarse tuning, it might find a following. In reply, I first note that aesthetic understanding works both ways. Jonathan Edwards stresses the beauty of the Christian message (Smith 1992). In addition, we might provide something a bit like the Ontological Argument: the most beautiful of things must exist, and this 'all understand to be God'. Moreover, the appeal to many universes is warranted only in the context of simplicity-driven reasoning. Aesthetically it has little appeal. Rather than go down those intellectual paths, I urge that we have only a qualified endorsement of inference to the best explanation. To be sure, it is how we naturally tend to reason, and that makes it innocent until proved guilty. Nonetheless, truth and understanding are not the same, and our hope that what would be the best way of understanding things if it is true will in fact turn out to be true, should be constrained by the austere principles of probability, including the principle that simpler theories are more probable. As far as the truth is concerned, we should back Occamist preference for simplicity over an aesthetic preference for a suitable balance of simplicity and complexity.

Theists are in a position to endorse inference to the best explanation in all areas other than metaphysics, where, I have urged, simplicity rules. For, given theism, we might well expect God to create in ways that are beautiful, and, as previously mentioned, where the beautiful is identified with the elegant, it implies fundamental simplicity.

Granted that an appeal to aesthetics does not undermine the argument from coarse tuning, we may now add to the confirmation of theism by appealing to the theistic explanation of the beauty of the universe. Consider the anecdote about the salad that Barbara Kepler made for her husband. He is said to have asked her, 'If since Creation tin plates, lettuce leaves, grains of salt, drops of oil and vinegar, [etc.] . . . had been floating in Space, could chance have brought them together today to form a salad?' 'But not as good', she retorted, 'nor as well made as this one!' (Rebière 1926). The moral of the tale is that although, given enough universes, we could explain why there is one suited to life, it is still improbable that we should be in such a beautiful one. For life is a necessary, but not a sufficient, condition for the sheer amount of natural beauty we find.

7. A PRIORI KNOWLEDGE OF SYNTHETIC TRUTHS

We have a priori knowledge of important truths about morality and rationality. An example of the former is that a self-centred life is morally inferior to one caring for others. An example of the latter is that simpler theories are not merely more probable, but significantly more probable, than complex ones. So although Kant had in mind quite other items of a priori knowledge, we can ask his excellent question, 'How is a priori knowledge of synthetic truths possible?' A thorough discussion of Kant's answer is beyond the scope of this work. Let me opine. Either the transcendental ego is God, in which case transcendental idealism is theistic, or it is not, in which case Kant's answer amounts to saying that we do not really have a priori knowledge of synthetic truths, which is a damn shame, so we should go on saying we do by calling our a priori beliefs knowledge. When it comes to a priori knowledge concerning morality and rationality, the evolutionary explanation is likewise deflationary (Forrest 1996*a*: 129–33). Thus, without some theistic supplement, evolution leaves it quite mysterious as to why our theory-choice reasoning is likely to lead to the truth on topics such as evolution itself (Plantinga 2003). So it seems we have an excellent opportunity to appeal to inference to the best explanation and use a priori knowledge as a datum to support theism.

So it might seem. I disagree, because it is the status as knowledge (or at least being highly probable that it is true) that lacks a naturalistic explanation, not the fact that we humans have these convictions. As I said when discussing beauty, austere considerations of probability should win out over inference to the best explanation where they differ. And what we know a priori cannot be considered a priori improbable. So a priori knowledge does not confirm theism.

It is, however, important to note this inference to the best explanation of a priori knowledge, for together with the argument from beauty we have a constructive dilemma. Either we back simplicity-driven probability theory, so can argue from coarse tuning and beauty, or we back inference to the best explanation, so can argue from a priori knowledge and by means of a cosmological argument.

8. THE *SENSUS DIVINITATIS*

This is the joker in the pack. The claim that we humans have a natural tendency to believe that there is a God might be taken as cheating, or might be taken as a sober estimate of how we arrive at beliefs, cutting through the inconclusive discussion of arguments for theism. Now I take it that both Calvin and the reformed epistemologists such as Plantinga think of this *sensus divinitatis* as a tendency to orthodox theism (Plantinga 1983). Both familiarity with those around us and such confidence as we have in the reports of anthropologists suggest, however, that there is indeed a *sensus divinitatis*, but that it is a tendency to something more vague than theism. What seems common, if not universal, is spirituality or a sense of the transcendent or the holy or something of that very general kind. In conversation, Chris Baker once described it to me as 'the great swirly Tao'. That just about captures it.

The *sensus divinitatis* tends to confirm any metaphysics that sustains spirituality or implies the existence of something transcendent. It disconfirms naturalism unless we think that a pantheistic naturalism is tenable. I doubt that it confirms the hypothesis of the Primordial God significantly, except indirectly by undermining naturalism.

9. A PRELIMINARY EXAMINATION OF THE PROBLEM OF EVIL

Perhaps God has undergone some change before creation, or perhaps creation is part of the first divine act. We are entitled to hypothesize the latter. In that case the Creator might well act in a way that would be considered morally right in a consequentialist moral theory. I submit that the same features as make the evils around us intuitively not the work of a morally righteous Creator count against consequentialism as an account of moral righteousness. There is, then, no evidence against the thesis that the Creator was a consequentialist. For instance, there was a time when left-wing intellectuals tried to defend Stalin. That was before the full extent of his killings became known, and maybe exaggerated. But suppose we were confident that the death of millions and the suffering of a whole people were both necessary and sufficient in the circumstances to establish a properly functioning socialist society.

Perhaps a tough-minded Stalinist would say that they were justified on consequentialist grounds, but our reaction to that would no doubt be, 'So much the worse for consequentialism!' Likewise, if the divine plan promotes human freedom to the extent of allowing the gross evils that occur on a daily basis, we might say that this is not the work of a morally righteous God, even if justifiable on consequentialist grounds. My response is that to posit moral righteousness that goes beyond consequentialism is to complicate the hypothesis of the Primordial God, unnecessarily. Let me brazen it out. The Primordial God is not good in the sense of morally righteous. If God is now a morally righteous God, then that is, I submit, something that God chooses to be subsequent to creation.

There is some plausibility to a variant of this account, one which insists that God has always had a loving disposition but, as above, asserts that if God is morally righteous, that is something God chose to become after creation, perhaps because loving relations with human beings require abiding by the same moral principles. On this variant, it is said that the disposition to be loving cannot manifest itself prior to creation because God cannot love merely possible creatures as individuals.

Either on the account I am giving or on the variant, it is important that, for the sake of morally responsible agents, God sets up laws that permit no easy or automatic intervention. Now I hold that God intervenes repeatedly in history whenever it is a loving thing to do, but the kinds of intervention I consider possible are restricted to the Incarnation and to the non-coercive inspiration emphasized in process theology. It is because of these restrictions that it so often seems as if God is neither morally righteous nor loving, but only good in a consequentialist sort of way.

10. CONCLUSION

Let me summarize the case for the neoclassical Primordial God. First, we should either reject reductive materialism or at least not have confidence in it. Hence we should attach a non-negligible probability to theism of some sort even before looking at the evidence. Various familiar kinds of evidence increase that probability, and especially likely is the simplest version of theism, belief that the Primordial God existed. The Problem of Evil is no serious threat to this belief because the Primordial God behaved like a good consequentialist.

APPENDIX ON THE CLASSIFICATION
DEPENDENCE OF SIMPLICITY

The coarse-tuning argument depends quite critically on the principle that simpler theories are significantly more probable than more complicated ones. It is thus vulnerable to the classification-dependence objection. This asserts that were we to classify things differently, quite different theories would be considered probable. This kind of objection threatens not merely the coarse-tuning argument but the whole of probabilistic metaphysics. It is therefore worth replying to in some detail. To do this, I shall concentrate on the version raised by Mark Colyvan, Jay Garfied, and Graham Priest (2005). This is aimed at the argument from fine tuning, which I shall now defend from their criticism. My defence applies equally to coarse tuning.

Bertrand's Paradox

Fine-tuning debates concern physical constants whose values have to be rather precise if there is to be life. I shall illustrate this with an imaginary example, supposing the constant in question to be an angle x taking a value between 0 and 90 degrees. There are various simple values an angle might take—for instance, 30, 45, or 60 degrees m and if x took one of those values, we might find that unremarkable. But suppose x were found to be 0.3782 degrees, and suppose that if x differed from that value by as much as 0.0001 of a degree, the universe would be unsuited to life. Then given one universe naturalism, we might say that the probability of its being suited to life is 1 in 900,000. Previously I have supposed that this sort of argument commits naturalists to the many universes hypothesis, but Colyvan, Garfield, and Priest disagree, taking Bertrand's Paradox to provide a defence of one universe naturalism.

Bertrand's probability theory paradox is that we could choose a different constant, y, where, say, $y = \cos x$. Suppose that all the different values of y were equiprobable. It would follow that if x takes values from 0 to 90, then y takes values from 0 to 1. For life we require y to be between 0.999978226 and 0.999978203, which gives a range of 0.000000023 and hence a probability of about 1 in about 40,000,000 which is significantly less than the previous figure of 1 in 900,000. I have chosen this example because initially there would seem to be no reason to say that the angle x is more natural as a constant than its cosine, y. The point of the example is that although both of the constants considered, x and y result in rather small probabilities of a universe suited to life, they differ considerably, suggesting that there is no one correct choice of tuneable constants.

Some of the constants that are fine-tuned for life take an infinite range of values. For instance, the energy of the Big Bang has no obvious upper bound.

In that case we have the additional problem noted by Colyvan, Garfield, and Priest: namely, that uniform distribution gives infinitesimal probability to any finite range of the constant in question.[5] So we would obtain quite spurious fine-tuning arguments. For instance, we could argue that merely because there had to be some bound on the energy of the Big Bang for there to be life, then the probability of that happening given one universe naturalism is infinitesimal. It makes no difference if 0.001 per cent more energy would prevent life or if life could not have occurred unless the energy had been 10^{10} times as much. And that is absurd.

The moral that Colyvan, Garfield, and Priest draw seems to be that until there is a way of assigning coherent logical probabilities that avoid both Bertrand's Paradox and the problem of the infinite range, then the argument from fine tuning is defective. With standards like those, I fear for their survival. But this is a challenge I shall nonetheless take up.

The infinite version of Bertrand's Paradox has been around for a long time, but it is usually stated as showing that for any positive integer N the probability of an integer chosen at random being less than N is zero. At that level of abstraction, it does not require an answer. Instead, we could simply say that probability theory does not cover such absurdities. Its application to fine tuning puts it, however, on the list of compulsory questions.

Swinburne's handling of Bertrand's Paradox

I endorse the way in which Swinburne would handle my example of x and $y =$ cos x. He would say that we have two different theories, both about as simple and hence as probable, and that we calculate the probability of life accordingly. If we have different theories T_1, T_2, etc. with probabilities Prob(T_1), Prob(T_2) etc. then the probability of life given one universe naturalism, Nat, is:

$$\text{Prob(Life/Nat)} = \text{Prob}(T_1) \times \text{Prob(Life/Nat \& } T_1) + \text{Prob}(T_2)$$
$$\times \text{Prob(Life/Nat \& } T_2) + \dots$$

Hence, in the above example we could ignore the theory using y, because it makes a negligible contribution to the probability compared with the theory using x.

Now, we can find a gerrymandered function of x, designed to give a much higher probability for life. For instance, we might consider $z = (\cos (x - 0.3782))^{1,000,000}$. Then z takes values from 0 to 1, and the universe is suited to life if z is greater than about 0.15, which, taking the z-theory to be T_3 gives us Prob(Life/Nat & T_3)= 85 per cent. But this is no support for one

5 That is, if we do not impose countable additivity. Given countable additivity, there can be no uniform distribution.

universe naturalism, because the corresponding Prob(T_3) is very low for such a gerrymandered theory.

I anticipate the objection that what I am pleased to call distinct theories hold of all the same worlds and have the same models, if that is not the same thing. So, on the semantic view of theories, there is just one theory (Suppes 1960, 1967). Or even if we reject the semantic view, they are logically equivalent theories. So how could we assign them different probabilities?

This is an interesting objection, but it turns on the assumption that what we are considering here is a scientific theory, whereas what we should be considering, I say, is a scientific-cum-metaphysical theory, and one of the key concepts of contemporary metaphysics is the idea that some properties and relations are more natural than others. I would say that this is itself just a question of some being simpler than others. But no matter how we choose to explicate it, we need this distinction. The different formulations of the same theory are based upon different judgements as to what the natural properties and relations are. So let us return to the example of the constants x and $y = \cos x$. Suppose the angle x is the value of a quantitative relation, R. There is another relation R* that has the value $\cos x$ whenever R has value x. The difference, then, between what I have been pleased to call two distinct theories is, rather, that they are two distinct formulations of the one theory, corresponding to two distinct judgements as to which is the more natural relation, R or R*. Hence it is not, strictly speaking, a scientific theory which we are judging as more or less probable, but a scientific theory together with an assessment of the naturalness of properties and relations.

Next suppose that some quantity w takes any real value, or to postpone discussing the infinite case, any real value in the range $\pm 10^{110}$. And suppose that for life w has to be in the range $\pm 10^{10}$. In spite of the large range for w that permits life, this could be taken as a case of fine tuning with the probability of life relative to one universe naturalism being the extraordinarily low figure of 1 in 10^{100}. But then consider the quantity v, the angle in degrees whose tan is w. Then the range for v is ± 90, and the probability that there is life turns out to be almost 100 percent, for the angle whose tan is 10^{10} is 90 minus a negligible amount, and the angle whose tan is -10^{10} is -90 plus a negligible amount. So it looks like fine tuning has been undermined. Moreover, this re-scaling would work even if the range for w covered all the real numbers. We might judge however, that the theory stated using w is a bit simpler, and therefore more probable, than that stated using v. Quite generally, we may have to trade off a high probability of life given an unlikely account of naturalness with a low probability given a more likely account of naturalness. In this case it is fair to suppose that the theory with v in place of w is significantly more probable than 1 in 10^{100}. So in this case the re-scaling is definitely worthwhile.

The moral is that the quite extraordinary cases of fine tuning, like Roger Penrose's estimate of a 1 in $10^{10^{123}}$ probability of a universe as smooth as ours are partially undermined (Penrose 1989: ch. 7). For there will be an alternative theory that, while itself somewhat less probable, gives a much greater probability for life. Fine tuning is not the brain-fryer we might have thought. Of course, since I am not relying upon it in the first place, that does not concern me. All I need is the corollary that different hypotheses as to what is the natural classification must be considered separately. Hence probabilistic metaphysics generally, and coarse tuning in particular, are not undermined.

6

God Changes

In the beginning there was the Primordial God, the God of the philosophers, Pure Will: an all-powerful, all-knowing, impersonal agent. The Primordial God chose to become the God of Abraham, Isaac, and Jacob; chose to become the triune God of orthodox Christianity; chose not to be impersonal; and chose to love individuals. That is in outline the developmental theism that I am proposing.

1. HOW NOT TO DO PHILOSOPHICAL THEOLOGY

Here is a spurious solution to the Problem of Evil, a parody of a certain way of doing philosophical theology. God is omniscient, omnipotent, and necessarily good. It is granted by the post-Plantingan atheologian that the existence of such a God is consistent with abundant evils such as we find around us. Now, God being omnipotent can bring about any consistent situation, including that granted by the atheologian, and if God does so, then there are such evils without God ceasing to be good. Moreover, because God is necessarily good, that act must itself be a good act. Now God's acts are constrained only by divine goodness, which admits no degrees, being perfect. Hence the act of bringing about a world with the evils around us is just one of a large number of possible acts of creation, none more and none less good than any other. There are no other constraints on God's act, so creating a world like ours is no more or less probable than creating any other. Hence the atheologian's admission of consistency has undermined any probabilistic argument from evil.

This is spurious, because all that is granted by the atheologian is that there is no *formal* inconsistency between the existence of a good, omniscient, omnipotent God and abundant evils. The atheologian argues, with initial plausibility, that it is rather improbable that a good God would create a universe like ours. Hence, if God is necessarily good, then in fact the atheologian is arguing that probably it is impossible that God create such a world as ours.

The moral, I take it is that when doing philosophical theology, it is unwise to suppose that just because it is in some sense conceivable that God can do X, then in fact God can do X. Now I am claiming that the Primordial God abdicated some power; but to show that the Primordial God had the power to abdicate power, I will not appeal to God's omnipotence defined as an ability to do everything it is conceivable that God do.

2. HOW, THEN, DOES GOD CHANGE?

Just because it is conceivable that God changes in various ways, it does not automatically follow that God has the power to change. What I have assumed, and will continue to assume, is that the Primordial God is an agent whose power is unlimited of its kind. And I am looking for a way in which God can change. Now, given substance dualism, it would be very hard to say much about God, because the correlation between the mental and the physical would then be under divine control, and so not something we may assume holds for God. I suppose that substance dualists might appeal to the doctrine that we are created in the divine image and likeness. But I am going instead to suppose the moderate materialist hypothesis that the mental is correlated with the physical in a metaphysically necessary fashion, where the physical includes not just the actuality of all that is now fixed but also those possibilities that are not yet fixed. In the context of the Primordial God's first act, then, all possible physical universes are still possible.

God's power as an agent is the power to bring about states of affairs that restrict the range of what is still possible. It follows that God does not just change things, but itself changes in bringing about physical states of affairs. For instance, if God had brought about the state of affairs that there was never to be anything physical, then this would amount to total abdication of power. Moreover, it would also, as far as I can see, have been tantamount to the choice to cease to exist. For there would no longer be anything possible or actual for the divine mind to depend upon.

At the other extreme, if God never brings about any state of affairs that governs anything but the immediate future, then God creates anew each moment, and Occasionalism would be correct. In that case the Primordial God continues to exist. Moreover, it changes, if at all, only by accumulating knowledge of what has been the case.

The Primordial God can undergo a more significant change by acting in ways that constrain the future histories of physical universes. In particular, God can change by ensuring that many universes that were once possible are no longer possible. Presumably these include all those in which suffering definitely exceeds joy, and probably all those in which joy does not exceed suffering. What corresponding change occurs to God? Previously God could entertain the possibility of creating a universe in which suffering outweighed joy. This has now become unthinkable, not in the sense of not being understood by God. For might-have-beens have whatever status our metaphysics grants them, and they may well, therefore, be understood by God precisely as might-have-beens. Rather, these universes are unthinkable in the morally relevant sense of not being such as we could decide whether or not to do it. For various acts to have become unthinkable is for God to have acquired a moral character, that of a virtuous consequentialist, whereas previously the divine consequentialism was not the result of a virtuous character. This illustrates how a change in which universes are still possible implies a change in the divine character.

3. THE NATURAL ORDER

For agents to be responsible in their interactions with each other, they need a stable environment and, moreover, one they can manipulate. God could provide stability merely by re-creating the universe moment by moment in a regular fashion. In that case Occasionalism would be correct, but I have already rejected that. Among other motives God might have for not creating in this fashion is that genuine persons must persist in a way that requires at the very least that later stages are causally influenced by earlier ones. Perhaps you retort, 'Persons, schmersons! Who cares?' I submit that if we were merely a succession of selves with the illusion of causal connections, we might be none the wiser, but it would give God less joy to know it than if there were genuine persons. Hence, I say, God's act of creation causes there to be either laws or something else constraining the future. These laws ensure that things have *existential inertia*, a tendency to persist. As a corollary, I see no need for the traditional thesis that God sustains the universe.

I shall now argue that if creation was part of the act of the Primordial God, then God has subsequently no power to overrule the natural order. I shall argue this in a negative fashion, by considering in turn the only four ways I can think of as to how God might overrule it. But before I do so, I make explicit the positive case for a God-constraining natural order. Admittedly, this case depends heavily on religious tradition, but that is significant, since the insistence that God does have power to overrule the natural order is itself largely based upon tradition. This positive case is based upon the premiss that God created the universe for a purpose that required there to be a natural order. This in turn requires that God decided that certain generalizations hold in the future, generalizations that are either about events or about powers. An example of the first kind would be the generalization that whenever particles interact at a point, energy and momentum are conserved. An example of the second kind might be that no positron has the power to decay into a proton and a neutron. Now I say that either God initially had power over the future, in which case such generalizations hold with the same sort of necessity that the past holds (accidental necessity), and God therefore no longer has power over the laws, or this generalization is merely the result of a divine intention to go on constraining nature in the same way. The latter, unlike the former, leaves scope for God to break the laws of nature. But it is open to the objection that if the natural order were the result of repeated divine decisions to institute it the same way, then God must share with us the blame for our wrongdoing. For unlike the supposed case of a natural order in which God could intervene, but which does not have to be renewed, we should not say that God is merely permitting the evils we do. And a blameworthy God is quite contrary to all religious traditions. To be sure, from a consequentialist point of view it makes no difference whether we think of God as permitting the evils or being a cause of them. But I am assuming that we theists assert that God is (now) morally righteous in more than the consequentialist sense.

I anticipate resistance to the idea that even God is constrained by the natural order. For it is contrary to divine omnipotence understood roughly as the thesis that God can do anything it is conceivable that a unique God can do. I say, however, that this doctrine is the conjunction of two theses. The first, which is the religious tradition, is that God is not limited in power except by not being able to do the impossible. The second, which is a piece of metaphysics, is that any description of a future whose conjunction with the description of the present and past is conceivable may be brought about. I reject the latter, not the former.

So much for the positive case. I now examine and criticize some ways in which it might seem that God could indeed ordain a natural order that would hold without renewal, while it remains the case that God could overrule this order. The first suggestion is what we might call the *Genesis hypothesis*. On it, God commands (in thought), 'Let there be such-and-such a universe!', and as a result, there is such-and-such a universe. Presumably on this hypothesis any coherent command is effective, so God could easily command that there be a universe with various DV (God willing) laws—that is, laws that hold, provided God does not intervene. This hypothesis might perhaps hold for a creative act by God, but only if it was after the initial act. For it requires a complexity that was not there in the beginning. Thus it requires that God have thoughts. Moreover, it requires as a meta-law the principle that God's commands are effective. For all I know, the Primordial God could bring about just this complexity and subsequently create in this Genesis fashion.

The next suggestion that comes to mind is that God subsequently intervenes by acting like any other agent, only with more power. Agency is a mystery that I accept prior to thinking about God. So there is no additional mystery if God intervenes by acting like any other agent. That suggestion fails, because agency within our universe has to operate within the constraints of the natural order. Indeed, it is as much part of the natural order as are physics, chemistry, and biology. When we freely choose to act rightly rather than wrongly, then that is possible not because we can overrule deterministic laws. It is possible, I say, because the laws are not deterministic.[1] So this suggestion does not imply that God can overrule the natural order, merely that God operates within it. Otherwise put, God can intervene, albeit subtly, without overruling the natural order.

The third suggestion that comes to mind is that what *we call* 'the natural order' does not consist in everything brought about by God's creative act, but rather consists in those aspects of the *genuine* natural order that are suitably regular and capable of systematic investigation. Hence, it is suggested that God acts in ways that we ordinarily think of as overruling the natural order. For example, God might as part of the initial act of creation ensure that if circumstances X arise, then in those circumstances an event Y occurs if and only if person S prays for Y. For example, God might ensure that in the circumstances in which Anne, a recent Ph.D., has to decide which job offer to accept and is perplexed,

---

[1] If the laws of physics appeared to be deterministic, I would adopt a many universes theory in which the very similar universes have slightly different initial conditions. Free action would then involve the termination of many of the universes, leaving many others (Davis 1991; Forrest 2001, 2006c).

that a normally shy but wise colleague, Barbara, is prompted to advise her if and only if she prays to God for guidance. I have no objection to this way of overruling the natural order except that, strictly speaking, God is still constrained by the initial creative act, and so there is an abandonment of divine power.

Finally, if we think that the natural order is the result of created things having causal powers, it might seem obvious that God could intervene just by being more powerful. Thus, if the orbits of the planets are the result of various gravitational forces, God could, we might think, increase the force between Jupiter and Saturn so that they start to orbit around each other. Either this is appealing to the supposed power of God to overrule the laws of nature, and so not a way in which that power might be explained, or we are thinking anthropomorphically and taking God to be physically pushing the two planets together. The latter might just be possible given a divine incarnation in some physical form that we cannot even imagine, but absent such peculiarities, it is open to the objection that without a body God cannot push or pull anything. We might at this point recall the silly argument against substance dualism from the premiss that a non-physical thing cannot interact with the physical. As Karl Popper (1966) has pointed out, this is based on a clockwork model of the universe in which all interactions are pushes or pulls. The valid residue in the silly argument is that it does require a body in order to interact by pushing or pulling. Hence a theory of causal powers, once it is purged of anthropomorphisms, offers no support for the idea of God intervening by breaking the laws of nature. God has to act relying on the laws, just as we do.

I infer that if a universe of our type was worth creating by the Primordial God, it was created without any possibility of subsequent overruling the natural order. This inference is far from conclusive, but the point of it is to make fairly probable the hypothesis that I take to be the key to theodicy: namely, that God is now constrained by the natural order when intervening to put things right that have gone wrong.

4. AN OBJECTION

I have argued that God's subsequent intervention in the universe is constrained by the natural order, which is itself ordained by God. I anticipate the objection that not even God can directly affect the future in this way, and hence the natural order is the result of continued divine will, in which case God is not constrained by it. For, it is widely held, an immediate effect must occur as soon as the cause does. This, the temporal analogue of the principle of no action at a distance, does, I grant, have intuitive appeal. But the objection fails even supposing it. For the objection exploits an ambiguity in the concept of the direct effect of an action. When God creates a universe, God does so directly, in the sense of not intending any intermediaries. It does not follow that God intends there to be no intermediaries. In particular, in creating a universe because of the joy contained therein, God brings about a natural order—say, one based on laws of nature. God does not have to calculate that such-and-such laws have desirable consequences. God does not have to, and maybe the Primordial God cannot, think about these laws. But in creating a universe of a certain type, God brings about these laws. And these laws operate immediately. So there need be no temporal gap between the creative act and the existence of the future-constraining natural order.

To say that the natural order is future-constraining is to assert that it does not just consist in a series of regularities brought about by God. Now there is no shortage of anti-Humean metaphysical theories according to which the natural order consists of more than mere regularities.[2] But regularities brought about by God are not mere regularities, and they might seem to be good candidates for laws, so why should theists believe that the laws are anything other than regularities that owe their continued occurrence to God's continued will that they do so? The answer, I say, concerns the issue of just who is responsible for acts that result in harm to others. If the so-called laws of nature have to be renewed by God each moment, then that puts the responsibility partly on God for the harm done. It is quite different if God, for the general good, ordains general laws that, among other things, permit the malicious intentions of creatures to result in harm to others. I submit, therefore, that theists should reject the otherwise attractive thesis that the so-called laws are just regularities brought about by repeated divine decree, not because it fails

---

[2] Probably the most popular anti-Humean theory is that laws of nature are relations between universals (Dretske 1977; Tooley 1977; Armstrong 1983). My own preferred theory is that laws are general facts that pre-exist their instances (Forrest 2006*b*). (See also McCall 1994).

to capture the intuitive necessity of the laws, but because it fails to exonerate God from the harm we humans do to each other and to other animals.

5. CREATING OTHER AGENTS

How can God bring it about that there are creatures who are agents, and hence who are made in the image and likeness of God? The answer might seem easy, given moderate materialism: just create the right sort of physical things in the right environment, and they must turn out to be conscious agents, for that is what we are. But it is not quite so simple. For the right environment, some would say, includes the absence of any being, whether God or just a creature of great power, who can interfere with our actions. Sartre seems to have thought that, and he is not alone.

The problem of divine interference may be illustrated by means of the example of Jacob wrestling with God, as in Genesis. To the onlooker this might look as if Jacob was drunk and struggling to maintain balance. But what would have been going on was that God and Jacob both had the power directly to bring about or prevent the very same event in the very same way: namely, Jacob falling down because of a series of neural processes resulting in muscle contractions. It might seem that Jacob, because weaker, would have had no power to act. Not so. God and Jacob would have had the very same power over Jacob's normal nerve activity. Of course God can, and in the story does, cheat by using the divine power over other things, making Jacob lame. But without such cheating we have incoherence if we say that both God and Jacob had power over the same neural processes. But whether God wins or we have incoherence, it follows that Jacob had no power. The problem, of course, is that if God retains power over the whole universe, then all our acts would seem to be like that. There is a solution, though. We may say that to exercise a power is to act, but that not to exercise it is precisely inaction, not action. In that case we could say that if the agents disagree, then the action occurs because one of them is not doing anything. Either this or the less plausible hypothesis that if the agents do not act in the same way, then nothing occurs, will solve the problem.

6. WHY WE MIGHT NONETHELESS SUPPOSE THAT GOD HAS RELINQUISHED SOME POWER TO OTHER AGENTS

Now let us consider what this solution does to responsibility. It is not here a case of God permitting wrong acts by choosing not to act subsequently—for example, by altering the trajectory of a bullet. That is another issue. The problem is that every time a human being does a wrong act with bad consequences, then the human being alone has acted. God has chosen not to act in spite of the bad consequences, presumably for the sake of human responsibility.

We may grant that having responsibility for our acts is either a source of joy or a condition for some other source of joy. But there is a class of wrong actions where the suffering is vastly greater than the joy of responsibility. These Marilyn McCord Adams (1999) calls horrendous evils. They, or at least the ones I am here concerned with, occur when a rather slight wrong inaction, say a momentary lapse of attention, a cowardly panic, or the failure to question a supposedly lawful authority, results in quite catastrophic evil. So if God has the power to act in these very cases, then God would act, causing the same behaviour as would result if both the human being and God had acted. Or if God does not act, then divine inaction is responsible for the horrendous evil, just as human inaction is.

By contrast, if God chooses to relinquish some power for the sake of us having responsibility collectively for our lives, then the evil that God permits in this way has to be averaged out over all of history. In addition, because, I assume, God lacks knowledge of what creatures will freely do until they do it, then even the expected evil of individual inactions has to be balanced against the expected good from the likely actions. Hence, if God decides that the overall consequences of a partial abdication of power to agents is worth risking for the sake of moral responsibility, then there might well be many individual cases in which, had God retained power, God would have acted.

The conclusion I reach, then, is that although it is perfectly coherent for God to retain power while creating other agents, resulting in dual control, the occurrence of horrendous evils forces us to say that God chose to abdicate some power to give agents sole control over and responsibility for their actions, which is what I mean by autonomy. The question of why autonomy is worth having, as opposed to dual control, is something I return to in the next chapter.

7. THE GENERATION OF PERSONS

I have argued that a sense of the gravity of our acts forces the conclusion that, in giving us freedom, God abdicates power, so our acts are not the joint acts of God and ourselves. But how is this possible? The moderate materialist hypothesis that I am operating with prevents me from baldly declaring that God abdicates power. God can do so only by affecting the physical, where this includes what is still possible for universes. My idea here concerns what constitutes a single mind, rather than several minds, and what constitutes a person. I take it that to be a person requires there to be not only a mind, in the sense of a unified conscious thing, but also the *first-person perspective*, as Lynne Rudder Baker (2000) calls it, and that this, in turn, requires the distinction between self and other, both in the present and extending in to the future. I shall also suppose that a mind suitably integrated with its environment can act, but that to be a person requires that the action be free. For present purposes, however, we may ignore the power of minds or of persons to act, since that would seem to follow of necessity from their being unified conscious things suitably integrated into a suitable environment. I shall concentrate, then, on two aspects of personhood: the unity of the mental, which is something required to be a mind, and the consciousness of self as distinct from others, which is required to have the first person perspective.

The unity of the mind could, perhaps, be ensured by positing a self related to various appearances. Or, as in an earlier work of mine, we could rely on a Kant-inspired idea that the unity derives from the integration of the appearances themselves (Forrest 1996a). We human beings are incapable of being aware of several unconnected things simultaneously. So the totality we are aware of forms a gestalt. The Kant-inspired idea is that this is a necessary feature of any mind, even the divine mind. Hence, if there were two things of which there was conscious awareness, then there would, at least momentarily, be two minds. This way of accounting for mental unity has the advantage of not requiring that the self be posited. Instead, the self is analysable as the unity of the mental.

The unity of the mental requires, I am assuming, a certain kind of unity in what the mind is aware of. Otherwise we would be simultan- eously aware of two things, not one, which I consider impossible. As to the kind of unity, we have some clues provided by altered states of consciousness. One of the more frequent of these is the type that Walter Stace called nature mysticism, where the distinctions are not attended to, and so the whole of that which you are in some sense aware of becomes the one object of attention (Stace 1955, 1960). By contrast, distinctions and clarity result in a focus on just one thing, in the foreground as it were. We should speculate, then, that the Primordial God sees all possible universes as a single thing, which appears a certain way, just as we can see a landscape as a whole in spite of the many details that make it up. There would be no self/other contrast in such total awareness.

In this case the only necessary condition that I can think if for the primordial unity of the mental is the absence of significant boundaries between possible universes. And therein lies the obvious objection. Isn't each possible universe distinct from each other one? Isn't each species of universe distinct from other species in its initial conditions and tuneable constants? Even more problematic is the distinction between different genera of universe distinguished by different kinds of law and different kinds of space-time, with, say, differing numbers of dimensions. The obvious objection is, I believe, the result of thinking of the plenum of possible universes as discrete, with each possible universe represented by a point with a minimum distance of separation from all other points. I suggest instead that we should think of the possible universes as packed together to form a many-dimensional continuum, where the properties of universes vary continuously as we move from point to point in the representation. There is not much difficulty in the idea of initial conditions and constants varying continuously across the space of possible universes. Even the laws can vary continuously, because between any two laws there is a continuum of statistical laws. Thus, between a law that all electrons attract each other and the actual law that they repel each other, we could pass by small degrees through various proportions of attraction, down to none attracting up through various proportions repelling. Alternatively, the force of attraction could be gradually weakened to zero, and then gradual strengthening forces of re-pulsion could be introduced. Neither is dimensionality a problem. How do we pass from a five-dimensional to a seven-dimensional universe? We use seven extra dimensions so as to bundle the five-dimensional ones into a twelve dimensional collection of universes, which is then altered continuously along some further, thirteenth dimension until it becomes a twelve dimensional bundle of seven-dimensional universes, themselves arranged in five dimensions. Moreover, because any smooth manifold can be embedded in a Euclidean one, it would seem that the space of all possible universes is connected.

To be a person requires more than being a mind. It requires the first person perspective, a sense of I and mine, which is opposed to the other, the not-self. It is hard to see how the Primordial God could have this, and subsequently God becomes, I believe, three Divine Persons, not one. The Trinity is not, however, our concern in this chapter, which is to understand how it is possible for God to arrange for the separation of some creatures as islands in the divine ocean. Part of what is required is that there be various sub-systems with the physical basis upon which the sense of self versus other supervenes. That, presumably, is something the neuro-philosophers, the psychologists, and the cognitive scientists can inform us about. It is also fairly easy to describe in terms of the, presumably supervenient, ontology of appearances.[3]

But in addition, I have required that morally responsible creatures be organisms over which God has chosen to have no power. This requires that there be a certain lack of unity between these sentient creatures and the rest of the universe. Otherwise the whole universe should appear as a whole to God with God retaining power over the morally responsible agents. It may well be the case that God also withdraws from other, non-responsible creatures, such as higher animals and small children. I am committed, however, only to the divine withdrawal from normal human beings (at the age of reason). This requires that the remainder of the universe, the portion other than the beings from whom God has withdrawn, itself forms a system with the necessary conditions for personhood (ignoring the Trinity in this chapter).

Here there is a gap in my account: just how does the remainder of reality, the divine ocean or, more prosaically, the divine Swiss cheese, necessitate a system of appearances as required both for the unity of the mental and for self-consciousness in such a way that the islands or

---

³ Elsewhere (Forrest 2005) I have analysed the way things appear in terms of the person to whom they appear standing in a relation of awareness to the complex relational property that corresponds to the way things appear to that person. It is easy to postulate that the person is aware of only one thing at a time, by insisting that the awareness holds between the person and the conjunction of all the complex relational properties that the person is simultaneously aware of, as opposed to the awareness holding between the person and these complex properties taken one by one. Self-consciousness then arises when this awareness of the conjunction is itself one of the conjuncts. This near-trivial difference between awareness of a conjunction and conjunction of awareness is all we need in an ontology of appearances to give an account of the unity. The neurophysiology of all this is not within my competence.

the holes are excluded. A satisfactory answer would exhibit the physical basis for the rest of the universe having the required unity. In Section 8 of Chapter 3 I suggested that the physical basis for the unity of the mental must be the holistic character of the physical system on which the mental supervenes, and I noted the holistic character of quantum-theoretic systems. What is required, therefore, is that the whole universe supports many sub-systems, each with a holistic character, while leaving the remainder of the universe with its holistic character. Will quantum theory come to my rescue again if I say the magic word 'decoherence'? All I can honestly say is that it is too early to decide one way or the other whether physics will support my hypothesis.

If God creates many universes, each with the requisite unity to support self-conscious mental unity, it would follow that God has split into many gods, one in charge of each universe. It is hard to argue against this, even using revealed premises. Some readers might be relieved, however, to hear that I think we have no reason to draw this conclusion. For I do not require that each actual universe (treating creaturely consciousnesses as holes) is a single system with the requisite unity. It is enough that all the actual universes (with holes in) taken together form a single system. Previously I suggested that the system of all possible universes is a connected space. I am now suggesting something similar: the system of actual universes minus the holes is still connected well enough to form the basis of a single divine mind.

8. ACQUIRING CHARACTER

One of the marked differences between the God of the philosophers and the God of various religious traditions is that the latter has character. Now it is easy to criticize the misapprehensions of the human beings who participate in these traditions. For instance, the Old Testament God is often despotic. Nonetheless, a critical examination of Hebrew religious tradition might well reveal some divine character traits. Among these are that God is not merely loving but loving in a properly jealous fashion, that God laughs at pompous self-important people, and that God is concerned with every individual, and not just with the common good.

If we grant the moderate materialist hypothesis that the nature of the divine mind depends on what has occurred and what is still possible for the physical order, then God can acquire character simply by choosing to foster some possibilities while excluding or at least making less frequent some others. But why should God acquire character? Or, I might add, if God is triune, why might the three Divine Persons acquire somewhat different characters?

The answer lies in the arbitrariness of complete power. Even given that God will in fact act so as to produce good consequences, there is much variety in what God could choose to do. God could make repeated choices, intervening in so far as previous decisions allow intervention. These choices, by constraining the remaining possibilities, influence the outcome of later choices. If those influences are systematic, then God acquires a character. For example, any decision which ties human fulfilment to a relationship with God and not, as would have been as appropriate, just to relationships with fellow humans will incline God to make further decisions which in one way or another proclaim that false gods will not be tolerated. Thus God acquires a properly jealous character.

9. AND LOVE?

I now come to the most important theme of developmental theism. God changes so as to become a loving God. The obvious objection to this is that the divine behaviour towards us is not loving. That objection is a consequence of the mistaken idea that to say God is loving is to say that the divine behaviour resembles the behaviour of a loving human being. Instead, I start from an analysis of what it is to be loving. Time was when philosophers sought to analyse familiar concepts. Knowledge got a great deal of attention, I recall, but curiously not much was said about love. Was that because if you decided that other human beings were loved only under a description, you ended up spending the night on the couch? Anyway, for want of precedent, I shall simply give an analysis of love of things, places, non-human animals, or persons. X loves Y if X has a disposition joyfully to mix X's flourishing with Y's, for better or worse. Here the familiar phrase 'for better or worse' is a conjunction, not a disjunction. So fair-weather friendship which is only for better counts as only a partial form of love, as does the suffering parent syndrome where the parents' flourishing is always vulnerable to the child's, but the parent never rejoices when things go well with the children. Love that is limited to specific activities, such as lovers who care very much about each other's sexual gratification but find each other's worries about tenure a complete bore, is partial and limited in another way. Love that is not partial is a risky business. For in cases in which Y is not flourishing, then the joy in the joyful mixing is outweighed by the suffering shared.

I say that if Y is the sort of thing that can experience joy, then Y flourishes if (1) Y experiences joy not outweighed by Y's own suffering, and (2) Y's state is a direct source of joy rather than suffering, to those aware of it. If Y cannot itself experience joy or suffering, then it flourishes if its state is such as to be a direct source of joy rather than suffering to those aware of it. Joy is a direct source of suffering when the joyful person is living in a fools' paradise ignorant of the truth. So the fools in their paradise are not flourishing. By contrast, the envious person suffers at the good fortune of others indirectly, because the others' good fortune combined with the envious person's lack of good fortune is itself a state of inequity, which is a direct source of suffering.

A distinction is often made between conditional and unconditional love. I take it that unconditional love is a willingness to go on loving in spite of the suffering due to lack of reciprocation. Whether that willingness is itself motivated by love or something else is, I suppose, a further distinction we might choose to make. Unconditional love might arise out of the virtue of fidelity rather than itself be motivated by love. Is the unconditional character of love good in itself? I suggest that it is not, but that, rather, the conditional character of much love is symptomatic of timidity. We admire the thorough mixing of flourishing even when imprudent. That the divine love is unconditional is important, I suggest, as a sign of its whole-heartedness.

I anticipate the objection that my analysis of love is defective because it makes no mention of the unity of lover and beloved. I am unmoved. To be sure, if those who love are able to co-ordinate their actions, they will trust each other and so act as one, but such acting as one is the acting of the individuals. For a unity to form out of various individuals, they would cease to be individuals. Hence they would not act as one; rather, there would be the one super-person acting. It is, I think, sloppy and sentimental to talk of unity as the product of love.

I have done the analytic thing, then. Now back to God and creation. I argue that the Primordial God will anticipate the joy of loving and so ensure the situation in which there is love between individual persons. First, I note that love multiplies joys by adding the joy of sharing joy to the shared joy. Moreover, this can be iterated with shared joy, at the sharing of joy and so on. Love also multiplies suffering; contrary to the proverb, a trouble shared is double the trouble. So it requires hope for human beings to see the value of being loving; but since the Primordial God creates for the sake of the likely overall balance of joy over suffering, it can anticipate that to become a loving God and to give creatures the opportunity to love will increase the likely balance of joy over suffering. Hence it will do so unless being loving gets in the way of other, greater sources of joy. We cannot entirely exclude the possibility that there might be some such source of joy, but the joy-multiplying character of love makes that rather unlikely. So we have reason to expect the Primordial God to come to be loving.

The proposed analysis of love makes it coherent to say that God, or a human being for that matter, loves humanity as a whole, rather than individual human beings. The difference, at least as regards God, is that to love humanity is to derive joy at the flourishing of human beings generally, which could be increased if the many flourish at the expense of a few, or even if a few flourish greatly at the expense of the many. Consider, then, a God motivated by love of humanity, or even by the love of all animals taken collectively, including humans ones. Such a God will not differ greatly from a consequentialist God, and would be as likely to create a universe of our kind as would a consequentialist one. But when we say that God is loving, we mean that God loves individuals, except perhaps any who freely reject the divine love. To love an individual is to love that person with her or his history, and not just any person who is now of the favoured type.[4] And this requires the mixing of divine flourishing with the flourishing of these individuals taken one by one, not just the flourishing of them taken as a whole. This in turn seems to require that the divine flourishing be mixed with the flourishing of the least well off of all those individuals whom God loves, including presumably, all those human beings who do not reject the divine love. In fact, it is hard to see how a loving God would be in an overall state of joy rather than suffering, given the state of many human beings, especially those who, in McCord Adams's phrase, commit horrendous evils while not rejecting the divine love. A God who genuinely loves each individual must, it seems, be a suffering

---

[4] Strictly speaking, I submit that we do not love individuals as such, but for you to love that person is to love any person sufficiently similar to that person now and with a sufficiently similar history. We call this love of an individual if there is no other actual person meeting that sufficient similarity condition. If readers think more (or even somewhat less) is required for loving individuals, so be it. It will make no difference. (Compare Brown 1997.)

God, which implies a remarkable kenosis. It also implies that God bring an end to this present state, which is rather wretched for those who love much, and bring about a future in which all whom God loves flourish.

So what is so joyful, then, about God loving individuals that it makes all this worthwhile? My answer is in two parts. The first part is that love, whether of individuals or of humanity as a whole, is worthwhile because of the potentially infinite joy of reciprocated love, in which X derives joy from sharing joy with Y, and so Y derives joy from this joy that X has, which in turn gives X more joy, and so on. This is a source of joy that, I believe, a purely consequentialist God can achieve only indirectly by becoming one who loves. The second part of the answer is that creatures who did derive potentially infinite joy from being loved by God as a collective rather than individuals would have to be ones that united to form a single super-person, whom God loved as an individual. Maybe God has ensured that on some planet there are such creatures, but, I say, we are not like that, and God has as good reason to create beings like us as those other creatures.

A consequentialist God would not have to change in order to become motivated, after creation, by the love of humanity taken as a whole. For after creation, other motives, notably the aesthetic, become less significant. This is not because there is no longer aesthetic joy, but because there is less opportunity for God to bring about beauty, having already done so by setting up the natural order. Now we know all too well that we humans often turn the beautiful into the ugly, which must be a source of suffering for God. But if the natural order has been set up in such a way that whether or not we love God and each other has a greater influence on the divine hedonic tone, then we may say that God has come to be loving of humanity. At least we may do so if God still has opportunity to affect creation.

We may assume, then, that after creation God loves humanity as a whole. In addition, the way in which reciprocal love multiplies joys provides a motive for a consequentialist God to become one who loves individuals in addition to loving humanity as a whole. There is a further motive if the flourishing of even a Divine Person is promoted by the acquisition of character, perhaps as a pre-condition for interpersonal relations of an especially joyful kind. Then the Primordial God, which lacks character, might nonetheless act so that the subsequent Divine Person or Persons has character. If we also grant that a vicious or neutral character is not going to promote the joy of the person who has it any more than a virtuous one, then for the sake of the good of creatures, the Divine Person or Persons would come to have a virtuous character. There are several different ways of being virtuous, but the Christian teaching is that a certain sort of loving disposition (*agapē*) is the greatest of virtues, and non-Christians of various kinds are eager to deny that this teaching is peculiarly Christian. It should not be too controversial, then, that for the sake of acquiring some character, and taking into consideration the good of creatures, God would acquire a loving character. In that case the Divine Person or Persons would perhaps be such as would not have created in the first place a universe with so much opportunity for suffering.

10. OBJECTIONS TO A LOVING GOD

Am I being too anthropomorphic in attributing sources of joy to God like those of us humans? In answer, I repeat my claim that the hedonic tone of a mental state, at least one that we are attending to, depends of metaphysical necessity on the content of the state. This claim is more easily illustrated with suffering than joy. There are only three possible ways of removing the suffering due to pain: remove the stimulus completely, remove its painful quality while retaining other aspects of the stimulus, or cease to attend to the stimulus. There is no fourth method: namely, enjoying pain as such. Masochists enjoy something else associated with pain. This holds even if it is conceivable that there be a pure masochist, who finds pain an immediate source of joy. Moderate materialists deny that the conceivable is in general possible, and I deny the possibility of such pure masochism, even though it is conceivable.

A second objection is that a being as powerful as God cannot love creatures, because, on the one hand, there is no genuine mixing of flourishing if the creatures are not free agents but rather divine puppets; but, on the other hand, a loving God would strive to win over those creatures who reject the divine love, even if that requires eventually overcoming their freedom. Many theists respond to this with a compromise, assuming that God will eventually, after death, overcome all creaturely rebellion and hate. This compromise attests to the problem without solving it.

This is a difficult objection to assess, for the thought that God would strive to overcome hatred if necessary by taking away freedom is not obviously correct. But one of the advantages of developmental theism is that it has a solution to this problem, assuming it is genuine. The solution is that the Primordial God is aware of the potential joy of love, but that this does not entail that it is loving. So it creates a universe with free creatures even if that allows for final damnation, but this is not something a loving God would do. Having created in this fashion, the loving God that develops then strives to save all, but might not be able to, if, as I argued above, the Primordial God sets up a natural order that cannot be overruled.

The next objection is not that God cannot love creatures, but that God has no reason to. For in the Trinity, which I take to be a development from the primordial state, the mixing of flourishing is there. So why love creatures who can disappoint by making incorrect choices? Some might say that this is because there is a special excellence in unconditional love, and that within the Trinity reciprocation is predictable with certainty, so the excellence of unconditional love is vacuous. I disagree, since I have suggested that unconditionality is good merely as a sign of whole-heartedness, which the love exemplified by the Trinity is. So why love creatures, as opposed, say, to ensuring that creatures have the joy of loving each other? The answer is that the consequentialist motive I have assigned to the Primordial God is not the motive of filling a perceived lack or need. I am not even sure what that would mean in the divine case. So, no matter how much joy there already is, the consequentialist has reason to bring about some further joyful situation. Assuming there is joy, for creatures and also for God, in loving relations with creatures in addition to the joy of love between Divine Persons, on the one hand, and love between creatures on the other, that is sufficient motive for the Primordial God to become a loving God. This is in spite of the risk of non-reciprocation, and so we may say that God's love for us is unconditional.

11. A SUMMARY OF THIS CHAPTER

The Primordial God has, I have argued, motive to undergo various kinds of kenotic abdication of power. When it created the universe, the natural order was set up so that not even God could overrule it. In creating free agents, God has, I argued, also restricted the divine power, contracting, as it were, away from their spheres of direct influence. I am supposing that the nature of the divine mind depends both on what is the case and what is still possible. So these restrictions affect what it is like to be God. Moreover, if one divine choice results in a situation in which another of the same kind becomes probable, we may say that God has acquired personality or character. And this is not a behaviourist analysis of personality, to do with future choices. The mind of God is itself influenced by this acquisition of personality. For instance, instead of saying that God tends to behave in a properly jealous fashion, we should say that God has acquired a mind such that God will behave in a properly jealous way. Last, and most significant, I have explained how the Primordial God changes from an agent that is motivated aesthetically to one that loves individuals.

7

Understanding Evil

The kenotic developmental theism I have been outlining provides additional resources to understand evil. That is the topic of this chapter, in which I continue the discussion begun in Chapter 5. If, however, you ask me to put my hand on my heart and say what I actually believe, I would have to say that I believe the disjunction of my kenotic proposal and something more orthodox. Hence it is of some importance that a great deal of what I say about the understanding of evil would apply to the hypothesis that God has always had a loving nature. As far as the problem of evil goes, I put forward kenosis as a fall-back position, saying, 'If, like me, you have doubts as to whether this universe is the creation of a loving God, then here is an alternative.' I am not arguing, therefore, that kenosis provides the only way to understand evil, although it would be neater intellectually if I could in honesty do so. My case for denying that God has always had a loving nature is based only on my preference for simpler hypotheses.

1. THE HEART AND THE HEAD

Economics may be dismal science, but epistemology is more dismal yet, and I had hoped to avoid it. Unfortunately, the problem of evil demands epistemological reflection. Consider the following story. Daniel Howard Snyder relates how when he told someone in the English Department that he was writing his thesis on the problem of evil, she replied, 'Isn't that old hat? I mean, what more can be said after Ivan Karamazov?'(Howard-Snyder 1996: preface). Either this is a stupendous *non sequitur*, betraying a total lack of understanding of how we ought to reason, or it tells us something important about epistemology. I suggest the latter. Consider another story, true or not: namely, that the Germanic tribes of 2,000 years ago used to debate issues twice, once drunk and once sober. There are, I would submit, two complementary ways of reasoning: the sober and the drunk; the analytic and the intuitive; the dispassionate and the passionate; the general, or, as people say abstract, and the particular or, as people say, the concrete. How are these related? It will not do to say that the passions lead us astray. They surely do, but we also feel in our bones that general or abstract reasoning is often beside the point.

I submit, and invite you to agree, that neither the head nor the heart is functioning very well. So it is foolish to rely solely on one or the other. We are in poor health both intellectually and emotionally, but we are well enough to correct our own errors if we try hard and do not deny our sickness. Maybe you disagree, but even if you do, I invite you to agree that if the different modes of reasoning, the drunk and the sober as it were, point in different directions, we have an intellectual dilemma. It is not a straightforward matter of one trumping the other.

Now let us return to the problem of evil. If we think passionately and consider particular cases, we do have an enormously powerful urge to reject the goodness of God, as this is commonly understood. No amount of careful analysis of the inference from 'God is good' to 'God would not allow such evils' undermines this. For it is not as if some correctible fallacy of equivocation has been made. The inference is immediate and seems quite persuasive.

To many there is a similar dilemma concerning the existence of God. For they hold, incorrectly, that the intellectual arguments fail, but that in their hearts they find that theism somehow makes sense of their lives.

As this mention of making sense suggests, also relevant is the relation between Bayesian reasoning with probabilities, on the one hand, and inference to the best explanation, on the other. I suggested earlier that we do not love the truth; we love understanding and, hopefully, fear falsehood. Now understanding combines the purely intellectual with the emotional in a way that probabilistic calculations do not. Hence inference to the best explanation, although it might seem redundant to Bayesians, remains important. Theistic conclusions reached by probabilistic calculations alone without a sense of understanding will seem abstract and strangely unconvincing—as if proving God by algebra.

We need, then, to understand evil. My proposal, in outline, goes like this. The God who created did not love individual creatures, was not such as should be likened to a good parent, and did not act in ways that we humans call morally good. Creation itself can be understood in terms of God acting for the sake of good consequences, where the goodness in question concerns the hedonic tone of both God and creatures. Maybe we can say that the Creator loved creation as a whole and loved humanity as a whole, but we should not say that the Creator loved the individuals who would be created. Either this is because God did not at that stage have a loving disposition or because, for some reason, merely possible creatures are not suitable objects of love.

The second suggestion requires comment. It is not, I think, their non-existence that excludes possible beings as objects of divine love. For possible beings could be loved as instances of precisely characterized types, with precisely characterized histories, and I doubt that we humans do anything different when we love. The difficulty, rather, is that there are too many precisely characterized histories of merely possible creatures, at most one of which will ever come about. And those that do come about do so partly as a result of divine choice and partly as a result of creatures' choices. Even if God can predict the creatures' choices, it is incoherent for God to predict the divine choices. (See Hunt 1997.) Therefore, prior to creation God does not know which possible life histories would be actualized. It follows that prior to creation either God loved all the possible creatures with all their distinct histories or God loved none of them. My objection to saying that God loved possible creatures as individuals is that the set of all possible histories of creatures lacks natural division into subsets, each corresponding to the possible histories of one individual. Instead, there is a continuum between one possible individual and the next. So if, prior to creation, God loved all possible creatures in all their immense variety and loved them as individuals rather than loving the whole *en bloc*, then God would love each variant of each individual, rather than loving each individual. Hence, God would create instances of all the variants on each possible individual. Not only is this intuitively absurd, it conflicts with my conviction that we are, and are intended to be, autarchic creatures who decide which of our variants comes to exist. Hence even if at the time of creation God knew all possible individuals with the precision required for love, we should assume that God was not loving in the sense of loving individuals. Therefore we may understand evil provided we can understand why the Primordial God acting in a consequentialist fashion would create an evil-prone universe like ours, and provided we can understand why a loving God permits these evils once there is an evil-prone universe in place.

2. WHY THE PRIMORDIAL GOD MIGHT WELL CREATE OUR KIND OF UNIVERSE

First, why would the Primordial God care at all about our well-being? When Shakespeare says in King Lear, 'As flies to wanton boys are we to the gods', he expresses uncommonly well a common sentiment. Why would God be bothered with us? The answer is that a good consequentialist takes the joy of any creature into account, no doubt using the *sparrow* (short for mean flourishing sparrow) as a unit, with human beings rating in the mega-sparrow range.

The Primordial God's motive for creating a universe suited to human beings, and extraterrestrial persons perhaps, is the joy to be derived from their loving each other, and loving God, provided various sources of suffering, both creaturely and divine, are taken into consideration. This is a motivation additional to the aesthetic for creating a life-filled universe. You may take the importance of love either as supported by tradition or as a plausible hypothesis or both. And I submit that the Primordial God might be motivated by love in two ways. One is the broadly speaking aesthetic pleasure in being aware of love. You might object, 'Public displays of affection among students in spring bring a smile to our lips, but why presume that God is like us?' The answer is that moderate materialism tells us that the connections between hedonic tone and the content of awareness are not decreed by God; they hold of metaphysical necessity. Those who do not smile at public displays of affection are either offended, because they think that such displays should be private, or saddened, because they are no longer romantically inclined. So, as elsewhere, I take it that the love between others is a direct source of joy to the beholder, but might be outweighed by indirect suffering. The second motive is the one I have elaborated in the previous chapter: namely, that the love between individuals can result in a positive feedback with a potentially infinite increase of joy.

Does love necessarily require suffering? I think not. There could be creatures for which it was true that so-called evils were mere privations of expected goods. Such creatures might be free to bring about either less or more joy, but live and love without suffering. Love does not, then, require suffering, but there is a connection. We admire whole-hearted love, which in the human case occurs only when those who love are willing, unconditionally, to share the suffering of those they love. And we rejoice when loving relationships that are thus tested by suffering reach a happier conclusion. Moreover, it is reasonable to suppose that those who love whole-heartedly are capable of greater joy than those who do not. In addition, there is joy in having autonomously come to be one of those who love whole-heartedly. Hence those human beings flourish the most who have autonomously come to love each other in a whole-hearted fashion, and so are prepared to share the sufferings as well as the joys of others. And, repeating the qualification 'at least in the human case', to come autonomously to be that kind of loving person is a process of growth, whereby some degree of love is manifested, and so love increases. Hence, reminding ourselves that God might well have created rather different persons as well as us, God has reason to create beings of our kind who cannot fully flourish without some sharing of the suffering of others. This does not imply the more suffering the better—the connection between freely acquired dispositions and their manifestation is not like that.

I am thus proposing an Irenaean soul-making theodicy as an answer to why God created an evil-prone universe. God creates so that various creatures, including ourselves, have the opportunity to make their own 'souls'—that is, to have autonomously become beings that are loving towards others. Here, by autonomy I mean autarchy (having freedom) together with the absence of any other agent who can exercise control over our actions. I am not submitting that autonomy is a good thing in itself; merely that it is better to have come to be loving autonomously than to have been predestined to do so. Therefore some suffering is good for us.

Now I accept the common opinion that autonomy is lacking in Heaven, where the freedom, because it is perfect, is constrained by the sheer irrationality of doing anything displeasing to God or anything expressive of hatred to others. This point is only an objection to those who consider that full autonomy is for ever a good thing. But because full autonomy is the good of making yourself the person you are, it is best when complete, and so a state of having made yourself who you are. So it is not a continuing good.

It is better, I say, to come to be loving in this autonomous way. Better, but riskier. For creatures like us, acquiring a loving character autonomously must involve some suffering. It would not be risky for God to create beings capable of suffering and inflicting suffering who were free—that is, have autarchy—but not autonomous. For then there would be dual control, with God permitting wrong acts only in so far as the good of acting freely on some occasion outweighed the consequences of the act. The dangerously risky combination is a situation with autonomous creatures capable of suffering and hence, we may suppose, of causing others of their kind to suffer. There is a way of preventing this risk by complicating the laws of nature, to exclude all brain processes correlated with dysfunctional suffering. I assume, however, that such unnecessary and *ad hoc* complications would lessen the divine aesthetic joy and that of creatures with whom God shares this joy.

In short, to create our type of being with the opportunity for autonomous soul-making without risk leads to excessive complexity. So I am repeating the unpalatable theodicy that, at least when considering creatures like us, some suffering is good, and no matter how human history had gone, we would have suffered. I am not, however, suggesting that the suffering that some, especially some children, undergo is productive. Here it is not the amount of suffering that is at issue, but its nonfunctional or even dysfunctional character. Given that the joy of having autonomously come to be loving creatures lasts throughout the afterlife, any amount of suffering that really does help us come to be this way is worth it, and would be tolerated by a loving God. We may go so far as to say with Richard Swinburne (1987) that it is good to suffer for the sake of others, even if the others are not loved by us. What we find hard to accept is that a loving God would have permitted an excess of suffering that has no apparent purpose, is sometimes even contrary to the development of the individual, and of no help to others. My claim is that the Primordial God risked the excess of suffering for the sake of the right amount.

That there is some dysfunctional, and hence excessive, suffering has been denied, for instance by Swinburne. Since no one thinks that we should not relieve severe suffering, then the function of much suffering must be to provide opportunities for relieving it. Serious but bearable suffering provides, however, as much opportunity for relief as does unbearable suffering. So the function of providing opportunity for others to relieve it cannot show that there is no dysfunctional suffering.

One risk that God took is that, at least in our part of this universe, collective wrongdoing would result in a non-functional or even dysfunctional excess of suffering and in the handing on of vice from one generation to the next, without deliberate malice nonetheless perpetrating horrendous evils. Perhaps there was an even more serious risk. Few of us, I fear, make the most of the opportunities given to us to become loving and virtuous. Moreover, the harm done to us by others, or sheer accidents, also results in our limited growth as persons. To some extent God might make good the defects that are not our fault. But even that might be too much like destroying the person in question, and then creating an improved version, which is certainly not a loving thing to do. So there is the risk of partial or even complete failure. The sort of consequentialist Primordial God that I am considering as Creator would take such a risk, for the sake of there being individuals who come to have the joy of freely and autonomously having come to be loving. Maybe in other universes, or just on other planets, God creates beings that achieve this without the risk because they are not autonomous. But since they are not like us, there is no question of God creating them instead of us. Maybe God has created them as well as us. All I am saying is that we were worth creating in spite of all the suffering we can inflict on each other.

This way of understanding evil is incomplete if we do not adjoin to it some explanation of why God can intervene in human history only in ways that do not break the laws of nature and why God did not bring about more complicated laws with various loopholes allowing the breaking of the apparent laws, with the true, more complicated ones hidden from the scientific method.[1] I have already offered an account of laws as unbreakable, so the crucial question is why God did not bring about complicated laws with various built-in exceptions to the simple approximate laws that we are able to discover. I find it ironic that so many theists want to defend the miraculous in the sense of violations of the laws in so far as we can comprehend them, even though it is only by denying the miraculous in this sense that, I say, theists can understand evil.

The question, then, is why God did not bring about more complicated laws, ones with many apparent exceptions designed so that God could repeatedly intervene to prevent or remove dysfunctional evils. The obvious answer is a harsh one: in either positive or negative ways the divine hedonic tone depends partly on the beauty of things. So either we say that there is joy in contemplating elegant laws or that there is suffering in contemplating *ad hoc* modifications. Either way, God is motivated to create a universe with simple laws rather than a counterpart that is very like ours but in which the apparent laws have loopholes to allow subsequent divine intervention if things go too badly wrong. Moreover, if part of the joy of Heaven is that God shares this

---

[1] What I have called apparent laws would then correspond to the *lossy* laws that Braddon-Mitchell (2001) discusses.

joy at the beauty of creation, which is, I say, the beauty of God, then this valuing the aesthetic is for our potential good also.

A less obvious answer is suggested by a solution to the problem, to be discussed below, of how God can choose between an infinity of possibilities. It is that in order to make a choice between possible universes suited to life, God maximizes some source of joy that can be maximized, even though this is less than some other sources of joy that cannot be maximized. And one source of joy that can be maximized is that which derives from the simplicity of the fundamental laws. For among the life-friendly laws there will be finitely many than which there are no simpler.

To summarize: we may understand evil as the result of a risk God took in order (1) to create autonomous agents like us capable of love; and (2) to do so elegantly. Fortunately, this is quite compatible with, and less joyful without, an afterlife in which among other shared joys is the joy of having come to be a loving person autonomously and the joy of contemplating the divine beauty, which is the beauty of creation.

Our emotional response is that it is both wrong and unloving to risk so much for the sake of elegance. And the risk here includes the risk of us coming to the afterlife with deformed characters as a result of the wrong we do or the wrong done to us. That would make us lesser beings than we might have been, even though we shall flourish perfectly as such beings. The emotional response in question should be analysed. Why would it not be loving to create in just the way I have described the Primordial God as creating—that is, taking a risk because it would be inelegant not to do so? After all, there seems to be a certain arbitrariness in just how much God creates, so why is it unloving to risk a human being becoming morally or emotionally retarded when it is not unloving to risk one fewer human being and one more dugong, say? It is something to do with taking risks with others. We think that it is morally acceptable, and maybe even compatible with loving others, to risk our own lives, doing things such as mixing every recreational drug available downtown or climbing Mt Everest, but neither moral nor loving to risk others—for instance, by giving your adolescent children a cocktail of recreational drugs or forcing them to join you in the climb. Previously I suggested that universal divine love requires the divine hedonic tone to be linked to that of the most miserable of creatures, not to the average or the total of happiness. In addition to all the things that love does and does not do, so admirably listed by St Paul in 1 *Corinthians* 13, it would be a nice touch of bathos to add that love does not maximize expected utility. I think we can extend this to say that the loving person is concerned not just with the individual as that individual now is but with that individual in the future. So the concern for the least well off that characterizes love extends to the concern for the least well off of all the future persons that the individual who is loved might become. To be sure, sometimes we have to take risks with others, and we all know that the over-protective parent, by trying to avoid certain risks, exposes the child to other sorts of harm. But the over-protective parent lacks wisdom, not love. Love is protective, cherishes the beloved, and is therefore risk-averse.

Likewise, a great deal of morality is concerned with side constraints on consequentialist reasoning, and the chief of those side constraints is not sacrificing individuals to the common good. I would suggest that this too extends to being risk-averse. For instance, we grant that it is immoral to sacrifice one chosen innocent victim for the sake of the whole people. It seems somewhat less immoral to have a lottery, to choose the victim, but unless all consent to the lottery, it is still contrary to our sense of justice.

Such risk taking is one of the obnoxious consequences of consequentialism, and so no objection to the hypothesis that the Primordial God would create that way. I hope it helps to explain the emotionally charged intuitive reaction to the evil around us: namely, that regardless of the reasons for risking dysfunctional suffering and horrendous evils, it is not a loving thing to do.

It is ironic that an unloving God would prize love so much as to risk creaturely suffering for the sake of autonomously coming to have a loving character. This irony would, however, be an inconsistency only if we held that a God who prized love so highly never became loving.

3. THE WORST-CASE SCENARIO

So what is the worst case? That in spite of all God's efforts, including the Incarnation, some, many, or even most of us are damned. Now up to the very last moment, God might use every method, including much pain and suffering, to try to win back the lost. But if it was too late, we should not expect any further pain at God's hands. Maybe justice requires that fellow creatures be entitled to inflict pain on those who have done them harm, although I suspect that this is an entitlement which only the damned, if such there be, would exercise. But in any case it would be finite. Afterwards God would sadly resign the damned to whatever sort of futile pleasures they could enjoy without harming others. However pleasant, this would be a total failure for them and a partial failure for God.

A consequentialist God would risk dismal failure for the sake of glorious success. And I think we need to take quite seriously the possibility not merely that we ourselves may be damned, but that our own actions harm the prospects of salvation for others. I agree that this is not a risk that a loving kind of creator would have incurred, but what I have been proposing is that kindness and love came later. God, having decided on some general features of our universe, is no longer all-powerful. But the up-side is that the sort of love God has exhibited in the Incarnation is not something that would ever have arisen had God not previously thought in an unloving, consequentialist fashion. If eventually all are saved, then we may say that our own failings have been a *felix culpa* because they occasioned the Incarnation. But the prospect of damnation—not to pain, but to pleasant futility—remains, even given the commodious doctrine of Purgatory.

4. IS THE DIVINE LOVE UNCONDITIONAL?

Love is a gamble, for by mixing your flourishing with that of others, you risk loss as well as gain. The difference between the love of people taken collectively and the love of individual persons is that the latter ties your well-being to that of the least fortunate.[2] When Pete Seeger sang 'A country is no richer than the poorest of its poor', he was adopting the idealized perspective of a nation grounded on love. Unconditional love accepts that risk, and hence accepts the risk of being held hostage by someone who exercises power by being miserable, and so making others miserable. Hence, if the divine love is unconditional, then someone, Satan maybe, could make God and all those who love God miserable just by means of self-inflicted suffering. I suspect that being unconditional is a mark of thoroughness in love, and that whatever motive God has to love, God's love would be unconditional. But God, at least the

---

[2] If we could measure flourishing, we could distinguish between the maximum extent of flourishing that a being is currently capable of and the percentage of the maximum that the being currently enjoys. To love another seems to increase the maximum capacity for flourishing, but if the one who is loved has a low percentage of flourishing then the one who loves likewise has a low percentage. I shall spare readers the formula.

Primordial God, is no fool for love's sake, and so would ensure that there is an end to the suffering of all creatures. What, then, happens to any who make themselves miserable to exercise power over God? That is surely irrational, and a loving God can intervene to force people to see what is rational without damage to their character. That is because irrationality is not as such a character trait. Rather, it is the consequence of various traits, some virtuous but most vicious. God might well choose never to alter someone's character except in a gradual and willing fashion. To show them the truth in ways that force rationality upon them is not, however, such an alteration. So we may anticipate that, after some sort of divine judgement which forces rationality upon us, any who have freely rejected God, will be lesser beings enjoying themselves without loving others. Given what they have become, they would be flourishing, in much the way that the aardvark or the platypus flourishes. To lower yourself, rejecting everything that gives human beings dignity, is the ultimate failure; but provided it does not involve suffering, it is compatible with flourishing as the sort of being you have chosen to become, and so does not detract from the joy of those, God and the blessed, who love even the damned as much as they love the aardvark and the platypus.

5. A SUMMARY OF THE PROPOSED UNDERSTANDING OF HOW EVIL CAME ABOUT

For the sake of the joy that love will give, the unloving Primordial God does something that probably no one would do out of love: puts both itself and creatures in a risky situation and limits its power to do anything about it. Perhaps these goals could be achieved in less risky ways by creating different kinds of being from us or by tinkering in *ad hoc* ways with the laws of nature. To the first suggestion, I say that God might well have created these different universes in addition to ours. To the second, I say that *ad hoc* laws would cause God aesthetic suffering. Having created in such a way that there is a natural order that cannot be overruled, the opportunities for God to intervene are limited. So although we would expect the by-now-loving God to intervene as much as possible to alleviate suffering, we can understand God's failure to remove non-functional suffering as a result of the limited divine power. In fact, it might well be that the only opportunities for divine intervention are by means of the Incarnation and inspiration by the Holy Spirit.

To those who find the problem of evil otherwise insoluble, I say, 'You may very well be right that no morally good or loving, all-powerful, all-knowing God would risk the dysfunctional suffering that humans experience, or the horrendous evils that normal human beings perpetrate.' However, I reply that when God was all-powerful, it was neither loving nor good except in a rather obnoxious consequentialist fashion. Subsequently God has become loving, but is no longer all-powerful.

6. REPLIES TO SOME OBJECTIONS

Why Value Autonomy?

I have assumed that it gives more joy to become a loving person as a result of autonomous choice than to have a loving character thrust upon you, or to acquire it by means of a restricted freedom. It could be objected that we should value autonomy only as a means to the end of getting what we want, rather than what others think we should want. Moreover, it could be asked what joy autonomy ever gave anyone. Is it not, rather, a burden?

My response is that autonomy as such does not give joy. Rather I am submitting that the achievement of a loving character autonomously is a greater source of joy to you, to other human beings, and to God, than its happening to you without your autonomous action. Moreover, it would not affect the proposed understanding of evil if I fell back to a weaker position: namely, that the joy in question derives not from the autonomy as such, but from the fact that this loving character may be interpreted as a gift from God. For the theist, the difference is between God offering us a gift and God forcing us to become loving.

The Love Drug

In a rainforest somewhere, about to be discovered, is an undistinguished looking climber whose berries contain a powerful love-inducing drug. And I do not just mean an aphrodisiac. The drug company will fail to make any profits, because the executives after sampling it will decide to offer it free to all. No one has to take it. So those who take it freely will freely attain a disposition to love, even if sheltered from all suffering. This is a putative counterexample to my claim that for beings like us some suffering is required for us freely to acquire love in the full sense, a love that is prepared to share suffering as well as joy.

My reply is that this is one of those imaginary examples that seem possible merely because we are not given enough details. In fact, we already know of the drug in question. It is oxytocin, but, like any other drug that affects the nervous system, we become tolerant of it. The same problem would hold for any easy way of freely becoming loving. That still leaves the prospect of elaborate voluntary microsurgery. But I doubt whether you would survive as the same person. For that would interfere with a necessary condition for persistence as a person: namely, that the main cause of the way you are at each time is the way you were shortly before.

The Objection to Multiple Universes

There is a problem in positing many universes for just the one God. For if, as I have suggested, the division of the mental into distinct minds is a consequence of the division of that of which there is consciousness, then it would seem that if many universes are created by the Primordial God, then this God has undergone fission into many gods, one for each universe. But without believing in multiple universes, we may no longer concentrate, as I have, on why God would think this universe worth creating. I would have to tackle the more difficult question of why God did not create a better type of universe, a question that I dismiss by saying, 'Perhaps God did as well'.

In Chapter 6 I considered the threat of divine fission, and I suggested that a system of many universes might still form a whole, a unity. Another reply is that, for all we know, God has undergone such fission. I am aware, however, that there are those who think I misread the offer to give the Wilde Lectures as an offer to give the wilder lectures or even the wildest lectures. And we can see why we should be reluctant to go that wild. For, given moderate materialism, the products of such divine fission would be isolated from each other, and it is plausible that the Primordial God would not choose to become several isolated gods. I will therefore give a more orthodox answer. A single universe governed by simple fundamental laws may contain many distinct domains or sub-universes governed by somewhat different derived laws. Thus, instead of saying of a better species of universe that God might have created it as well, we may say that our universe is a rather large one, containing within it copies of many species of smaller universes. The copies would not, however, go back right to the beginning, because the initial conditions for the species in question would be the starting-point of a given sub-universe. Moreover, the laws of nature operating in the sub-universe would be derived laws, based upon both the ultimate laws of nature and the circumstances holding in the sub-universe.

And if that strikes you as still too speculative, I have a fall-back position. Our universe is very large, perhaps vastly larger than the visible universe. So even if the circumstances for advanced life forms to occur are extremely rare, there may well be extraterrestrials. When we come to consider the problem of evil, a better world that God could create as well as ours does not have to be a whole universe. A planet around a star so distant that it cannot be infected by the evils on Earth would do just as well. So the conversation need not go, 'Why did God not create a better universe?', 'Perhaps God did as well as a ours'. It might, more modestly, go, 'Why did not God create a better course of evolution?' 'Perhaps God did as well as ours'.

The Taint of Evil

Another objection is that some evils taint any consequences, so that these consequences are not in their context good, although had they arisen in some other way, then they would have been good. Perhaps, as my wife has suggested to me, the Coliseum should be razed to the ground because its value as a monument is for ever tainted by its use. Likewise, suppose that the consequences of a war turn out to be such that had they occurred in some other way, they would be immensely beneficial. It is not just that we would ask whether it was worth it. We might hold that it could not be worth it, because these are tainted consequences that do not have the value they would otherwise have. In terms of hedonic tone, this would be an organic unity effect. The whole is a state of suffering, even though, if we tried to add up the tones of the parts, we would say that it was on balance joyful.

The tainting of otherwise good consequences might seem to undermine the common point that we cannot tell simply by observing whether ours is a creation-worthy universe. Such tainting could be taken as the intellectual articulation of Dostoevsky's rejection in *The Brothers Karamazov* of the way an afterlife might reconcile us to evil. For any afterlife, however fulfilling it might be in many respects, is, the objection goes, tainted by the evils of this life. And we may suppose that the blessed in Heaven would have the utmost sensitivity to such tainting.

I am not sure how seriously to take this objection. It smacks of the deliberate cultivation of moral refinement. Nonetheless, it can be answered. For the objection carries within it the seed of a reply. If tainting evil is possible, then so is its exact opposite, absorbing good. This is a good that does not merely *cancel out* evil, but, in Roderick Chisholm's (1990) terminology, defeats it. So let us return to *The Brothers Karamazov*. A Heaven in which a good time is had by all, who greet each other in friendship, is not sufficient to absorb the cruelty exhibited by the landowner who hunted the child to death with his hounds. Something of a qualitatively different kind is required, and this is provided by the way in which God's love for creatures has been demonstrated in the Incarnation. Something happens that has the opposite effect of tainting. At least provided all are saved, and this is the result of the Incarnation, we may say that even the most horrendous evil turns out to be *felix culpa*. For we will then be able to say that, had it not been for these evils, there would have been no Incarnation. If not all are saved even with the Incarnation, it might well be the case that both human and divine joy in an afterlife are for ever tainted. That might be one of the risks the Primordial God took.

The No-afterlife Objection

God took a risk of excessive suffering, but the initial divine plan was of moderate suffering, because it is good for us. This is, I take it, the familiar Irenaean soul-making theodicy, as presented by John Hick while he was still a Christian (Hick 1966) or by Richard Swinburne (1987). The objection to be considered is that a soul-making theodicy requires an afterlife, but an afterlife is not possible. Quite why a soul-making theodicy requires an afterlife is not immediately obvious, but here is an argument for that conclusion. The Primordial God might have risked excessive or dysfunctional suffering, but on a soul-making theodicy the aim was to ensure enough suffering for humans to come to have loving characters. Now both the joy in having and the joy in being aware of a loving character would be greater if there was an afterlife. So we may draw the conclusion that, if possible, the Primordial God would have ensured an afterlife. A corollary is that belief in God should make us hope for an afterlife if an afterlife is possible. We may not, however, draw the conclusion that because, it is said, an afterlife is impossible, then we should reject a soul-making theodicy. For the conclusion that there will be an afterlife is itself conditional upon the possibility of one. If an afterlife is not possible, then the Primordial God might have intended something like this: the young tend to be selfish, but after some hard knocks they settled down to become loving citizens, parents, and grandparents, dying fulfilled but without any afterlife. That is not what we find, but the Primordial God is not risk-averse, so that might have been what was intended.

For any who think, as I used to, that an adequate theodicy requires an afterlife, any objection to an afterlife is thereby an objection to theism. But what is the objection? It is based upon the rather strong requirement on personal identity that to be the same person in an afterlife requires having the same body, and that to have the same body requires that there be neither a gap in Time nor discontinuous motion in Space. How is that possible? If we require, however, neither spatial nor temporal continuity, then one way in which there would be an afterlife is for God to have brought about a law of nature ensuring that everything that happens in this present epoch is reflected in a suitable form in another epoch.

If we do require spatial or temporal continuity, the 'How is it possible?' question may still be answered. Here is a development of Peter van Inwagen's suggestion that God removes the dying, replacing them by corpses (van Inwagen 1978). If we postulate an extra spatial dimension, then such removal could be achieved by moving sideways in this dimension, and it need not even be a direct divine act. This idea has the advantage of making sense of the accounts of the risen Jesus, who seemed to appear and disappear, yet was solid. That would easily be understood in terms of moving sideways in another dimension. An alternative speculation involves many parallel universes (Forrest 2006c).

Pie in the Sky

If we grant that an afterlife is possible, and so required as part of a theodicy, there is a further objection that such an afterlife renders this life trivial. And, as part of a properly anthropocentric metaphysics, I take the significance of life as a premiss and so I am committed to rejecting any theory that trivializes life, whether it is fatalism or 'pie in the sky bye and bye'. But I say a soul-making theodicy is as far from trivializing this life as possible. While it is good to be always joyful, always in love, it is better to have come to that state after moderate suffering, moderate moral struggle, and loving without being in love. Hence the joy of an afterlife is increased by the schooling of this life, provided we do achieve this result in an afterlife.

The Animal Suffering Objection

We can understand how a divine plan that calls for moderate suffering as the means for moral growth might go wrong with the perpetuation from one generation to the next of sin and misery. As part of this risk, we can understand how it comes about that humans have inflicted suffering on other animals. That too is part of the risk. But the initial plan seems not merely to have been to take a risk, but to have included the suffering of animals without the possibility of their moral growth. For they existed before there were any autonomous creatures, and hence before things got out of control.

There are two complementary answers to this question. The first is that the divine aesthetic joy in a world in which organisms evolve exceeds the suffering that is involved in such a world if creatures who are persons and who are capable of suffering are to evolve. The second answer is that the pain of those animals that are not sufficiently person-like to be compensated in an afterlife is not the suffering of those animals so much as the suffering of God. For they, unlike us, are not holes in the divine. I hope I do not offend Hindus by suggesting that most animals are divine avatars. This divine suffering is offset by the divine joy in creation.

The borderline cases are those animals, apes and monkeys perhaps, that are sufficiently like us to be holes in the divine, but not sufficiently like us for their lives to be enriched as a result of moderate suffering. Now just because the mental depends of necessity on the physical, it does not follow that supposedly gradual physical evolution of human beings results in a corresponding gradual evolution of the mental. So it is not obvious that there are any such borderline cases. But if there are, their suffering is, I suppose, part of the price for our evolution. If an afterlife is possible, as I believe it is, we may suppose that they are compensated.

The Problem of Arbitrary Divine Choice

Is there a unique best possible act of creation? More accurately, is there a best if we ignore moral constraints on consequentialism and assume that the Creator does not as yet love creation? One suggestion would be that the best is to create just one instance of every possible species of universe that is *creation-worthy*, where a creation-worthy species is one that God would create if there were a choice between creating it or not, regardless of what else is created, and where I stipulate that two possible universes belong to the same species just in case their initial state and laws of nature are the same.[3] The above discussion of the argument from evil is an extended defence of the creation-worthy character of our species of universe with its risk of excessive suffering. If there is a best possible act of creation, and it is to create every species of creation-worthy universe, then it suffices to defend the claim that our universe is creation-worthy. I need to consider, however, some arguments to the conclusion that there is no best possible act of creation.

It might be said that a system of one instance of every species of creation-worthy universe would lack the unity required for God to remain a single god. That would occur if creation-worthy species of universe form two or more islands surrounded by ones that are not creation-worthy.

A different objection to there being a best act of creation is based upon the following dilemma. Either there is something aesthetically offensive about universes that are too similar to each other or God would create multiple copies of universes. In the first case it is not clear whether there would be a best possible choice of a system of not too similar universes. In the second, whatever number, finite or infinite, that God created of a universe of a given species, God could create more, which would be a better act of creation.

We have no way of knowing, therefore, whether there is a best possible act of creation. Hence I should not rest a case for theism on the supposition that there is one. Suppose, then, there is not. What follows? If God has the capacity nonetheless to select arbitrarily one system of individually creation-worthy universes, then it seems to me, as it has to many, that God would do so, and that there is no reason to say that God would not have created a universe of our species as part of this system (Robert Adams 1972; Schlesinger 1977; Swinburne 1994). But William Rowe, for one, disagrees, claiming that a morally unsurpassable God could do no other than create the best (Rowe 2004). While others, such as Frances and Daniel Howard-Snyder (1994), have resisted this claim I am prepared to concede, that if there is no best possible act of creation, then, as Rowe argues, it is not possible that there be a morally unsurpassable Creator. Not surprisingly, I respond that the Creator I am positing is not even morally righteous, let alone morally unsurpassable,

---

[3] If there is no initial state, then two possible universes belong to the same species if they share the same laws of nature, and as we go back in time, they approximate each other better and better.

and it would be unreasonable not to create at all just because you could not create the best.

There is, however, a more pressing problem. How is God *able* to choose between an infinity of possible acts of creation in a random fashion? The result of so doing would be that each possible act was equally probable. Yet it might well be that there are infinitely many possible acts of creation to choose between. If this is the smallest infinity—namely, the number of integers—then there is no way of assigning equal probabilities adding up to one, not even by assigning each one an infinitesimal. If it is a larger infinity, there may well be a way of assigning equal probabilities, but it will depend on how the possible acts of creation are arranged. Now there is one case where this will cause no trouble. If the only requirement is to choose one species from a given genus of universe, then among those that are creation-worthy we might expect to find some parameters corresponding to the initial conditions or the constants in the laws. If a given parameter varies from *a* to *b* (for creation-worthy cases), there is a natural equal probability distribution for that parameter. Even in this case, it is still somewhat difficult to see how God would make the random choice. Come to think of it, it is rather difficult to see how anyone makes a genuinely random choice. But we do, and rationally. Buridan's ass starves, not a martyr to rationality but a warning to ditherers.

The principle governing arbitrary choice seems to be this. If we cannot find what is, all things considered, the best, then we find the most important kind of value we are able to maximize and use that instead. Even if all motives are ultimately hedonic, we may distinguish different kinds of joy and suffering, and so choose by maximizing those kinds of joy that can be maximized or minimize those kinds of suffering that can be minimized.

To take a highly idealized example, suppose that the possible acts of creation could be assigned a negative, positive, or zero whole number that measured their goodness. So God would not create any to which a positive number had not been assigned. Then there is no best act of creation. What is God to do? If there were acts that resulted in the minimum suffering (or no suffering at all), and there was a best among these, then God might choose that act, but I find this implausible. There is, however, a salient choice. It is to create the simplest among the universes that has an infinite amount of the greatest source of joy. I believe that there is a greatest source of joy—namely, love—and I believe that ours is the simplest kind of universe suited to the existence of creatures whom God can love and who can love God.

Simplicity here is invoked as a tie-breaker, not an enormously important source of joy in itself. But it has to be a source of joy even to act as a tie-breaker. So I return to the theme of the aesthetic motive: there is joy in an elegant creation, using the least means to a given end.

Therefore, if there is no best act of creation (or if there is no best that does not result in divine fission into distinct gods), God would probably choose to create one or more universes, of a given genus, based upon the simplest life-friendly laws. If there is need for a random choice of parameters among equally simple life-friendly universes, then perhaps God would be able to choose one or more values of some parameters at random. Whether God chooses in this way to create many universes or just one would depend on whether life-friendly universes of this genus are infinite or not.

My conclusion, then, is that if there is a best possible act of creation, then there is no reason to suppose that our universe would not have originated from such an act. If there is no best possible act, it is quite likely that our genus of universe is of just the kind that God would bring about, involving the simplest laws that are life-friendly. Assuming that God creates a universe of our genus, the only reason for not creating a universe of our species would be if some other choice of the parameters (constants or initial conditions) resulted in a universe without the risk of excessive evils. I cannot myself see how this could happen.

7. 'DID HEAVEN LOOK ON? AND WOULD NOT TAKE THEIR PART?'

The Primordial God created with the risk that the combination of creaturely autonomy and the capacity to suffer would go badly wrong. And it did. So why did God not do something about it at a later stage? I assume that God does know and hence shares our sufferings, and so has a motive to remove those sufferings that are not functional.

My reply is that God no longer has enough power to remove these sufferings, because the natural order, although ordained by God, now constrains God as much as it constrains creatures. This leads, however, to a rejoinder: namely, the *quantum problem of evil*, as I shall call it. I have been assuming that the Primordial God took a risk by setting up a universe with laws that prevent subsequent miraculous divine intervention. But it is widely held that contemporary physics shows that many things previously considered impossible, like the sudden change of a certain mass of water into the same mass of wine, are just highly improbable. Hence God could work such miracles without breaking the laws of nature. Rather than considering ourselves vindicated by this, we theists should rend our garments. For if such miracles can occur, then a loving God could intervene repeatedly to answer prayers or just out of compassion, without prayers. A certain amount of suffering is no doubt good for us. Far be it from me to suggest, for instance, that I be preserved from the suffering that the learned world's reception of this book will no doubt cause me. But we might expect the miraculous cure or even prevention of all unnecessary suffering. And that we do not find.

One solution to the quantum problem of evil is to brazen it out, by insisting that there is more to the natural order than quantum theory predicts, and hence that most of the highly improbable possibilities are contrary to the natural order that God sets up. Brazen though this might be, it has the support of common sense, and it is what we would expect from a creator. For the sort of autonomy we have, where in this life we make ourselves the sort of beings we will for ever be in the next, cannot be one based on dual divine/human control, which would force God to prevent our unloving or morally wrong acts. For the sake of this autonomy, God must be like Ulysses chained to the mast at his own order, so as not to jump into the sea on hearing the Sirens. The Primordial God has to prevent subsequent divine intervention for the sake of human autonomy, knowing that subsequently, out of both love and moral righteousness, God would intervene if it were possible. Hence the laws of nature must be tuned not merely to permit life, but to permit creatures like us, whose actions are not determined, but which are not such as to be too easily influenced by divine intervention. This leaves room for subtle divine interventions, in the form of the Incarnation and the indwelling of the Holy Spirit.

Less brazen is the many worlds or parallel universe interpretation of quantum theory of David Deutsch (1996), which, as I develop it (Forrest 1999), retains the intellectually attractive feature that the probability of a type of event X is the proportion of sub-universes in which an X occurs. Because of the problem of defining proportions among infinite populations, this interpretation is more acceptable if there are only finitely many sub-universes. In that case the predicted quantum-theoretic probabilities will be only approximations to the actual proportions, and if the predicted probability is very small, the actual proportion might be more or it might be zero. In the latter case the event occurs in none of the sub-universes, and hence it is no longer possible for God to bring it about. For, given this interpretation, we have a model for agency, whether human or divine, as the termination of some but not other sub-universes, or as I prefer to call them universe-fibres (Forrest 2006c).

8. COLLECTIVE AUTONOMY

I have been discussing the problem of evil as if human beings were themselves merely individuals. This is because a loving God will, I hold, be concerned with our well-being as individuals. There is, however, an alternative understanding of why God does not intervene, at least not as much as we might expect. Although we are individuals, we are 'essentially' social beings.[4] I shall be discussing the related concept of collective responsibility in the last chapter. Here it suffices to note that for social beings like us there is joy or suffering for the individual in what a community to which that individual belongs has done. I prove that empirically by exhibiting a footy fan.

In addition to the joy of having made yourself a loving person, there is the joy of participating in a community that has made itself a loving community. Respect for collective autonomy would tend to restrict the ways in which God influences human beings to, I think, four situations. One is to prevent our annihilation. The second is where the human moral state is so grave that some intervention is required, otherwise human beings have no opportunity for improvement. The third is where the human beings in question freely invite divine inspiration. In that case it is a rather delicate matter as to when the inspiration interferes with collective autonomy. Finally, God can intervene by becoming one of us, as in the Incarnation, because in that case what God incarnate does is part of our collective history of growth towards a loving community.

As far as individuals are concerned, suffering is often quite dysfunctional. I have previously accounted for this by suggesting that God took

---

[4] Essentially social in the sense of 'essence' that is used by those who reject what they call 'essentialism'. An essence in this sense is an *axiological* essence, not an *ontological* essence. It is ontologically essential that a person have a self/other distinction, but this could be the case even if humans over the age of puberty lived all alone except to mate. In that case there would be no society as we understand it. By an *axiological* essence I mean a prerequisite for living a good life.

a risk, setting up a non-deterministic system with autonomous creatures and with many opportunities for suffering as part of the divine plan. We may supplement this account of dysfunctional individual suffering by assuming that God is also concerned with humanity's collective responsibility, provided we can explain why we find ourselves morally and intellectually unhealthy in the first place. For collective autonomy is fostered by our working out our own salvation. What I have in mind as an explanation of why we find ourselves morally and intellectually unhealthy is a sanitized doctrine of Original Sin transmitted from one generation to the next. This is not original guilt, but concupiscence, by which I understand the situation of fragile virtues and robust vices that is such a distressing feature of the human condition. The problem is why a loving God would let things go so wrong in the first place. Given that we became bogged down by these vicious tendencies, it is plausible enough that a loving God would exhibit a light touch in helping us make moral progress.

Developmental theism provides a way of understanding Original Sin. The Primordial God created us with the risk of just such an eventuality, a risk resulting from the dangerous combination of suffering and autonomy. The God of love inherited this situation and is guided by respect for collective as well as individual autonomy.

9. WHY NOT SATAN?

Granted that we need to understand evil in an emotionally satisfying way, it might seem that I should have *Alvinized* you by talking of Satan. Now I am quite agnostic about the existence of angelic beings, if by that we understand beings whose physical systems are not material objects. While I think that no child should be allowed to read Philip Pullman's nihilistic books, his idea of angels as beings whose bodies are made of light is along the right lines (Pullman 1996). Much that is physical is not material. So why not invoke Satan as the source of evil inspiration. We can tell a story of how God, while concerned with our well-being, is even more concerned with that of angels, including Satan, who are worth not mega-sparrows but giga-sparrows. Our sufferings are thus collateral damage in a cosmic struggle among angels. This hypothesis also has the advantage of providing creatures with whom the divine aesthetic joy could be shared at the moment of creation, reinforcing the aesthetic motive of the Primordial God, to which I have repeatedly appealed.

I have no serious objection to Satan theodicy, but it requires us to grant something the probability of which is hard to assess: namely, that there are physical but non-material systems capable of supporting agency and consciousness and of influencing us. Moreover, it too requires developmental theism. For Satan is not one of us, so no account of collective autonomy links our fortune with Satan's. If God eventually brings about Satan's repentance, the blessed in Heaven will rejoice for God's sake, but not because it completes our collective history. Hence if God intertwined our history with that of the angels, it is once again a case of the consequentialist sacrificing of the little people—us—to a greater good. It might be loving of God towards angels, but not towards us. I submit, then, that Satan theodicy requires us to say that God changes and comes to be loving towards us. Moreover, without some abdication of divine power, a loving God would remove the excess of suffering that results from natural evils.

10. SUMMARY

Kenotic theism provides additional resources for understanding evil, notably by means of the development from an all-powerful but unloving God to a loving God with limited powers of intervention. Either the act of creation was the best possible, or else it was salient because the simplest among an array of good possible acts among which there was no best possible. The only reason we could have for thinking that our universe was not likely to result from such an act would be if there was either a simpler set of life-friendly laws or as simple a set that resulted in a universe without the risk of things going wrong, as they seem to have done with ours. In that case, if there was an argument to show that there is no best possible act of creation, this might be used to support the case for a salient choice among acts of creation that did not result in our universe. My conjecture, however, is that further research will show that our universe has the simplest possible life-friendly laws.

8

The Trinity

1. DEMYSTIFYING DOGMA

Most Christians are committed to the doctrine of the Trinity, but too humble to explain it. I am not impressed. But for those who are, I would like to note some awkward consequences. First, and most obvious, it makes it hard to explain why they remain Christians rather than adopt a unitarian religion, such as the Baha'i faith, which I commend for its tolerance. Second, it makes it hard to say just what formulation of the Trinity is being believed in. What about the Athanasian Creed promulgated by a local council in Gaul and based upon St Augustine's thought? This has come to have some standing in Western Christendom because of its clear exclusion of various heretical positions, and its inclusion in *The Book of Common Prayer.* For that reason I shall have something to say about squaring my own account with the Athanasian Creed at the end of this chapter. It is, however, of limited authority, and if necessary, we could ignore it while still calling ourselves orthodox Christians.

As far as I can see, the only way to decide just what formulation of the Trinity is required by Christianity is to check whether the proposed formulation is consistent with the traditional motivations for the doctrine, which seem to be these: insistence upon the genuine divinity as well as the full humanity of Jesus; the acknowledgement that Jesus spoke to the one he called his father; and, more recently, the widespread acceptance that a loving community is a better sort of thing than a single, individual, Divine Person. That motivation is in turn related to the tradition that God's creation of a universe with sentient life was something extra, as it were, something which if *per impossibile* we had been around before creation we could not have predicted with certainty. For unless there is the opportunity for love within the Godhead, we might assume that creation was required so that God could love others. A further influence is the fidelity of Christians to the earlier Hebrew monotheism, combined with respect for Islam, to which tritheism is abhorrent.

We require, then, an account of God in which the Persons are sufficiently distinct to have the joy of loving relations between then, but sufficiently united to prevent the charge of tritheism. And there are two questions here. How is this possible? And how did it come about? The latter question is important, because unless there is an explanation of the origin of the Trinity, then Christians, by holding that God has always been a Trinity, would be proposing a rather complicated ultimate explanation; whereas given an impersonal Primordial God, we can understand how a multiplicity of Divine Persons would come about because of the anticipated joy.

2. SELFHOOD AND PERSONHOOD

The Primordial God may for convenience be described as a self, if that just means that which is conscious and exercises power. Strictly speaking, we can adopt a no-self theory and re-describe consciousness and the exercise of power in such a way that there is no centre of consciousness or exerciser of power. But this hardly differs from saying that the self does exist but is constituted by its consciousness and power. And in any case, we are not here engaged in the project of analytic ontology, so it is convenient, as I have said, to think of the Primordial God as a self, and make the distinction between selfhood and personhood. Interestingly, a rather similar distinction has been made in Hinduism between *atman*, the self, and *jiva*, the person. And in certain forms of Buddhism, while it is denied there is a self, the person, which is given the pejorative term *pudgala*, is recognized. The distinction or something like it transcends cultural barriers, which should encourage us to take it seriously.

A person, I take it, can sensibly ask the question 'Who am I?' and reply in terms of character, interpersonal relations, and, especially, the history of how that character and those relations were acquired. This reply requires a distinction between self and others. Given my Occamist prejudices, I say that the important differences between persons are not due to some indefinable thisness, but the history, as just mentioned. So the idea that you should love someone for her or himself amounts to a recognition of the importance of that person's history, shared with your own, and which a substitute, even a soul mate, would lack. In this connection I note that Richard Swinburne (1994) has argued that even if, as he believes, we humans have thisness, divine beings do not.

Now for some folk psychology: love increases personhood, but decreases selfhood. Here there is ample material for a sermon, which I shall spare you. Love I have analysed in terms of the act of mixing flourishing. Flourishing was not quite the same as joy but was defined in terms of joy, so that to flourish is not merely to experience joy but to give joy to others as a result of their being directly aware of your condition. The more the flourishing of X depends on that of Y and vice versa, the more X and Y will, if rational, act in harmony so that their joint actions will tend to be like a single agent that comprised both of them. If the act of mixing flourishing is not itself free then this results in a diminution of personhood as in a dystopic society modeled on a beehive. Freely mixing and continuing to mix your flourishing with another results, however, in growth of personhood, but at the expense of selfhood. There might even be a tendency to speak in terms of 'we', not 'I', although that is ambiguous between love and the exercise of power over another. Hence we might say that three Divine Persons making up a perfect community of love would have such perfect harmony that they would behave as if they were a single God. That is, I suppose, a tritheistic position, but one without any suggestion of the polytheism which personified various aspects of the natural order as gods and goddesses. It is, I think, the position of the Church of Jesus Christ of the Latter-day Saints. If in some way we can moderate this near-tolerable tritheism so that we can truly say that there is just the one God, then we have a genuine social trinitarianism.

Here, then, is a strategy for trying to understand the Trinity. First, speculate about how a perfect community of three divine beings, three gods to put it bluntly, might arise. Then, out of respect for the tradition and the commitments of Jews and Muslims, work out ways of moderating the resulting position so that we cease to describe it as tritheism. The key to this is to note that there is a difference between a joint act in the sense of a single act performed by more than one Divine Person and three co-ordinated acts. It is the former that occurs when God exercises control over the universe. If, contrary to my previous suggestion, creation occurs after the formation of the Trinity, then creation will itself be a case of a single act jointly performed. Otherwise, these joint acts are restricted by the laws of nature. If, then, we define God as the creator and controller of the universe, we may truly say there is but one God.

Here is an analogy that might be helpful. A federation of states retaining total autonomy on all internal matters might nonetheless be constitutionally bound to be a single agent in external affairs. Hence they would constitute a single nation, as opposed to a mere alliance.

3. GENERATION VERSUS FISSION

Swinburne's account is that there was one Divine Person, who generated the second, and so on (Swinburne 1994). I have a difficulty with this. Either there is a first moment, or there is not. If there is a first moment, then at that moment the First Person exists, but the other Divine Persons do not. To be a person requires at minimum either character or interpersonal relations or a history, which would distinguish that person from other possible persons (if there are no other actual persons). At the initial moment God would therefore not be a person unless there is a divine character. But to posit a character that has not been acquired complicates the hypothesis considerably. So we may safely say that on Swinburne's account there is no first moment. This has two awkward consequences. The first is that quite generally unless we posit a continual development of God, then whatever motive God has to act, God already had that motive earlier. The second is a particular but especially troublesome case of this. It is a trilemma. Either (1) we are to think of the Second Person as continually growing in some other way, perhaps by being given an increasing share over the divine power, or (2) the Second Person is continually brought into being, or (3) the causation of the continuing existence of the Second Person is always redundant because it has always already occurred. The only trouble with (1) is that if it is possible, and I think it is, then it provides such a good model for the life of the Trinity that we should say that the other Divine Persons' love of the First will be expressed by the continual returning of power, which thus circulates. That is incompatible with the growth of the Second Person. In that case we have to treat the Trinity as a whole as the basic metaphysical hypothesis, rather than saying that the first cause is the First Person alone. So we have an increase in complexity.

The suggestion that the Second Person is continually brought into being is incompatible with the identity over time of the Second Person, who then becomes nothing but a recurring type of self.

The third suggestion leads to a paradox.[1] At each moment the First Person has no motive to bring into being the Second Person, who already exists. So there would be no such act of bringing another Divine Person into existence. But since that holds at all times, the Second Person would never have existed. A solution to this paradox is that by being aware of it, the First Person does have a motive to act. And that solves the more general problem that, whatever motive God has to act, God has already had that motive and acted. If there is no first moment, then God repeats the same act, an act that is quite redundant, and repeats it precisely because God is aware of the paradox in question. But thinking about a paradox requires planning, with a means to an end, and to posit such structure in the first cause would be extravagant. So if the First Person has such structure, that would require an antecedent change in the Primordial God so as to become a more complicated kind of being. But now exactly the same problem holds for that antecedent change unless there is a first moment.

My reason for rejecting this modified Swinburnian account is that it requires the Primordial God to have a motive to become a more complicated being who can then think about paradoxes, but not a motive directly to generate a community of persons. Now, if the only way of generating a Trinity was the one Swinburne suggests, then that would make sense; but if my account of divine fission (Forrest 1998c) is possible, then the Primordial God would have reason to undergo fission in the initial divine act, thus pre-empting the possibility of a Swinburnian generation.

It could be objected that fission is contrary to the Nicaean Creed, which asserts that the First Person *begot* the Second. My reply is that on one variant of my account the Trinity as a whole will turn out to be identical to the Primordial God, but on another variant the First Person will turn out to be identical to the Primordial God. Moreover, fission, not being ordinary creation, is as good a candidate as any for the process of generation. To be sure, I then have to subscribe to the letter of the Arian formula that the First Person preceded the Second in time, but I

[1] Compare again the Assassin Paradox.

take it that Arianism is the heresy of assimilating the generation of the Second Person to creation, which fission avoids even more clearly than Swinburne's generation account.

4. THE MECHANICS OF FISSION

On either Swinburne's generation account or my fission account, we should ask, 'How does that happen?' If we could simply appeal to divine omnipotence understood as the capacity to do anything it is conceivable that a unique god could do, then there would be no problem. God could do it. But the developmental theism I am proposing is based upon a moderate form of materialism, the idea that consciousness and agency occur at all and only the situations where the physical possibilities are appropriate. The Primordial God, I am assuming, has a consciousness and agency appropriate to the maximal range of possibilities of which this God is aware and in which it can choose. How can such a God limit the range of possibilities to produce three divine beings? My answer is that because the initial range of possibilities is infinite, it contains within it multiple copies of itself. This is quite general, but is most easily demonstrated on the supposition that every possible universe has a first moment. Then, given types of events A, B, and C, and a possible universe U, we may consider: (1) a universe $A + U^*$, which begins with an A and is then followed by an exact replica U^* of U; (2) $B + U^{**}$, which begins with a B and is then followed by an exact replica U^{**} of U; and (3) the universe $C + U^{***}$, which begins with a C and is then followed by an exact replica U^{***} of U. Notice that the set of all possible $A + U^*$ universes is a subset of the set of all possible universes, likewise for the set of all $B + U^{**}$ universes, and the set of all $C + U^{***}$ universes. And these three subsets are disjoint. If the Primordial God acts so that only $A + U^*$, $B + U^{**}$, and $C + U^{***}$ universes are still possible, then after the first event there are three copies of every universe that was possible initially. The primordial consciousness of all possibilities might in this way undergo fission into three divine beings with power over the ranges of possibilities which began with an A, with a B, and with a C respectively. (Readers with an enthusiasm for mathematics might like to compare the Banach–Tarski theorem. See Wagon 1985.)

That is a sketch of an account of the Primordial God's fission into three. But some difficulties remain. First, are we really to hold that everything happens in triplicate, and if so, what point would there be in that? My suggestion here is that because the harmony between these universes holds of necessity, created agents (such as us) do not have counterparts in other universes. Rather, our bodies are extended across all these so-called universes that do not differ significantly at the macroscopic level from ours. Elsewhere I have called them *universe-fibres* and have called the universe a *bundle* (Forrest 2006c). That is to emphasize that these universes are not spatially separate from one another, as genuine universes would have to be. In fact, we might suppose that there are not just three but very many such universe-fibres and that they form a bundle composed of three sub-bundles each of which has the right sort of unity for there to be a distinct Divine Person aware of it.

There is no objection to saying that the three sub-bundles can grow or shrink by the transference of universe-fibres from or to another sub-bundle. Nor can there be any objection to the idea that initially one sub-bundle was much larger than the others. The growth or shrinkage of sub-bundles provides a way in which the Divine Persons can express their love by gifts. Whether the three sub-bundles start off approximately equal, or one is much larger than the others, affects whether in addition to saying that the Primordial God is the same God as the Trinity, we say that even though it was not a person, we may say in retrospect that it was the first stage of something that was the same self, even though not the same person, as the First Person.

5. THE CO-ORDINATION PROBLEM

The three Divine Persons would not constitute the one God unless we could say that in some situations they perform a single act. Later, I shall posit a necessary harmony, but first let us consider any sort of harmony. This raises the co-ordination problem. Consider three people, only one of whom may go through the door at a time and only one of whom may open the door for the others. If they are all deferential to each other, then confusion results as surely as if each wants to be deferred to by the others.[2] Once they understand that each wants to hold the door for the others, and would prefer to go last rather than first, there might then be a sort of reverse of preferences in which each decides to give to another the privilege of doing what they want. Confusion still results. The lesson is that good will does not remove all co-ordination problems.

---

[2] I owe this example to Barry Smith. Phillip Pettit has made a similar point.

In the case of three Divine Persons each with control over a distinct bundle of universe-fibres, the problem will be who decides first. For the sake of harmony, the others will then copy the one who acts first. Here is a solution to the co-ordination problem. Each person offers precedence to one of the other two. There is then a fifty/fifty chance of no decision (because A offers precedence to B, B to C, and C to A), but also a fifty/fifty chance of agreement (B and C both offer precedence to A, C and A both offer precedence to B, or A and B both offer precedence to C). So the three Persons go on offering until they reach an agreement. Notice that if co-ordination is reached in this way, there must be more than two Persons involved. So, as Swinburne points out, a Binity is more problematic than a Trinity (Swinburne 1994).

6. FURTHER MODERATING SOCIAL TRINITARIANISM

The speculation given ensures that all three Persons act in harmony. A further moderation, and a consequent lessening of the tritheistic flavour of the speculation, is provided by (1) denying that the Divine Persons can exist independently of each other, and (2) denying that they can disagree so that they fail to act as one when acting on the universe. In that case we could say that they have but one will in matters relating to the qualitative character of physical events. Hence, although we might be able to analyse the divine action upon the universe in terms of the harmonious intentions of the three Divine Persons, there are not three distinct acts in the sense that one could occur without the other. For the harmony is necessary. Hence we may say that there is but a single divine act.

A divinely caused necessity, like a law of nature, could subsequently put constraints on the Divine Persons so that they cannot disagree on how they act upon the universe, and so that if one of them were to choose to cease to exist, so would the others. The physical expression of this harmony is a law that the three sub-bundles contain qualitatively similar events, although perhaps differing in the number of universe-fibres.

Let us now return to the co-ordination problem, which I solved in terms of intentions regarding precedence. If these intentions are, as I am assuming, encoded in what has occurred physically, and what is still possible, then how can an intention be formed without some physical correlate? The answer is that this is not possible. What, then, would be a physical expression of an offer of precedence to another Divine Person?

It would be like a law of nature, except that it would govern only the immediate future. It would consist of states of affairs of the form: universe A, under the control of one Divine Person, is to be copied in universe B, under the control of another. If the three Divine Persons find themselves in a deadlock as described above, then these laws will simply tell us that whatever happens in any world happens in the others too, without any one universe being singled out as having precedence. But where there is no deadlock, then the result is an asymmetry to the effect that whatever happens in universe A must happens in universes B and C without the converse being necessitated. That communicates the giving of precedence to one of the three Persons.

Previously I noted that a harmony that was not free was an exercise not of love, but of power. On my account, though, it is the Primordial God that ensures harmony, in a way that we would call paternalistic. There is no exercise of power over each other within the Trinity, where the love is expressed not by the necessary harmony concerning action on the universe but by the offering of precedence to the others, as well as by the shifting boundaries between the three sub-bundles.

The advantage of this account over Swinburne's hypothesis that there is a division of responsibilities is that by saying that the Divine Persons cannot fail to act harmoniously on their respective universe-fibres, we are entitled to say that they act as a single agent.

The prior necessities governing the correlations of universes would be the result of an act by the Primordial God for the sake of some good end. But what end does it serve? Surely this is not in order to validate the monotheistic intuitions of human beings many billions of years later. This is related to another question I have difficulty with: Why does the Primordial God not undergo fission into many gods, each with control over a single universe? My only answer is that there is an organic unity effect whereby for a given richness and diversity there is greater aesthetic joy in its being a unity rather than a mere collection. Provided, then, the same diversity can be achieved without fission into quite distinct gods, there is a motive not to undergo fission.

7. OBJECTIONS

What is the Physical Correlate of Divine Love?

I have proposed that there are laws ensuring the harmony of the Divine Persons when acting on the universe. Now there must be things that the Divine Persons do to express their love. And I suggested that the continual giving up of power over their sub-bundles of universe-fibres would provide one way of expressing love. But what is the physical correlate of the love, as opposed to its effect? If there is none, then my moderate materialist account breaks down.

The required correlate is, I say, nothing more than the possibility of a different division of the whole bundle into its three sub-bundles. The problem, then, concerns only the requirement that the universe-fibres are somehow related to each other in ways that allow different divisions into sub-bundles. The most economical way of ensuring this is for them to be spatially related using extra dimensions.

From Fairy-Tales to Science Fiction?

This objection is one I touched upon in the Introduction, but it is only now that I have given enough details to state the objection with any force. It is important because it strikes at my whole methodology.

Magic consists of a powerful person saying words that produce effects. I have already argued that the Primordial God would not have created in this way, which I called the Genesis hypothesis. I have, moreover, avoided ascribing to God the sort of quasi-magical power derived from omnipotence characterized as the ability to bring about any state of affairs that it is conceivable that a unique god could bring about. Hence the charge that religion seems like a fairy-tale is not one I need to worry about. On my account, things do not just happen; they happen because God acts like any other agent. This requirement to look at the physical details of God's acts has led me to a novel account of the Trinity, in which the three Divine Persons act on different universe-fibres, but in harmony, so that both we and other familiar material objects extend across the fibres. The objection is that I have avoided a fairy-tale only by engaging in science fiction. Very probably this conjecture of universe-fibres spread out in a higher dimension with varying boundaries between sub-bundles is fictitious. So what point is there to it?

I have two answers. The less cautious is that I can use the universe-fibre conjecture to provide an account of the afterlife, to explain how agency works and to interpret quantum theory (Forrest 2006c). Note especially that if our universe consists of many fibres—that is, parallel universes with differing initial conditions—then free will could be exercised by bringing to an end various fibres, even if the conditional laws operating in each fibre (if this fibre continues to exist, then . . .) had deterministic consequents. Moreover, we may think of each universe-fibre as corresponding to one of the many possible stories of the universe told from the perspective of possible person X. This strikes me as a rather natural way for God to create a universe, by, as it were, telling its story many times from each perspective. All these features encourage me to think that my conjecture might not be so very improbable.

My more cautious reply is to grant that probably I am wrong, but that if mine were the only moderate materialist explication of the Trinity then it would not be so bad as to make moderate materialism and orthodox Christianity an implausible combination. In that case my account would be fairly probable. If there are other and better stories to be told, then the combination of moderate materialism and orthodox Christianity is all the more likely. Hence my story-telling serves a purpose.

The Wrong Grade of Necessity?

The proposed persisting unity of God based upon necessary harmony and interdependence is nothing more than the result of a decision by the pre-fission God, a decision that binds the future. This assimilates the necessity of the interdependence of the Divine Persons to the sort of necessity that the laws of nature have (I say!): namely, the necessity which holds because of God's future-binding decision (Forrest 2006b). Is that a strong enough glue to join three Persons into a single substance? Is it not mere nomological necessity, and do we not need metaphysical necessity in these matters? Not so. Necessity does not come in degrees, provided it is a genuine necessity that admits no exceptions. So the recent past caused to be the way it is by the most insignificant of agents is as fixed, as strongly cemented into place, as the necessity that binds and has always bound even God. Hence, in discussing the necessary coexistence of the Divine Persons, all that is required is that ever since they have existed, they cannot exist without each other.

In further support of my conjecture I note an analogy made several times in the literature between the identity of the Persons in the Trinity and the identity of a human being at different stages of his or her life. The first instance of this that I know of is in the intriguing, witty, but sacrilegious story by Gore Vidal, *Live from Golgotha* (1992). But in serious philosophical discussion we owe it first to Brian Leftow.[3]

[3] When giving a paper in June 2001 at the Conference on the Doctrine of the Trinity in Moscow (Forrest 2003), I was informed that Brian Leftow had already used this example, subsequently published in Leftow 2004.

Anyway, the analogy is between the three Divine Persons and time-travellers who live in the company of their earlier stages. In my version we imagine A who, having reached fourscore years, instead of dying takes a time machine back to become B, who does something similar, becoming C who, on reaching fourscore years, becomes A. A, B, and C live their lives simultaneously, and in fact are reared as triplets. Each remembers being the other, and each knows what they will all do. This story is quite fanciful, and of course quite incompatible both with the requirement that there be a causal explanation of later stages by earlier ones and the requirement that we have genuine autonomy incompatible with our decisions being fated. Nonetheless, we might say of such a case that the three simultaneous person-stages were stages of the one person.

What this weird and wonderful example shows, other than the perverted minds of philosophers, is that the sort of identity that a person has over time would be enough to glue three Divine Persons into a single God. When it comes to human persons, we might well require endurance without temporal parts, but then the question arises as to just what conditions are required for this endurance to be possible. And in the human case it suffices that the stages of the person's life are related by causal connections that arise from the natural order. Metaphysical necessity is not required. Likewise, I say, there is no need for metaphysical necessity when it comes to the bonds between the Divine Persons. Hence I claim that if the three Divine Persons depend on each other by a necessity that they have no control over and that resulted from a previous decision by the pre-fission God, that is enough to show that the three are one God.

8. THE ATHANASIAN CREED

The Athanasian Creed tells us that each of the three Persons is God, yet there are not three gods. Conversely, the Christ is one person, yet both divine and human, where being divine and being human are contraries. Not much is uncontroversial in philosophy, but I take it that van Inwagen (1976) has shown that the Athanasian Creed is perfectly coherent if we accept Relative Identity, the thesis that when we say X is the same as Y, we invite the question 'Same what?' Now relative identity is plausible when we are talking about identity over time. If in the middle of some discussion of abortion I were to say that I am the same as a certain foetus that came to exist about 14 days after conception, then someone might well say, 'Well, yes you are the same living organism, but not the same person, for you were not a person back then.' Likewise, although I do not believe in reincarnation, many do, and so they might say, 'I am the same as someone who lived a thousand years ago.' They mean 'same person' not 'same living organism'.

Likewise, if we ask whether the Divine Persons are the same or distinct, we may disambiguate between same god and same person. And as above, we may appeal to the analogy with identity over time to establish that this is appropriate. At this point we might either provide a further account of how the relative identity comes about or simply declare it a mystery. The latter unfortunately complicates our account of God, rendering it less probable. Therefore we should seek to understand relative identity. This we may do if we reject the thesis that to persist is to be an enduring thing that lacks temporal parts. In that case all we need is the harmless Lockean thesis of relative persistence. In particular, if I refer to myself, I refer to myself by referring to my present part. So my reference is ambiguous between various wholes of which my present part is a part. That is why we should sometimes ask the question 'Same what?' For there is both a living organism and a person of which my present part is a part.

I conclude that either talk of relative identity, although demonstrating coherence, complicates the doctrine of the Trinity, or it is best under-stood as the consequence of part/whole ambiguity in reference. Hence I arrive at a rather tame interpretation of the Athanasian Creed. Consider the names 'God the Son' and 'Holy Spirit'. Someone ignorant of Christianity asks innocently enough, 'Are they the same?' The orthodox answer is 'Same God; different Divine Persons'. The phrase 'God the Son' refers to *whatever* St John was referring to at the beginning of his Gospel by 'the Word', and the 'Holy Spirit' refers to *whatever* St John was referring to towards the end of his Gospel when he has Jesus mention 'another Paraclete'. In both those accounts of how the names refer, I used the word 'whatever', which could be expanded as either 'whatever per-son' or 'whatever god'. Hence the answer 'Same God; different persons'. But the ambiguity of reference is not a difficult metaphysical issue, just the ordinary part/whole ambiguity of reference in any ordinary language.

SUMMARY

I have obtained the following admittedly speculative account. The Prim-ordial God chose to split into three Divine Persons who are constituted by the three different sub-bundles of universe-fibres they have control over. These three Persons are one God in the following respects:

1. Necessarily they cannot disagree concerning their action upon the universe.
2. All familiar objects, including ourselves, exist spread out across universe-fibres under the control of different Divine Persons, so the three Divine Persons jointly act on the one universe.
3. No Divine Person can exist independently of the others.

9

The Incarnation

This work is based upon three themes: the physicality of God, the divine development, and kenosis. But up to now the kenosis discussed has been of a rather moderate kind: God brings about laws that cannot be broken, and God grants agents space to be their own soul-makers, which required a divine retreat from the areas of which we are in command. This leaves God the power to act like any other agent within the constraints of the laws. In this chapter I want to defend a much more radical kenosis. Following Gottfried Thomasius and Charles Gore, I take the Incarnation to be one of the Divine Persons temporarily undergoing a radical diminution of power and knowledge to become human. (Compare Forrest 2000.)

This raises three questions. Is it not some abominable heresy? How is it possible? And what would the point of it be?

1. IS KENOSIS HERETICAL?

There is quite proper antipathy to any position that makes Jesus out to be merely human. But to be merely human is not something that holds of the rest of us solely in virtue of what we are here and now. That Jesus remained the very same person as he once was when he had full divine status shows, therefore, that he at no time was *merely* human. This point that being merely human depends on your origins follows from a more general thesis that the kind of thing that something is depends on the origins of that kind (Kripke 1977). Being human is a kind, and I take it that being *merely* human is a sub-kind.

One minor qualification: I am assuming that God became incarnate as a human being only once. This is like my assumption that there are only three Persons to the Trinity. In principle it is negotiable. I note, however, that Hindu avatars are not described as incarnations in the sense that Jesus is. Another qualification: none of this prevents us from saying that at some other time the second Divine Person became incarnate as an extraterrestrial, but this cannot happen simultaneously with the incarnation as Jesus. Anyway, if there were other incarnations of the second Divine Person, then that further affects the kind of being Jesus is, as well as raising problems with the Trinity, which I shall now discuss, apologizing for the digression.

If the best possible kind of universe has an infinity of autonomous communities in which there is a divine incarnation, then presumably God creates a universe of this kind. But if the Trinity has a fixed, finite number of members, as it might be three, then at least one Divine Person undergoes an infinity of incarnations. This is perfectly coherent provided there have been only a finite number of incarnations so far, and hence only a finite number of communities of autonomous sentient beings so far. That has the consequence, however, that the blessed in Heaven will from time to time cease to be perfectly happy while God, whom they love, is suffering, for two reasons: because some of these communities undergo suffering, and because God is suffering as a result of an incarnation. If that seems counter-intuitive, or if it is believed that the universe, being spatially infinite, already contains an infinity of communities of autonomous creations, then we might be driven to the thesis that the Trinity contains infinitely many Divine Persons. The problem with such an Infinitary is that although co-ordination may be achieved, there is no way for each member to be offered precedence by the others. Nor is it easy to achieve co-ordination. So there is much to be said for a finite Trinity.

The general principle that kinds are constituted in part by their origins is usually established by fanciful thought experiments. One of these concerns Swampman and Marshwoman, who by an incredible fluke are formed by random combinations of chemicals to be exactly like humans except not with the usual origins (Davidson 1987). They and their offspring, the Bogfolk, are not of our kind.[1] Here is a similar story. Adam and Eve were specially created by God, whom they did not disobey. Their descendants still live in Eden, also known as Shangri-la and located somewhere in Tibet. The rest of us evolved from apes. We

---

[1] Donald Davidson's example concerned Swampman only. Swampman was originally a replica of Davidson, and would not only have taken the place of that famous philosopher but have thought he was Davidson. Subsequently Swampman has come to be thought of as just any person formed by a random combination of chemicals. I added Marshwoman not just because it is 'not good for [Swamp]man to be alone', but because I wanted the Bogfolk to have offspring without human ancestry.

are capable of interbreeding with the descendants of Adam and Eve, but never have. So they and we are of different kinds. Should we interbreed in the future, there would be hybrids, constituting yet another kind. The third example is the least fanciful. All life in our galaxy is descended from proto-bacteria that came to exist by chance somewhere. On another galaxy thousands of millions of light-years away, different proto-bacteria came to exist by chance, and among their descendants some of the simpler ones exactly resemble some of the bacteria on Earth. Because the ancestry is different, they are not of the same kind, just a similar one.

Maybe these examples are not totally convincing. If not, it might be because we have several different concepts of a kind, and the Bogfolk example concerns just one concept. Even so, the examples should undermine any intuition that if Jesus's earthly life was exactly like that of an ordinary human being, except quite without sin, then Jesus was, excepting sin, just an ordinary human being. On the kenotic account, he was a human being who was the very same person as one of the three Divine Persons, and so, on one valid concept of a kind, not of the same kind as the rest of human beings. Thus Jesus was *fully* human, but not *merely* human.

Is there, then, anything lacking in the kenotic account that might be found in the more traditional one? If you hold, as I do not, a strict doctrine of divine eternity, the traditional doctrine of hypostatic union is very like the kenotic account. For in the traditional doctrine the divine nature occupies an eternal realm that is not comparable to human time. The human nature is, however, in human time, so the divine and human natures are not strictly simultaneous. They have to be united in a *sui generis* fashion, of which the best human analogue concerns distinct stages of a human being's life with non-simultaneous bonds. On the kenotic account, there is likewise a non-simultaneous bonding of the pre-incarnational and incarnational phases of one person. I conclude that if kenotic incarnation is contrary to the spirit of Christianity, then so is the traditional account involving divine eternity.

2. A CASE FOR KENOSIS

If God is eternal, then kenosis is, I submit, indistinguishable from the traditional theology of the hypostatic union. If God occupies some but not all moments of our time, and in particular does not, *qua* divine, exist during Jesus's earthly life, then kenosis is, once again, rather like the doctrine of the hypostatic union. The most popular position, however, is that God existed at all times during Jesus's life. This seems to be required if we take seriously the idea of Jesus conversing with his heavenly Father. In that case there are only two possibilities. The first is that the second Divine Person acquires additional human attributes without losing divine power or knowledge. The second is that there is a loss of divine power and knowledge.

The problem with the former, traditional account is how, if at all, the divine and human attributes are integrated to make a single person. My claim is that either there is not enough integration, or the divine eclipses the human or the human eclipses the divine in a way that requires kenosis. Hence we should opt for kenosis.

First, suppose that we do not integrate the divine and the human. In that case we may distinguish a divine and a human agency in Jesus. Let us consider a quite mundane matter. A customer comes to Jesus's carpentry shop on a wet day, asking for a plough to be mended. Jesus wants to get the plough inside, but the door is narrow. So he has somehow to work out how to do it, either by trial and error or using geometric intuition. Various brain processes occur, and as a consequence, he tries a limited number of ways of doing it and gets it inside at the fourth attempt. Simultaneously, the divine nature, we are to suppose, knows exactly what to do. This should remind us of our previous problem with divine and (ordinary) human agency. If there is no integration, then Jesus can act as human or as divine, but for good reasons does not act as divine. How does this differ from the case of other human beings? I have previously suggested that, in order to make us truly autonomous, God has to withdraw from our little worlds, leaving us in complete control. So we may suppose that this is not the case with Jesus. With him, the divine nature, although it could be invoked, is somehow chosen not to. Perhaps, though, in less trivial matters there would be such direct divine inspiration. A picture is beginning to emerge of what this sort of incarnation is like. Jesus is a man possessed by God, one whom God has decided not to grant the usual autonomy. No doubt such a sinless being could be described as part of God, but in that sense so could non-human animals, assuming they are without sin too. God is, I say, in the non-human animals and the plants and in everything except us agents to whom he has given some autonomy. But the Incarnation is not just a matter of someone lacking autonomy.

To avoid that absurd conclusion, if we take God to be in Time, as we are, and if we deny kenosis, then we require the integration of the divine and the human; so even though we might reasonably talk of two wills, we have but a single agent. Perhaps this can be described coherently, but all attempts I know of seem to collapse into one of the three positions mentioned. Either Jesus was too divine to be human, or too human be to divine excepting kenosis, or there is dual agency and no real integration.

Here Swinburne (1994) appeals to the precedent of multiple personality. That is only a partial analogy, however. If the personalities take turns at being conscious, then we may integrate them into a single, albeit confused, person. But if in fact they are simultaneously conscious, and if such simultaneity is ongoing rather than episodic, then it is hard to see why the multiple personalities would not be several distinct persons with one body. To be sure, it is controversial whether human beings with multiple personalities are as distinct as we often suppose; but if not, the supposed precedent should be treated as a conceivable hypothetical example. Regardless of the correct diagnosis of one of the more fascinating psycho-pathologies, an example of genuinely simultaneous personalities is a precedent for distinct divine and human agents. I suspect that there is a tendency among Christians to think of Jesus as being human with occasional episodes of divinity, but if anyone took that seriously, they would have to opt for intermittent kenosis.

Should we say that divine knowledge and power were capacities that Jesus had but chose not to exercise? That sets up a dilemma: was there something Jesus had to do in order to exercise these powers, pray perhaps? If there was, which, incidentally, seems to fit Scripture better, then I fail to see how we could say that Jesus had the traditional divine attributes, so there was at least a partial kenosis. If not, then in the act of thinking what was the true answer to a question, or in deciding what to do, Jesus would automatically exercise his capacities, regardless of whether he has them *qua* divine or *qua* human, and so his divine nature would obliterate the human one.

3. PROBLEMS WITH ESSENCES

If Divine Persons are eternal, we should not ask what properties a Divine Person must retain in order to continue existing. So for an eternal being we cannot make the essential/accidental distinction in this way. The problem still arises, though, if we take the union of the two natures of

Christ as analogous to personal identity. In any case I am supposing that God is not eternal.

So let us talk of essences. Take Bertrand's Russell's example: we may ask whether a human being could become a poached egg without ceasing to exist. Presumably not, and that is because, intuitively, we belong to some kind that is essential for persistence and excludes being a poached egg. Most would say that either we belong to the kind *being a human animal*, to the kind *being a person*, or to the kind *being both a human animal and a person*. There is much to be said for the Lockean thesis that persistence is relative to a kind, so we can persist as the same animal but not as the same person, or vice versa. In the previous chapter I made that suggestion as a way of watering down the Athanasian Creed. In that case essences are relative to the kinds (or, perhaps better, the sortals) being considered.

The problem that essences pose for a kenotic account of the Incarnation is that it might seem that for a Divine Person to become a human being is no more possible than for a human being to become a poached egg. The only solution to this problem that I know of is to insist that Divine Persons and human persons are univocally persons. And if that is not what the great Church Councils had in mind, my response is that this is the emerging consensus of the faithful, and we know better because we, collectively, are older and wiser now. Granted the univocity of personhood, we may say that a Divine Person became human, retaining the essential kind attribute of personhood. As for divinity, that is essentially an attribute of God, not of the three Persons who make up God. Jesus is, then, a phase of the second Divine Person, one that began a little over 2,000 years ago and for which humanity is a necessary condition.

The rejection of univocal talk about divine and human persons lies, I suspect, at the heart of much rejection of the kenotic theory of the Incarnation. For kenosis requires that, quite literally, the Second Person of the Trinity and Jesus of Nazareth are the same person. Brian Hebblethwaite is an example of a theologian who sympathizes with the idea of kenosis, but finally rejects the sort of kenosis I am proposing on the grounds that we do not speak univocally of God and humans (Hebblethwaite 1987). A further reason occasionally given for rejecting the univocity of personhood is that it implies social trinitarianism, but I do not take that as a criticism.

If you hold that things persist by enduring as the very same thing without temporal parts, there is a further problem concerning fusion.

For Jesus the human being would seem to have existed as a foetus before he became a person, and the Second Person of the Trinity existed, we may suppose, at that time. If you are an endurantist, one solution is to adopt the theory of relative identity rather than the relative persistence substitute. Less radical would be to deny that the time that God is in is exactly the same as ours, with God perhaps being simultaneous with us only from time to time. Provided there was a nine-month or so gap in the times of divine/human simultaneity, there need be no fusion.

4. HOW IS KENOTIC INCARNATION POSSIBLE?

Even if it is not a sufficient condition, psychological continuity would seem to be a necessary condition for persistence as the same person. For consider the science fiction version of Locke's Prince and Cobbler story. We have the example in which all the connections between your neurons are rapidly dissolved and then re-established so as to make your brain a replica of some quite different person. You would be the same organism, perhaps, but not the same person. So the kenotic theory of the Incarnation requires a gradual process by which the Second Divine Person becomes Jesus of Nazareth.

Moderate materialism helps answer the question of how a gradual kenosis is possible. Initially, the Second Person has a body or brain *analogue*, consisting, I suggested in the previous chapter, of a sub-bundle of universe-fibres. So, to undergo kenosis, this has merely to contract over, say, the time of Mary's pregnancy so as to come to be that of which Jesus as a baby is directly aware. Previously I suggested that there has to be a withdrawal of the divine away from the domains of human agency, but here there is an exception. While for the other two Persons there is indeed such a withdrawal, the Second Person not merely has control over Jesus's domain, but for a while has control over nothing else. At that point, presumably before birth, the Second Person has become fully human like us in all things except that Jesus has a pre-birth history as the second Divine Person, and, I would suggest, some recollection of this pre-birth history, and a corresponding sense of the irrationality of sin. This procedure can go in reverse, no doubt, by a gradual process starting at the Resurrection and ending at the Ascension.

The Second Person can do this by gradually giving over control of a whole sub-bundle of universe-fibres to the other Divine Persons while gradually taking control over the portions of their universe-fibres from which they have abdicated power to provide space for the human being Jesus. This is a gradual process and has no physical implications beyond whatever physical connections unite the universe-fibres into the sub-bundles. That is all that has to be effected, and it is something we would not notice.

5. ARE THE INCARNATION AND THE RESURRECTION CONTRARY TO THE NATURAL ORDER?

One objection might be that the Incarnation would be contrary to the natural order and so, on my account, impossible. Not so, I say. All that is required is that God by carefully guiding human history ensures that there will be at the appropriate time a human being free from our sinful tendencies, who has a lively sense of the presence of the First and Second Persons, and who has the sort of memory of being divine that a human might be capable of. Then the Incarnation as such involves no disruption of the natural order. Without it, Mary would still have had a son who would have been very much as many non-Christians think of Jesus, a very good but sadly deluded person.

To be sure, the interference of God in human history by repeated inspirations to ensure that there comes to be such a human being would be quite significant and not ideal from the point of view of respecting our collective autonomy. As such, we may safely say that it occurred only because we were in such a parlous state that we could not get out of our mess by ourselves.

The Resurrection is impossible to reconcile with the natural order as it is currently described by scientists. But there is no reason to hold that this description is complete. And here I take some encouragement from the speculations of physicists concerning extra dimensions of Space or many universes. I suggest that we extend into a further dimension or so or across many universes, and that there are *ghostly* parts of us, the behaviour of which is guided by the parts that are more familiar—until, that is, the more familiar parts cease to exist. It is then, I speculate, part of the natural order that we continue to exist in a fashion that we will find hard to control. Negotiating that life, and even growing again the more familiar this-worldly parts, requires, we may suppose, trust in the divine, or trust in those who have such trust. Without that we would be helpless, because anything we do might seem like throwing ourselves into an abyss. So it is Jesus's trust in the Father that enabled him to come back to ordinary life. And one of the reasons for the Incarnation might be the inability of sinful human beings to have such trust in anyone who was not human.

6. KENOSIS AND THE SALVATION OF INDIVIDUALS

Our salvation is, I suspect, a rather complicated process. For the way in which human history was, and still to some extent is, a cycle of vice transmitted from generation to generation is itself a complicated problem without a simple solution. Moreover, salvation is available in all ages, not just in the first century and definitely not just in ours. So there is room for *accommodation*, by which I mean God dealing with humans in ways that make sense only because of the ways in which the humans at the time think. Thus Satisfaction accounts might seem wrong-headed to most of our contemporaries, but God may have allowed Satisfaction as one of the effects of the death of Jesus to accommodate cultures for which it was significant. Again, an adequate account of the Atonement would have to mention the concept of sacrifice, which has featured strongly in many cultures. In short, accommodation permits a qualified cultural relativism concerning how we are saved. Hence, unlike the Trinity, it is not just, or even primarily, a topic in philosophical theology.

Nonetheless, I shall be considering just two aspects of our salvation, one individual and one collective. I do this in order to offer more support for kenosis, by showing how it helps us to understand some aspects of the Atonement. First, then, let us consider individual salvation, starting with the Abelardian thesis that Jesus saved by means of example. This is too weak, because it ignores the complexity of the process by which vice is transmitted, which includes resentment of the good. A promising, and widely held, variant is that Jesus revealed the divine love for us. We can see how this revelation is salvific. For one fundamental moral problem is that we cannot bear to recognize our own moral failure. There are many devices for avoiding this recognition: comparing ourselves favourably with others—a dangerous exercise if they are not psychologically intimate to us; naturalizing wickedness as just a phenomenon like any other; glorifying it by calling it something else—ambition, or heroism, or an exercise of our right to happiness; grovelling in a pathetic way about the few minor sins we do acknowledge—like a swindler who occasioned many suicides confessing impure thoughts to a priest. The all-time favourite strategy is of course just brute self-deception—turning the blind inner eye to our sins.

Only the full, emotionally rich, acknowledgement of divine love for us enables us to recognize the depths of our wickedness. To be sure, there may well be many who are innocent, and for them no religion is necessary. We might well hope that the proportion of the innocent increases with time, and it is not for me to claim a large proportion of fellow sinners. I make bold to say that much of the good religion does—and I acknowledge that it does much harm too in one way or another—is to assure the wicked that they can attend to their own wretched state without falling into despair, because God loves them. Christianity is, I believe, superior to other religions not because it does less harm but because it does more good, by performing this function of assuring us of divine love. And it does this because Jesus not merely told us so and not merely gave an example of love—a prophet could have done as much—but because by becoming human a Divine Person demonstrated that love. St Paul and St John, of course, put it much better than I.

The point of that mini-sermon is that the Incarnation performs this function of revealing God's love only if, as all Christians in fact believe, becoming human and dying on the Cross are themselves astounding acts of love, ones which we would insist were totally extravagant until we see their purpose. The danger with more traditional accounts of the Incarnation that tells us that *qua* human Jesus suffered but *qua* divine he did not, is not that it requires a great deal of philosophy to make sense of the *qua*s, but that it threatens to undermine the capacity of the Incarnation to act as a revelation of divine love.

The advantage of the kenotic account is that it is plain to all that the Incarnation, including the willingness to suffer death, is a superlative act of love by the pre-Incarnation Second Person. The problem with more traditional accounts is that because of their intellectual opacity we have to take it on trust that the Incarnation shows us the divine love, which is scarcely different from taking it on trust that God loves us. Kenosis is clear enough, so that anyone who accepts it intellectually and is not emotionally defective will have a lively sense of the divine love. So it performs the salvific role to perfection.

7. PARTICIPATION

The above was a sketch of one way in which individuals are saved. But there is also a collective account. Consider collective action. What we do as a group, perhaps as the whole of humanity, is, I concede, exhausted by what we do as individuals. There is nothing over and above the individuals, nothing comparable to the way in which the mental, although necessarily correlated with the physical, is nonetheless irreducible. Yet the idea of collective action is morally significant. For the answer to the question 'What should we do?'—the political question—is not just the conjunction of the moral questions 'What should I do?' (Forrest 1998*b*). Often a situation arises in which each individual acts in a way that is morally acceptable, but collectively we do something wrong. An example might be the collective inaction over the genocide in Rwanda. We could point the finger at the Secretary-General of the United Nations, but in the circumstances it is not clear that he was to blame. If it was not all of us who are to blame, then it was the United Nations as such, a lazy organization made up of far-from-lazy individuals. This mismatch between individual and collective action arises either because individuals are unaware of the collective beliefs or because for us collectively to do the right thing requires heroic supererogatory goodness on the part of some individuals.

We are in a parlous state not just individually, but collectively, and this is the result of the way in which sinful tendencies perpetuate themselves from one generation to the next. Moreover, we participate in this collective sinfulness, but not by being individually guilty for what others did or did not do. That would be absurd: I am not responsible for the dispossession of the aboriginal inhabitants of Australia, although I must in all honesty say as a non-aboriginal Australian, 'We are responsible for this dispossession'.

A great deal of religion amounts to the attempt to say 'we' and to include God as one of us. The idea of a sacrifice, when it is not diabolical, is, I take it, the attempt to invite God to share a meal and so come to have the fellowship, the sense of 'we' that accompanies a shared meal. This is futile, but not because God does not literally eat. Hebrew prophets in effect explained that God enjoys our obedience as we enjoy good food and drink. The problem is, rather, that because of our participation in collective sin, we find ourselves unable to give God the required sacrifice of obedience. And this is where the Incarnation enables us to participate in divinity in a way that the old sacrifices failed to. The Second Person becomes part of the 'we' of at least two communities: the Church and the whole of humanity. Kenosis provides a way of understanding this participation in the collective, for although God as such is not one of us, one of the Divine Persons is. On more traditional accounts of the Incarnation, there is always the problem that we might have to say that the Christ *qua* human is one of us but *qua* divine is not, thus qualifying the participation.

I am thus partially endorsing the Anselmian idea of Satisfaction. It is not that Jesus makes reparation on our behalf. We make reparation for what we did wrong collectively, but we can do it only because Jesus is one of us, because the Sacrifice is obedience, and because Jesus was perfectly obedient. Just as the fans of a football club can say, 'We did it, no one believed we could do it but us, but we won', we can say, 'Yes, we did it, we made an acceptable sacrifice to God'.

A common objection to the Anselmian account is to deny that God would require reparation. My response is that God does not require it, but we do. Our kind of psychology cannot be at ease with God until we have made reparation. It is a fact about *us* that makes some sort of sacrificial atonement valid, not a fact about God.

8. THE EXALTATION

After his death the process of kenosis could have just gone in reverse as it were. But the Christian tradition suggests otherwise. It suggests that while Jesus came to reacquire control over a sub-bundle of universe-fibres, he also remained in control of a hole, as it were, from which the other Divine Persons had retreated in their bundles, as they retreated also from all other created persons to whom autonomy was granted. Jesus would thus be embodied in whatever heavenly realm the afterlife requires.

The domains of control that the risen Christ has thus divide into the whole universe-fibres that are his as a Divine Person and his domains within the universe-fibres of the other Divine Persons. These latter can be thought of as in an extended sense Jesus's body even if they include more than an ordinary human being has direct control over. So now, after the Christ's earthly life, we may talk of him *qua* divine and *qua* human, because of his having control over the physical in two distinct ways. It is thus possible to say that Jesus *qua* human is present in some places but not others, meaning that it is his body in this extended sense that is present.

9. THE REAL PRESENCE

This leads to the Real Presence of Jesus in the Eucharist, which requires metaphysical explication if it is not to be dismissed as conceivable but impossible. In this case there are three or four problems that must be addressed: the triviality problem; the multilocation problem; the union problem, and, perhaps, the time gap problem.

The triviality problem is that God is present everywhere, so is automatically present in the Eucharist. The solution is that we make a distinction between Jesus *qua* divine and *qua* human. It is the humanity as well as the divinity that must be present. All orthodox accounts of the Incarnation make this distinction in some way or other. What is noteworthy as far as I am concerned is that, as discussed above, the distinction can be made on my kenotic account even after the Exaltation. So let us concentrate on the other three.

The multilocation problem is that there are simultaneous celebrations of the Eucharist at which Jesus is present, as well as, it is assumed, having a heavenly presence. This is not the problem of whether there are scattered objects with separated parts, but the problem of how a human being can be wholly present in many places at once. As with Brian Leftow's example of the Rockettes (Leftow 2004), I would claim that time-travel is conceivable, and so a person may indeed be in many places at the same time. The problem, though, is not with the mere conceivability of human multilocation, but with providing a plausible enough metaphysical hypothesis. If Jesus is really present when the Eucharist is celebrated, it is then somewhat less important that his presence be tied to the consecrated bread and wine in such a way that Christians can literally eat his body and drink his blood. And without a solution to the multilocation problem, there can be no hope of any further doctrine of the Real Presence in the bread and wine.

The union problem concerns the connection between the bread and wine and the Real Presence. If Jesus is present whenever the bread and wine are consecrated in the Eucharist, that is, perhaps, the most important aspect of the tradition. But many Christians believe in a more literal understanding of Jesus's words, 'This is my body . . . This is my blood'. And that raises the question of just what the supposed connection is intended to be between the bread and wine, on the one hand, and Jesus's body, on the other.

Finally, we might well expect the doctrine of the Real Presence to identify the bread and wine not—or not just—with the Jesus now, but with Jesus as crucified and risen. How can the bread and wine be Jesus not just now but almost 2,000 years ago? This is the time gap problem.

Do the traditional theses of transubstantiation or consubstantiation provide adequate solutions to the three problems that I am concentrating on? The spaghetti effect discourages me from answering this question. An adequate answer might involve a discussion of centuries of argument and counter-argument, as well as the question of just how much of scholasticism is genuinely outmoded as a result of our vastly increased understanding of the physical. In an appendix, I shall, however, discuss these theses with just as much attention as is required to explain why I do not rely upon them to solve the three problems with the Real Presence. Leaving that to an appendix, I now totally ignore transubstantiation and consubstantiation and provide a speculation that, while it might well be described as miraculous, it is not a supernatural breaking of the laws of nature.

First I need a piece of conceptual analysis. What is it to be my *body* or your *body*? No doubt there is some ambiguity, but one, central concept is that of X's body as that thing over which X has direct rather than indirect control. I call this the *agency conception* of the body. By 'direct' I here mean without any intermediary that is itself an act. I do not mean lacking in causal intermediaries, such as nerve impulses. And control over is not to be taken to mean total control over. Thus few can directly increase their metabolic rate. Another analysis of the concept of a body is that it is a thing of the sort that human beings are usually considered to have direct control over. Let us call that the *parochial conception* of the body. It is not the one I shall be using.

What justification is there, then, for the agency conception of the body? First, it is not intuitively incorrect to think of a prosthesis as part of your body. Consider, for instance, an artificial hand that is operated by wrist muscles but which you learn to control directly. Secondly, we may consider the situation of the necessarily symmetrical universe in which whenever something happens on a given planet A, of necessity something of the same type occurs on planet B. We human beings live on one or both of these planets. So whatever any agent living on A or B does has effects on both A and B. And for any agent, there will be two exactly resembling human bodies, one on A and the other on B, over which the agent has direct control. Then I ask, who is the real agent, and which of A or B is Earth? I invite you to agree that in this, admittedly peculiar, situation the agent would have a body on both A and B, which would both be Earth. So both we and our planet would be multiply located. And that conclusion will hold even if the symmetry is not perfect, provided the differences are too small for us to notice. I doubt that we could directly apply this hypothesis to the Real Presence. What we may do is use this hypothesis to support the proposed analysis of a body and to show that in that sense a person can have many bodies. This example also shows that multilocated bodies are possible even without body/soul dualism.

In this connection I would also like to acknowledge Daniel Dennett's unwitting support of agency conception, and his consequent contribution to eucharistic theology—I am sure he will be thrilled on both counts. In his splendid paper 'Where am I?' (Dennett 1979), he does a good job of undermining the intuition that where we are is where our bodies in the parochial sense are. And I take this as support for the validity of the agency conception.

We obtain a sanitized doctrine of the Real Presence, then, if we speculate that Jesus, at some time during the period between the Last Supper and the Resurrection had direct control over whatever bread and wine would subsequently be consecrated. This is not to say that the control was causally unmediated, leaping across space and time as it were, but rather that Jesus directly intended the bread and wine to be consumed in his memory, which then occurred in a quite natural fashion. The only abnormal feature is the directness of the intention.

I am told, by Jeff Hodges, that in St John's Gospel (6: 50–8) the word for 'eat' (*phagein*) has connotations of chewing or gnawing, and that the word used for 'body' (*sarx*) means 'flesh'. So we might require a less sanitized doctrine, one that comes close to cannibalism. The general policy of replacing supernatural explanations by highly speculative physical ones may be used either instead of or to supplement the previous sanitized doctrine. We require an extra spatial dimension or dimensions, which, as previously mentioned, coheres well with accounts of the risen Jesus. Suppose that both we and Jesus have extension into an extra dimension, but that our senses only record what is going on in a slice so thin with respect to the extra dimension that it is as if three-dimensional—as we ordinarily think of the whole of Space. Then, while in this thin slice we are eating bread, further into the extra spatial dimension we might be eating Jesus's flesh and drinking his blood in whatever form these take. This appeal to further dimensions is not new, and the *Catholic Encyclopedia* article on 'Transubstantiation' notes it, but dismisses it because it is not supernatural.[2] That it is not supernatural in the sense of being contrary to the laws governing that world is an advantage, I say, not a disadvantage.

10. THE HOLY SPIRIT

God has retained some power over the universe, but if, as I have suggested, God has given us autonomy, then how can we be *inspired*? One suggestion is that there is a stage just at the point when we freely decide in which our attention is involuntarily drawn to various relevant considerations.[3] It would seem that God might, therefore, inspire by drawing our attention to what we would not otherwise notice, provided this is compatible with the laws of nature.

Christians, however, consider the function of inspiration to be the domain of the Third Person, the Holy Spirit, rather than all three Persons acting together. Why? Here is a speculation. The divine plan might have been that there were angels, who could act on human decisions by inspiration. For the sake of that plan, the Primordial God ensures a withdrawal not merely from the brain activity concerned with action but also from that concerned with attention. In that case the locus of inspiration—namely, the various things to which our attention is drawn—would be possible for angels, as part of the natural order, directly to control, but not for God. So for God to inspire would require an incarnation as an angel. We could then suppose that from time to time the Third Person has an angelic incarnation as the Holy Spirit, in

---

[2] The article 'Transubstantiation' in the *Catholic Encyclopedia* states: 'Nor does the modern theory of n-dimensions throw any light upon the subject; for the Body of Christ is not invisible or impalpable to us because it occupies the fourth dimension, but because it transcends and is wholly independent of space. Such a mode of existence, it is clear, does not come within the scope of physics and mechanics, but belongs to a higher, supernatural order.' <http://www.newadvent.org/cathen/05573a.htm>

[3] Richard Franklin (1968) has argued that the locus of freedom is the act of attention. He may well be right, but even so, there is a difference between choosing to continue to attend, which could be free, and something's coming to your attention in the first place.

order to inspire. This would explain St John's attribution to Jesus of the cryptic remark about the Paraclete not being able to come until he, Jesus, has gone back to the Father. For perhaps the divine life cannot operate with just one Divine Person. (In that case we have a good argument from tradition/revelation that there is a genuine Trinity, not a Binity.)

APPENDIX

The purpose of this appendix is to expound the traditional theses of transubstantiation and consubstantiation only in sufficient detail to explain why I reject them and seek a rather different account of the Real Presence.

Like the doctrines of the Trinity and the Incarnation, the Real Presence has been formulated in metaphysical terms using the concept of substance. Thus the Western Church at the Fourth Lateran Council in 1215 and the Eastern Orthodox Churches at the Synod of Jerusalem in 1672 separately stated transubstantiation as doctrine. At the Reformation, Luther and the Lutherans preached consubstantiation, and at the Counter-Reformation the Council of Trent reaffirmed transubstantiation. The reformers Zwingli and Calvin disagreed with Luther, considering that Jesus was not really present in the Eucharist, which was interpreted as a sign of Jesus's sacrifice. Because of the metaphysical vocabulary used, it is easy to confuse the doctrine of the Real Presence, which I accept, with a given metaphysical explication that not even a universal Council of the Church would have the right to pronounce on. It is precisely the latter, though, that might be proposed as a solution to the three problems mentioned, to do with multilocation, union, and the time gap. Hopefully it will prevent more confusion than it generates if I use the hyphenated 'trans-substantiation' and 'con-substantiation' for the metaphysical explications. Because Catholics are more likely to interpret transubstantiation as trans-substantiation than Lutherans are to interpret consubstantiation as con-substantiation, I shall discuss trans-substantiation first.

The religious doctrine of transubstantiation asserts that the bread and wine are somehow replaced by the Body and Blood of Jesus. Its metaphysical explication, trans-substantiation, is often accused of being outmoded, on the grounds that it requires a theory of substances that sustain accidents with causal powers, and yet the causal powers of bread and wine—for instance, to nourish and to relax—are to be understood in terms of detailed chemical properties and not, as medieval thinkers assumed, the powers of their accidents. To meet this objection, it is necessary to think of the familiar macroscopic properties of the bread and wine as *real* but, in all normal cases, *dependent* on the less familiar micro-structure, in much the way that many near-dualist materialists think of the mental properties as *real* but *dependent* on patterns of axon-spikings and synapse-firings. Such dependence implies, that of—metaphysical necessity—wherever there is the appropriate pattern, then the mental property occurs. We may then say the same about the structure of the bread, especially its chemical composition and the manifest properties that depend on that structure. These will include all the primary properties such as shape, size, mass, and so on. It is more controversial whether the 'secondary' properties, such as colour and taste, are included. We may also include various powers, for instance to nourish, among the manifest properties. Trans-substantiation includes the thesis that these observable features, *the accidents*, remain the same after the Consecration, but are no longer properties of anything. This is because God has intervened, breaking the natural order by destroying the atoms that made up the bread and wine or by rendering them temporarily unable to sustain the usual accidents such as the power to nourish. Therefore the accidents are not universals, which would remain as properties of similar unconsecrated portions of bread and wine. Analytic philosophers would call them *abstract particulars*, or, as a result of Donald Williams's joke, *tropes* (Williams 1953; Campbell 1990; Bacon 1995). Then the substances of scholastic philosophy would be concrete particulars: namely, sums of accidents together with whatever unites them. It is not easy to see just how they are united, but being in the same places at the same times, although good evidence for unity, is not sufficient for abstract particulars to be united. (If it were, the properties of light shining through glass would be united with the properties of the glass to make a single concrete substance.) Ordinarily, there is a close connection between a property belonging to a substance and a corresponding predicate being true of the substance. Thus, if the abstract particular *this sweetness* is part of the concrete particular *this portion of wine*, it follows that this portion of wine is sweet. I shall stipulate that this is always the case and so, a bundle of accidents unified in some way that severs the predication/property connection cannot be called a substance, strictly speaking. Such pseudo-substances can arise if that on which the accidents depend is not in the same place and the same time as the accidents. So a hologram is a pseudo-substance.

Since the scholastic theory of persistence was that of strict identity over time (endurance), and since it was supposed that substances persist, we should hold that both the abstract and the concrete particulars can endure for a while—say, a few days in the case of a piece of bread. As a corollary, the abstract particulars that make up the substance should be interpreted as imprecise—for instance, *being between 90 and 110 grams.*[4]

---

[4] There will be many candidates for the system of atoms on which the observable features depend. But even though a portion of bread or of wine will both gain and lose many atoms, many of these candidates do not contain transient members, and so may be said to endure as long as the observable features.

Trans-substantiation may be interpreted, then, as the thesis that (1) prior to the Consecration the accidents of bread are united in the normal way by all depending on the same structured system of atoms, so we may say that they are properties of the bread; but that (2) after the Consecration they are no longer united in this way or are properties of anything. Instead, they are united in a different way, by the presence of Jesus, forming a pseudo-substance. Until we are told how the presence of Jesus unites these accidents, we have not solved the union problem. For the mere co-location of the accidents of the bread and wine with Jesus is not enough to say that in eating the bread and drinking the wine we consume the Body and Blood of Jesus. It would show only that we consume the accidents of bread and wine. The reason why we cannot say that the accidents of bread and wine and the Body and Blood of Jesus form a genuine substance is that Jesus—being multilocated—would thus have inconsistent predicates. Nor will it do to say that Jesus *qua* divine may exercise the power of keeping these accidents in being, because to solve the triviality problem, the accidents of bread and wine are associated with the humanity, not the divinity, of Jesus. Instead, we must suppose that as a result of divine providence there is a hidden feature of the natural order that ensures that Jesus's intention to save humanity, some time around the Crucifixion, is the common cause of all these post-Consecration accidents of bread and wine, which would otherwise cease to exist. Hence we may say that after the Consecration the accidents of bread and wine form with Jesus's intention to save a pseudo-substance, which we may consume in much the way we may consume the substances of unconsecrated bread and wine.

The multilocation problem is then solved, because the many portions of consecrated bread and wine depend on the same thing: namely, Jesus's intention. The union problem is solved because after the Consecration the observable features of bread and wine stand to Jesus somewhat as before the Consecration they stand to the atoms. The time gap problem is solved because the accidents depend directly on Jesus's intention, the way in which the divine causation of laws of nature extends into the future.

It is not that I find the metaphysics of this version of trans-substantiation outmoded, but I reject miracles that violate rather than work within the natural order. And I see no way that trans-substantiation can avoid asserting either that the atoms that made up the bread cease to exist or, more plausibly, that they are rendered temporarily powerless to sustain the observable features of bread and wine. My conclusion is that there is nothing wrong with trans-substantiation except that it is supernatural in the sense of a violation of the laws of nature.

What about con-substantiation, then? Con-substantiation amounts to saying that prior to the Consecration the accidents depend on the system of atoms, but afterwards they depend both on the system of atoms and Jesus's intention. This would differ from the situation before the Consecration in that, if the atoms were to cease to exist, the accidents would endure. Con-substantiation, thus explicated, has the advantage over trans-substantiation of not violating the natural order by hypothesizing that the atoms cease to exist or lose their normal powers. Even so, I prefer trans-substantiation because on my explication of con-substantiation the difference made by the Consecration is only counterfactual: if the atoms were to cease to exist, then the accidents would remain. Such a purely counterfactual difference is not intuitively adequate for the doctrine of the Real Presence.

Concluding Remarks

Earlier I described myself as a sheep in wolf's clothing. The combination of kenotic divine development and moderate materialism might seem radical, but I have been able to show that it provides a metaphysics congenial to the central Christian doctrines. Somewhere along the line I surely pass from hypotheses that are about as likely as not to mere speculation. And I am under no illusion that speculations which might appear plausible to me might seem crazy to others, or that which seems plausible now might seem weird to future generations. The pessimistic induction (Newton-Smith 1981: 14) hits philosophy with a vengeance. Consequently, there is much that I have said that I neither believe nor disbelieve.

Here is a parody of Socrates that both says and shows my frivolous attitude to most things, including most philosophy, but not to the core traditions of Christianity: the unexamined life is a Soapie, the examined one a Sit Com. Bearing all this in mind, I claim to have exhibited some advantages that moderate materialism and a development kenotic theism have in the explication of theism generally, and Christianity in particular. The chief advantage is that by restricting the range of possible divine actions, it becomes easier to understand them. But it also helps generate answers to 'How is it possible?' questions, such as 'How is the Trinity possible?' and 'How is the Incarnation possible?'

Bibliography

Adams, Marilyn McCord (1999), *Horrendous Evils and the Goodness of God* (Ithaca, NY: Cornell University Press).

Adams, Robert (1972), 'Must God Create the Best?', *Philosophical Review*, 80, 317–22.

Armstrong, David (1983), *What is a Law of Nature?* (Cambridge: Cambridge University Press).

Bacon, John (1995), *Universals and Property Instances: The Alphabet of Being* (Oxford: Basil Blackwell).

Bigelow, John (1996), 'Presentism and Properties', *Philosophical Perspectives*, 10, 35–52.

_____ Ellis, Brian, and Lierse, Caroline (2004), 'The World as One of a Kind: Natural Necessity and Laws of Nature', in John Carroll (ed.), *Readings on Laws of Nature* (Pittsburgh: University of Pittsburgh Press), 141–60.

Braddon-Mitchell, David (2001), 'Lossy Laws', *Noûs*, 35, no. 2, 260–77.

Brown, Deborah (1997), 'The Right Method of Boy-Loving', in Roger Lamb (ed.), *Love Analyzed* (Boulder, Colo.: Westview Press), 49–64.

Byrne, Alex (2005), 'Inverted Qualia', in Edward N. Zalta (ed.), *The Stanford Encyclopedia of Philosophy (Summer 2005 Edition)*, URL = <http://plato.stanford.edu.archives/sum2005/entries/qualia-inverted>.

Campbell, Keith (1990), *Abstract Particulars* (Oxford: Basil Blackwell).

Chalmers, David (1996), *The Conscious Mind: In Search of a Fundamental Theory* (New York: Oxford University Press).

Chisholm, Roderick (1976), *Persons and Objects: A Metaphysical Study* (London: George Allen & Unwin).

_____ (1990), 'The Defeat of Good and Evil', in Marilyn McCord Adams and Robert Adams (eds.), *The Problem of Evil* (Oxford: Oxford University Press), 209–21.

Churchland, Patricia Smith (1986), *Neurophilosophy: Towards a Unified Science of Mind-Brain* (Cambridge, Mass.: MIT Press).

Collingwood, Robin (1940), *An Essay on Metaphysics* (Oxford: Clarendon Press).

Colyvan, Mark, Garfied, Jay, and Priest, Graham (2005), 'Problems with the Argument from Fine Tuning', *Synthese*, 145, 325–38.

Craig, William (1979), *The Kalam Cosmological Argument* (London: Macmillan).

_____ (2000), *The Tensed Theory of Time: A Critical Examination* (Dordrecht: Kluwer).

Darwin, Charles (1875), *The Movements and Habits of Climbing Plants* (London: John Murray).

—— (1883), *The Formation of Vegetable Mould, through the Action of Worms* (London: John Murray).

Davidson, Donald (1987), 'Knowing One's Own Mind', *Proceedings and Addresses of the American Philosophical Association*, 61, 441–58; repr. in Davidson, *Subjective, Intersubjective, Objective* (Oxford: Clarendon Press, 2001), 15–38.

Davis, Wayne (1991), 'The World-Shift Theory of Free Choice', *Australasian Journal of Philosophy*, 69, 206–11.

Dennett, Daniel (1979), 'Where Am I?', in *Brainstorms: Philosophical Essays on Mind and Psychology* (Hassocks: Harvester Press), 310–23.

Deutsch, David (1996), *The Fabric of Reality* (New York: Penguin, 1996).

Divers, John (2002), *Possible Worlds* (London: Routledge).

Dretske, Fred (1977), 'Laws of Nature', *Philosophy of Science*, 44, 248–68.

Ewing, Alfred (1973), *Value and Reality* (London: Allen & Unwin).

Feldhay, Rivka (1995), *Galileo and the Church: Political Inquisition or Critical Dialogue?* (Cambridge: Cambridge University Press).

Forrest, Peter (1991), 'Aesthetic Understanding', *Philosophy and Phenomenological Research*, 51, 33–52.

—— (1994), 'Why Most of Us Should Be Scientific Realists: A Reply to van Fraassen', *The Monist*, 77, 47–70.

—— (1996a), *God without the Supernatural: A Defence of Naturalistic Theism* (Ithaca, NY: Cornell University Press).

—— (1996b), 'Physicalism and Classical Theism', *Faith and Philosophy*, 13, 179–200.

—— (1998a), 'Answers to Prayer and Conditional Situations', *Faith and Philosophy*, 15, 41–51.

—— (1998b), 'Collective Responsibility and Restitution', *Philosophical Papers*, 27, 79–91.

—— (1998c), 'Divine Fission: A New Way of Moderating Social Trinitarianism', *Religious Studies*, 34, 281–98.

—— (1999), 'In Defence of Phase Space', *Synthese*, 119, 299–311.

—— (2000), 'The Incarnation: A Philosophical Case for Kenosis', *Religious Studies*, 36, 127–40.

—— (2001a), 'Actuality and Consciousness', in Uwe Meexnor and Peter Simons (eds.), *The Proceedings of the 1999 International Wittgenstein Symposium* (Kirchberg am Wechsel: Austrian Wittgenstein Society), 130–9.

—— (2001b), 'Counting the Cost of Modal Realism', in Gerhard Preyer and Frank Siebelt (eds.), *Reality and Humean Supervenience: Essays on the Philosophy of David Lewis* (Lanham, Md.: Rowman & Littlefield), 93–103.

—— (2003), 'The Trinity and Personal Identity', in Melville Stewart (ed.), *The Trinity: East/West Dialogue* (Dordrecht: Kluwer), 75–82.

_____ (2005), 'Universals as Sense-data', *Philosophy and Phenomenological Research*, 71, 622–31.

_____ (2006*a*), 'Epistemic Bootstrapping', in Stephen Hetherington (ed.), *Perspectives in Cognitive Science, Aspects of Knowing: Epistemological Essays* (New York: Elsevier Press), ch. 4.

_____ (2006*b*), 'General Facts, Physical Necessity and the Metaphysics of Time', in Dean Zimmerman (ed.), *Oxford Studies in Metaphysics*, ii (Oxford: Oxford University Press), 137–54.

_____ (2006*c*), 'The Tree of Life', in Peter Van Iwwagen and Dean Zimmerman (eds.), *Persons, Human and Divine* (Oxford: Oxford University Press), 301–18.

Franklin, Richard (1968), *Freewill and Determinism: A Study of Rival Conceptions of Man* (London: Routledge & Kegan Paul).

Gale, Richard (1991), *On the Nature and Existence of God* (Cambridge: Cambridge University Press).

Gasking, Douglas (1955), 'Causation and Recipes', *Mind*, 64, 479–87.

Gaus, Gerry (1990), *Value and Justification* (New York: Cambridge University Press).

Geach, Peter (1977), *Providence and Evil* (Cambridge: Cambridge University Press).

Gore, Charles (1922), *Belief in Christ* (London: J. Murray).

Gosse, Philip Henry (1857), *Omphalos: An Attempt to Untie the Geological Knot* (London: J. Van Voorst).

Griffin, David (2001), *Reenchantment without Supernaturalism: A Process Philosophy of Religion*, (Ithaca, NY: Cornell University Press).

Harman, Gilbert (1986), *Change in View: Principles of Reasoning* (Cambridge Mass: Bradford MIT).

Hebblethwaite, Brian (1987), *The Incarnation: Collected Essays in Christology* (Cambridge: Cambridge University Press).

Hick, John (1966), *Evil and the God of Love* (New York: Harper & Row).

Howard-Snyder, Daniel (1996) (ed.), *The Evidential Argument from Evil* (Bloomington, Ind.: Indiana University Press).

_____ and Howard-Snyder, Frances (1994), 'How an Unsurpassable Being can Create a Surpassable World', *Faith and Philosophy*, 11, 260–8.

Hunt, David (1997), 'Two Problems with Knowing the Future', *American Philosophical Quarterly*, 34, 273–85.

Jackson, Frank (1982), 'Epiphenomenal Qualia', *Philosophical Quarterly*, 32, 127–36.

_____ (1986), 'What Mary Didn't Know', *Journal of Philosophy*, 83, 291–5.

Kripke, Saul (1977), 'Speaker's Reference and Semantic Reference', in *Midwest Studies in Philosophy*, 2, 255–76.

Leftow, Brian (2002), 'The Eternal Present in God and Time', in Gregory E. Ganssle and David M. Woodruff (eds.), *Essays on the Divine Nature* (Oxford: Oxford University Press), 21–48.

Leftow, Brian (2004), 'A Latin Trinity', *Faith and Philosophy*, 21, 304–33.

Leslie, John (1979), *Value and Existence* (Oxford: Basil Blackwell, 1979).

—— (1989), *Universes* (London: Routledge).

—— (2001), *Many Gods: Infinite Minds: A Philosophical Cosmology* (Oxford: Clarendon Press).

Levine, Joseph (2001), *Purple Haze: The Puzzle of Consciousness* (New York: Oxford University Press).

—— (1986), *On the Plurality of Worlds* (Oxford: Basil Blackwell).

Lewis, David (1983), 'Postscript to "Mad Pain and Martian Pain"', in *Philosophical Papers,* i (Oxford: Oxford University Press), 130–2.

—— (1977), 'What Experience Teaches', in Ned Block, Owen J. Flanagan and Güven Güzeldere (eds.), *The Nature of Conciousnes: Philosophical Debates* (Cambridge, Mass.: MIT Press), 579–96.

Lockwood, Michael (1989), *Minds, Brains and the Quantum: The Compound I* (Oxford: Basil Blackwell).

Mackie, John (1977), *Ethics: Inventing Right and Wrong* (Harmondsworth: Penguin).

—— (1982), *The Miracle of Theism: Arguments For and Against the Existence of God* (Oxford: Clarendon Press).

McCall, Storrs (1994), *A Model of the Universe* (Oxford: Oxford University Press).

Miller, Barry (2001), *The Fullness of Being: A New Paradigm for Existence* (Oxford: Clarendon Press).

Morris, Thomas (1987), *Anselmian Explorations: Essays in Philosophical Theology* (Notre Dame, Ind.: University of Notre Dame Press).

Newman, John Henry (1870), *An Essay in Aid of a Grammar of Assent* (London: Burns Oates).

Newton-Smith, William (1981), *The Rationality of Science* (Boston: Routledge & Kegan Paul).

Parfit, Derek (1984), *Reasons and Persons* (Oxford: Clarendon Press).

Penrose, Roger (1987), 'Minds, Machines and Mathematics', in Colin Blakemore and Susan Greenfield (eds.), *Mindwaves* (Oxford: Blackwell), 259–78.

—— (1989), *The Emperor's New Mind* (Oxford: Oxford University Press).

Pinnock, Clark (1994) (ed.), *The Openness of God* (Downers Grove, Ill.: InterVarsity Press).

Plantinga, Alvin (1983), 'Reason and Belief in God', in Alvin Plantinga and Nicholas Wolterstorff (eds.), *Faith and Rationality* (Notre Dame, Ind.: University of Notre Dame Press), 16–93.

—— (1986), 'On Ockham's Way Out', *Faith and Philosophy*, 86, 235–69.

—— (2002), *Warranted Christian Belief* (New York: Oxford University Press).

—— (2003), 'Probability and Defeaters', *Pacific Philosophical Quarterly*, 84, 291–8.

Popper, Karl (1996), *Of Clouds and Clocks: An Approach to the Problem of Rationally and the Freedom of Man* (St Louis, Mo.: Washington University Press).

Price, Huw (1996), *Time's Arrow and Archimedes' Point: New Directions for the Physics of Time* (New York: Oxford University Press).

Pullman, Philip (1996), *The Golden Compass* (New York: Alfred A. Knopf).

Rebière, Alphonse (1926), *Mathematiques et mathematiciens; penses et curiosits, recueillies par A. Rebière* (Paris: Vuibert).

Rice, Hugh (2000), *God and Goodness* (Oxford: Oxford University Press).

Robinson, Howard (2003), 'Dualism', in Stephen Stich and Ted Warfield (eds.), *The Blackwell Guide to Philosophy of Mind* (Malden, Mass.: Blackwell), 85–101.

Rogers, Katherin (2000), *Perfect Being Theology* (Edinburgh: Edinburgh University Press).

Rowe, William (2004), *Can God be Free?* (Oxford: Clarendon Press).

Rudder Baker, Lynne (2000), *Persons and Bodies: A Constitution View* (Cambridge: Cambridge University Press).

Sanders, John (1998), *The God Who Risks: A Theology of Providence* (Downers Grove, Ill.: InterVarsity Press).

Schellenberg, John (1993), *Divine Hiddenness and Human Reason* (Ithaca, NY: Cornell University Press).

Schlesinger, George (1977), *Religion and Scientific Method* (Dordrecht: Reidel).

Smith, John (1992), *Jonathan Edwards: Puritan, Preacher, Philosopher* (Notre Dame, Ind.: University of Notre Dame Press).

Sorensen, Roy (forthcoming), 'The Vanishing Point: A Model of the Self as an Absence', *Monist*.

Stace, Walter (1955), *Mysticism and Human Reason* (Tucson, Ariz.: University of Arizona Press).

_____ (1960), *Mysticism and Philosophy* (Philadelphia: Lippincott).

Strawson, Galen (1994), *Mental Reality* (Cambridge, Mass.: MIT Press).

Stump, Eleonore, and Kretzmann, Norman (1981), 'Eternity', *Journal of Philosophy*, 78, 429–57.

Suppes, Patrick (1960), 'A Comparison of the Meaning and Uses of Models in Mathematics and the Empirical Sciences', *Synthese* 60, 287–300.

_____ (1967), *Set Theoretical Structures in Science*, Mimeographed lecture notes (Stanford University).

Swinburne, Richard (1986), *The Evolution of the Soul* (Oxford: Clarendon Press).

_____ (1987), *Providence and the Problem of Evil* (Oxford: Clarendon Press).

_____ (1994), *The Christian God* (Oxford: Clarendon Press).

_____ (2001), *Epistemic Justification* (Oxford: Clarendon Press).

_____ and Shoemaker, Sydney (1984), *Personal Identity* (Oxford: Basil Blackwell).

Tooley, Michael (1977), 'The Nature of Laws', *Canadian Journal of Philosophy*, 7, 667–98.

—— (1997), *Time, Tense and Causation* (Oxford: Clarendon Press).

van Fraassen, Bas (1980), *The Scientific Image* (Oxford: Clarendon Press).

Van Inwagen, Peter (1978), 'The Possibility of Resurrection', *International Journal for Philosophy of Religion*, 9, 114–21.

Vidal, Gore (1992), *Live from Golgotha* (New York: Random House).

von Wright, Georg (1971) *Explanation and Understanding* (Ithaca, NY: Cornell University Press).

Wagon, Stan (1985), *The Banach–Tarski Paradox* (Cambridge: Cambridge University Press).

Welch, Claude (1965), (ed. and trans.), *God and Incarnation in Mid-Nineteenth Century German Theology: G. Thomasius, I. A. Dorner, A. E. Biedermann* (New York: Oxford University Press).

Williams, Donald (1953) 'The Elements of Being', *Review of Metaphysics*, 7, 3–18, 171–92.

Wykstra, Stephen (1984), 'The Humean Obstacle to Evidential Arguments from Suffering: On Avoiding the Evils of Appearance', *International Journal for the Philosophy of Religion*, 16, 73–94.

Wynn, Mark (1999), *God and Goodness: A Natural Theological Perspective* (London : Routledge).

Zimmerman, Dean (1996), 'Persistence and Presentism', *Philosophical Papers*, 25, 115–26.

Index